PAUL'S MESSAGE OF FREEDOM:
What Does It Mean to the Black Church?

Amos Jones, Jr.

Judson Press ® Valley Forge

PAUL'S MESSAGE OF FREEDOM
Copyright © 1984
Judson Press, Valley Forge, Pa 19482-0851

Unless otherwise indicated, the Scripture quotations in this publication are from the Revised Standard Version of the Bible copyrighted 1946, 1952 © 1971, 1973 by the Division of Christian Education of the National Council of the Churches of Christ in the U.S.A., and used by permission.

Other versions of the Bible quoted in this book are:
The Bible: A New Translation by James Moffatt. Copyright 1954 by James Moffatt. Reprinted by permission of Harper & Row, Publishers, Inc.

The New Testament in Modern English, rev. ed. Copyright © J. B. Phillips 1972. Used by permission of The Macmillan Company and Geoffrey Bles, Ltd.

The New English Bible, copyright © The Delegates of the Oxford University Press and The Syndics of the Cambridge University Press 1961, 1970.

The Jerusalem Bible, copyright © 1966 by Darton, Longman & Todd, Ltd. and Doubleday and Company, Inc. Used by permission of the publisher.

HOLY BIBLE New International Version, copyright © 1978, New York International Bible Society. Used by permission.

Library of Congress Cataloging in Publication Data

Jones, Amos.
  Paul's message of freedom.

  Includes bibliographical references.
  1. Freedom (Theology)—Biblical teaching. 2. Bible.
N.T. Epistles of Paul—Criticism, interpretation, etc.
3. Afro-Americans—Religion. 4. Afro-Americans—Social
conditions—1975-   5. Afro-Americans—Economic
conditions. I. title.
BS2655.L5J66 1984   227'.06   83-23874
ISBN 0-8170-0840-3

Contents

Foreword **5**

1 Introduction **11**

2 Claim Your Freedom **27**

3 The Great Reversal **69**

4 Discipline: The Long Road to Freedom **113**

5 The Body of Christ: Unity in the Free Community **155**

6 Economic Independence as a Strategy for Freedom **203**

Notes **227**

Foreword

The reader of this book will probably find it interesting that a black theologian has written something about the apostle Paul's theological position on liberation. Very few black theologians have given the apostle serious consideration when they have sought to spin out their theologies of liberation from the Bible. Admittedly, I have taken on a pretentious endeavor.

Early in my studies at Vanderbilt Divinity School in Nashville, Tennessee, it dawned upon me that there was a deeply engrained antipathy within the ranks of black theologians for the apostle Paul. It appeared that they took seriously the statement attributed to Paul, "slaves be obedient to your masters." (The tenuousness of this situation will be dealt with in subsequent chapters.) When I first read Howard Thurman's *Jesus and the Disinherited*, I immediately became aware that Paul was not held in high esteem by Thurman. I began to raise the question of what basis these persons utilized to draw their conclusion that Paul was antiliberation and, therefore, not useful for the struggle for freedom by black people. Inasmuch as I had cast my theological career in the direction of New Testament exegesis, I drew the conclusion that black theologians such as James Cone and Howard Thurman surely had not based their judgment on the sound principles of form criticism and New Testament exegesis. I discovered that Howard Thurman could not embrace Paul because of the influence of his grandmother who disliked Paul. But Thurman's grandmother's dislike for Paul was due to sermons delivered by her white plantation preacher who erroneously attributed to Paul the statement "slaves be obedient to your masters." His grandmother's only fondness for Pauline Scripture was Paul's "Hymn to Love" in 1 Corinthians 13. As for black theologians such as James Cone, I drew the conclusion that these persons had not carefully considered the genuine writings and sayings of Paul vis-á-vis those attributed to him; rather, they flippantly accepted as genuine everything supportive of slavery attributed to the apostle in whatever translation they chose to use. I felt this was a grave injustice to Paul.

The more I read the black theologians of the sixties, the more I became angry with their renunciation of the apostle for what they thought was his antiliberation theological position. I began to study the genuine writings of Paul even more. I read and reread his works. I read all I could find about the apostle, especially that material which related to his position on liberation. I enrolled in practically every course offered at Vanderbilt Divinity School that had to do with Paul in any way. It was in my encounter with Paul in the classes of Dr. Leander Keck that the apostle came alive to me. Dr. Keck made Paul live; he stood Paul up as a courageous and indefatigable warrior for Christian freedom! His clarity of mind, his careful scholarship, and his ability to set Paul within the context of the historical *sitz-im-leben* (situation in life) of Paul's day made it altogether clear that it was Paul who provided the theological framework for the nascent church's struggle for freedom in an extremely hostile world.

It was during my study in the many courses taught by Dr. Keck that I undertook serious investigation of Paul's attitude toward civil courts and slavery. I came away from my investigation convinced that Paul was most radical in his positions on both civil courts and slavery, positions most difficult to deal with in our day. Through these classroom experiences with Dr. Keck, I became an enthusiastic disciple of the apostle Paul. The apostle revolutionized my entire perception of theology and liberation.

I quickly discovered, however, that I was virtually alone, as a black student, in my endearment to Paul. My black student colleagues, who were not engaged in biblical studies, could not understand the tenacity with which I embraced the apostle and his theology of liberation. I felt alone. It was a lonely journey.

The most profound experience, which proved to be the pivotal point that turned me in the direction of producing a written work on Paul's theology of liberation from a black perspective, was a visit to the Vanderbilt Divinity School campus by James Cone and Albert Cleage. These men's presentations to the faculty and student body virtually undressed Paul and set him out as an archadvocate of slavery and supporter of the status quo. I had the privilege of conversing intensely with Dr. Cone about his anti-Pauline position. In a vigorous exchange as we walked to the University Club on campus, I was rocked back on my heels by Dr. Cone's most challenging words, "You put in writing what you are saying to me about Paul, and I will respond to you." It was then that I gathered up all the determination within me to publish one day my thoughts on Paul and his theology of liberation.

When I began to develop my dissertation for the Doctor of Ministry degree at Vanderbilt Divinity School, I had no question what the topic would be. I entitled it *In Defense of Paul: A Discussion with James Cone and Albert Cleage*. What follows in this work is a spin-off of that dissertation. The first two chapters of this book are revised editions of the first two chapters of the dissertation. The remaining four chapters are new creations that emerged from my continuing investigation of the apostle's theology of freedom.

In the work that follows, I have tried to set a trajectory for the quest for the blessedness of liberation that Paul has provided for the church in general and for the black church in particular. I have tried to devise a logical development of thought, according to the apostle Paul, that would allow the church in general and the black church in particular to move from bondage to freedom. Sometimes along the course of preparing this work, I have thought that my most salient task was to vindicate the apostle Paul. The malignant castigation hurled at him by black theologians, save a few (e.g., Martin Luther King, Jr., and Latta Thomas), has made Paul appear to be, in the life and thought of black people, a back number, a byword, and a derision. So I suppose one of the things that is being attempted here is the task of redeeming Paul for the sake of the black church and black theologians. I hope I am successful. However, as I think soberly, the apostle needs no vindication; the liberator needs no liberation. If he is allowed to speak for himself, he will prove himself to be the great advocate and field general of Christian liberation. And so, in the final analysis, I have tried to allow Paul to speak for himself. In all of my strivings, this is what I have attempted to do. My hope is that I have been faithful to this task.

There are many people I must thank for their assistance in the initiation, preparation, and completion of this work. First of all, I must extend special thanks to Dr. Leander Keck for inspiring me to embrace the apostle Paul and for guiding me over a very rigorous but fruitful path. I am indebted to Dr. Kelly Miller Smith who, although disagreeing with me and my position on Paul's position on liberation, encouraged me to press on and even aided me greatly in the publication of this book. My gratitude is extended to Mr. Van Wilson for assisting me in sharpening my historical perspective in the chapter "The Great Reversal." I am grateful to Ms. Brenda J. Holland for reading and editing portions of the manuscript and to members of the Christian Education Department of the Sunday School Publishing Board for typing parts of the manuscript and tending to other very important clerical tasks. I am deeply appreciative of the members of Westwood Baptist Church, University Center, for bearing with me through the many months spent in the preparation of this work.

There are no words or verbal expressions worthy enough to express my indebtedness to my wife Grace for her understanding and for the many days, weeks, and months she sacrificed so that I might spend time in my study to pour out my thoughts onto paper. Finally, I wish to thank Reverend Harold Twiss, General Manager of Judson Press, for bearing with me through the many revisions and delays in the preparation of the manuscript and for his invaluable assistance. It is my hope that this work will make some contribution to those who, like myself, struggle to be free someday.

Amos Jones, Jr.
Nashville, Tennessee
April, 1983

1

Introduction

The New Testament of the Christian Bible is a tremendous set of documents. It is to the credit of the grace of God working through consecrated people that such a body of literature could be forged and canonized to withstand the flame and flood of trials through the ages. With remarkable genius, the early church culled out the excess and caught the essence of the theological and historical meaning of Jesus. Remarkably enough and surely because it must have been in the providence of God, what we know as the New Testament corpus has lasted to this day.

Freedom is outstanding among the theological motifs of the New Testament. Prodigiously encouched with the New Testament, the theology of freedom has endured the onslaught of ages of biblical tampering and scientific surgery. Neither the Dark Ages, the Age of Reason, nor the Space Age has diminished or altered the New Testament's attempt to offer persons the precious boon of freedom in Christ. In this discussion, we are interested in the freedom for which Christ sets us free.

The esteemed New Testament theologian of the Bultmannian

school, Ernst Käsemann, has recorded some telling words regarding the New Testament and freedom. He says, ''I see the whole of the New Testament as involving the cause of Christian freedom. . . .''[1] ''Freedom has become the real and the sole mark of the Christian and the church.''[2] For Käsemann, ''Jesus'' means ''freedom.'' Using the texts from Matthew to Revelation, Käsemann argues that the early church understood Jesus in terms of freedom: freedom not only from moral and spiritual sin, but freedom also from political and social oppression. So whether sin is understood to be moral bondage or political and social oppression, the message of the New Testament, according to Käsemann, is that ''Jesus'' means ''freedom.''

Wrestling with a Theology to Glean Freedom

Nowhere in the New Testament is the theological motif of freedom so vividly pronounced as it is in the theology of the apostle Paul. The theological motif of freedom is treated far more extensively in the writings of Paul than in any of the other writings in the New Testament. (The term for ''freedom,'' *eleutheria,* appears more than fifteen times in the writings of Paul, more than twice as many times as in the rest of the New Testament.) In effect, in order to deal with the theological motif of freedom as it appears in the New Testament, one is driven of necessity to deal with Paul, in whose work the preponderance of references to freedom is made.[3] Whether one is seeking theological answers for the question of freedom from sin, law, social or political bondage, or freedom from death, one must come to grips with the theology of Paul. When we wrestle with Paul's theology[4] of freedom, we discover that, in a very real and astounding sense, he provides for us today a road map which, if seriously considered and properly followed, could set the Christian church and the nation of America back on the road to freedom.

Paul's theology of freedom does not come down to us as an innocuous and untried theory; it comes out of the crucible of the apostle's struggles and anguish of both soul and body. The freedom Paul discovered in Christ's Spirit and Word gave him courage and power to stand, not only against religious authorities in

Jerusalem but also against principalities and powers. Likewise this freedom gave Paul the power to wrestle with the "beasts at Ephesus" (1 Corinthians 15:32), a reference to Roman soldiers who were so designated by the early church. An example of this is a similar incident, referred to by Ignatius of Antioch: "From Syria to Rome I am fighting with wild beasts, by land and sea, by night and day, bound to ten 'leopards' (that is a company of soldiers), and they become worse for kind treatment." (See Ignatius, *To the Romans,* V, 1.) Paul was truly free. So the road to Christian freedom as it comes from Paul the Apostle is one that was tried and proven to be functional and effective. The dust of indifference has not covered it beyond recognition; the storms of heresies and the quakes of theological controversies have neither destroyed nor washed away the road. The Way still stands. The strategies that Paul left to guide the Christians who would come after him along the road to freedom are yet etched on the pages of the Holy Bible.

Wandering Off into Bondage

How then, in such an ostensibly free nation as America, are black people and so many of the peoples within its coasts found sidetracked from the road to freedom and wandering about in their own wilderness of bondage? The answer may be found in our violation of a descriptive prohibition from the Proverbs of antiquity.

> Remove not the ancient landmark
> which your fathers have set.
> –Proverbs 22:28.

The ancient landmark has reference to the Law (the covenant) that Yahweh made with Israel; this was the medium to freedom for the ancient Hebrews. The salvation history *(Heilsgeschichte)* of the Hebrews is marked by the oscillating movement of rendezvous and rebellion. There were times when the Hebrews had a rendezvous with Yahweh and rallied around the landmark of God's covenant. These were times when Israel enjoyed tremendous freedom, peace, and prosperity. But there were periods in history when the pendulum swung in the opposite direction; in rebellion, the Israelites turned away from the landmark. With the landmark removed and nothing to guide them along the road, the Hebrews found themselves in the throes of idolatry. Weakened by their worship of idols, and wandering aimlessly in a waste and howling wilderness, they became prime candidates for bondage. Deep from the chambers of bondage, Israel cried:

> By the waters of Babylon, there we sat down and wept,
>   when we remembered Zion.
> On the willows there
>   we hung up our lyres.
> For there our captors
>   required of us songs,
> and our tormentors, mirth, saying,
>   "Sing us one of the songs of Zion!"
>
> How shall we sing the Lord's song in a foreign land?
> —Psalm 137:1-4

All this because the ancient landmark had been removed!

The embodiment of God's covenant appeared on the stage of history in Jesus. He established for all time the landmark of freedom:

> "The Spirit of the Lord is upon me
> because he has anointed me to preach good news to the poor.
> He has sent me to proclaim release to the captives
> and recovering of sight to the blind,
> to set at liberty those who are oppressed,
> to proclaim the acceptable year of the Lord."
> —Luke 4:18-19

Jesus' proclamation was that the truth which he brought to the world was sufficient to make men free (see John 8:32). The freedom that Jesus made available to men was irrevocable: "So if the Son makes you free, you will be free indeed" (John 8:36).

Jesus' coming into the world was God's initiative to establish once again and for all time the landmark of freedom. It is the writings of the apostle Paul, written long before any of the Four Gospels or any of the other writings of the New Testament,[5] which capture the meaning and method of the theological landmark of freedom that Jesus established. Centuries of inquiry and testing have proven that Paul accurately captured the meaning of ''Jesus'' as it relates to Christian freedom; and there is no question as to the clarity of Paul's statement regarding the freedom for which Christ has set us free. Thus, the conclusion must be drawn that either the landmark has been removed or America and blacks and others of America's people have wandered from the landmark of freedom. Both America and its people are experiencing their own kind of peculiar bondage, the kind which is at once invisible but vicious.

Examples of bondage in our society are almost too numerous to mention; but mention some we must. The Watergate fiasco was an indicator of the still prevailing bondage to the quest for political power. Movies, television, burgeoning peep shows, and adult movie houses all serve notice of a society in bondage to sex and violence. But possibly the most venal and vicious of all is the bondage experienced in America today by blacks.

Before he was assassinated in Memphis, Tennessee, on April 4, 1968, Martin Luther King, Jr., wrote his final work that placed before America the fundamental question *Where Do We Go from Here: Chaos or Community?* He asked the question, Will it be freedom and first-class citizenship for black people and peace and community for America, or will it be chaos for all? In that work, he graphically described the disparity between the Negro American and the white counterpart. He set forth some noble goals and lofty objectives in education, housing, rights, and employment, which should be sought by America in order to bring about community among its people, both black and white.[6]

When one measures the progress that has been made toward community, in the sense that Martin Luther King, Jr., understood it more than fifteen years ago, the conclusion must be drawn that we have not moved toward community but away from it and toward chaos. There is a move to make more certain, though subtle, the bondage of black people. The Supreme Court ruling in the Bakke case indicates an erosion in the sentiment that, inasmuch as America has done much to keep black people down, it must now do much to raise them up. Black peoples' stride toward freedom has been reduced to a crawl by soaring inflation and towering unemployment. Smug indifference among educators in public schools has driven to staggering proportions the number of dropouts and "push-outs" among black youth. Many see mandatory literacy tests as mechanisms to single out black youth as hopelessly ignorant. So though the times have changed, the chaotic conditions that sparked riots in Watts, Detroit, Newark, and Memphis in the sixties still remain; black people are now even more in a bondage that is both venal and vicious. The examples of people in bondage in America could go on and on, e.g., the Indians, the Mexican Americans.

How Responsible Is Paul for This Bondage?

What is the answer to this question of bondage in American society? Does Paul's understanding of Christian freedom provide that answer? Many people think not. This is the case with many theologians, many blacks, and many women.

Many contemporary theologians consider Paul to be an enigma. His theological value for liberation seems to elude them. In a theologically witty way, Wayne A. Meeks has styled Paul as the Christian Proteus, a term from Homer's *Odyssey*. Proteus, a sea god, had the uncanny ability of changing forms at will and escaping the grasp of his would-be captors. Similarly, Meeks's argument is that Paul has eluded the grasp of contemporary theologians. He says of Paul, "There is no figure in the first generation of Christianity about whom we know so much as about Paul—and precisely at the points where he reveals most about himself we are most puzzled."[7]

Theologians of the 1960s and Karl Barth and Dietrich Bonhoeffer before them tried to corner Paul as a secular theologian. Rudolf Bultmann saw him as the prime demythologizer of the New Testament. Joseph Fletcher attempted to paint the apostle into the corner of situation ethics. Jewish scholars charged Paul with being a traitor, a corruptor of the Law and covenant, and first in the line of Christian anti-Semitists. And of course, Albert Schweitzer was convinced that Paul was a mystic. In these contemporary theologians' attempts to capture and categorize Paul, it seems that his theme of liberation—particularly liberation from the kinds of bondage we face today—escapes them. For them, Paul remains an enigma.

Rather than be the solution to the problem of bondage for blacks, Paul for them has been the problem. For this, Paul has been anathematized by blacks. Black theologians, for example, malign Paul and treat him roughly for what seems to be his endorsement of the institution of slavery. Therefore, they say, Paul is culpable of contributing to and righteously sanctioning the vitriolic suffering that black people endured under the lash of the white oppressor in America.

Interestingly enough, blacks in American slavery, though pitifully but understandably illiterate because of the strong prohibitions placed upon them by the white oppressor, discovered forceful themes of liberation in the Old Testament and New Testament; but they did not find these themes in Paul's writings. In fact, it seemed that the writings of Paul, and certainly those alleged to be written by him by the white preacher and the white oppressor, gave sainted approval to the heinous bondage in which they found themselves. For this reason, black slaves in America vowed never to read the part of the Bible that contained the writings of Paul, and they held the apostle in righteous contempt. The grandmother of Howard Thurman is a good example. It was the writings of Paul that were referred to her by white preachers as biblical evidence that justified the rightness of slavery. Born in slavery, she vowed never to read that part of the Bible which contained the writings of Paul (with the exception of 1 Corinthians 13).[8]

Even when the slave chains were broken, black religious thinkers found it difficult to deal with Paul because of the opprobrious odium that had been placed on him by past generations of blacks.[9] As recently as the late 1960s, Paul has been held culpable by black theologians of making the burden of bondage heavier for black people. James H. Cone and Albert B. Cleage, Jr., have anathematized the apostle to the point of writing him off.[10]

The problem with this, however, is that Paul is accused of things for which he is not guilty. In all probability, the anathematization of Paul by blacks could very well be because of their inadvertent misreading of his writings, caused by their failure to wrestle with the man's theological thought or simply their acceptance of biblical statements alleged by others to be from Paul (when in all likelihood they are not from him at all). But more than this, blacks have failed to take seriously the flagrant misuse of Paul's writings and certainly those attributed to him by the white church to make a stronger case for slavery.[11]

The problem women have had with Paul is similar to that which black people have. Although women today are trying to find some usefulness in the apostle's theology regarding themselves,[12] for the most part they anathematize him for his seeming consignment of them to silence in the church. However, the problem could very well be that the church has failed to solve the problem of what Paul said and what he did not say about women and their liberated condition in the church. Because certain writings have been assigned to Paul's hand, writings whose Pauline authorship is questionable, there is no sharpness as to what he actually said about women in the church.

So the three examples cited, viz., Paul the theological enigma, Paul the problem for blacks, and Paul the problem for women, point up the virtual certainty that there is hardly any positive feeling, at least among some theologians, blacks, and women, that Paul provides an answer to the question of bondage in American society. At best he is an enigma to some and an anathema to others.

How Some Misread Paul's Vulnerability

The point of the foregoing argument could be taken another step: that Paul has not much to offer for the cause of liberation because of his vulnerability. This probably is the position of many black theologians and black people as a whole. For them understandably it could be said that if Paul is so vague on his position regarding slavery, then he has made himself vulnerable and subject to being misused and is therefore suspect (the discussion of Paul's position on slavery will be more fully discussed in chapter 2).

Overemphasizing the State

The same could be said about Paul's position regarding the Christian's attitude toward the state (Romans 13:1). Because it seems that Paul is vague and thus vulnerable on the Christian's attitude toward the state, there has arisen a tremendous and frightening spirit of patriotism in America. It is a kind of blind patriotism that is expounded by white, Anglo Saxon Protestants to the exclusion of all others. The extreme of this is seen in the rising conservatism in this country and the flurry of Ku Klux Klan activity across the land. It is not beyond imagination to conclude that this rising spirit of panting patriotism has been the result of truth spoken by Paul but twisted by knaves.

Also, the seeming vulnerability of Paul regarding his position on the state could very well be the reason for the American government renouncing the role of servant and assuming the role of master and lord. This fact has been the concern of many theologians and scholars, and for no small reason, for there has arisen in prodigious proportions a rival religion to Christianity, the religion of nationalism.[13] This phenomenon has grown to such proportions that during the presidency of Richard M. Nixon, the nation had on its hands its first imperial president.[14] Such a quest for religious as well as political supremacy led to startling and flagrant criminal acts by men such as Charles Colson, John Dean, John Mitchell, and Jeb Stuart Magruder—who for his part in the Watergate fiasco said he "lost his ethical compass."[15] Theologically speaking, it is inconceivable that such a bizarre politico-religious development could have happened, deliberately or not, without a misreading or misunderstanding of Paul's position on the state. So it could be that because of Paul's seeming vulnerability regarding the Christian attitude toward the state, many have brushed him aside.

However, the problem seems not to be with Paul at all but

with those who have interpreted him or who have failed to interpret him correctly. It is probably true to say that the church has failed to speak a clear word on Paul's true attitude toward the state. The failure of this is attributed to the church's failure to allow Paul to speak from the deeper meaning of Romans 13:1ff. as well as 1 Corinthians 6:1ff.

Abandoning Biblical Law

As has possibly been the case with Paul's position on the state, it is possible also that the age of permissiveness that has riddled our society for more than a decade could be attributed to what seemed to be Paul's relaxation of the legal code, i.e., the Law of the Old Testament. Paul's attitude toward the Law rendered him once again no less than vulnerable.

This misunderstanding of what Paul was doing with the Law caused serious problems with the Corinthians. Not understanding Paul's theological system of freedom from bondage but bondage in freedom, the Corinthians took Pauline freedom to mean freedom without responsibility, freedom without limits. Thus, the Corinthians became engaged in indiscriminate sexual activities, inordinate eating habits, and all sorts of opulent excess (this is what the Corinthians thought it meant to be free from the Law and to be in the Spirit). As a result, marriage vows were reprehensibly violated and the family structure was woefully weakened.

In the past decade in America we have seen similar indiscriminate sexual activity (inordinate and opulent excess, i.e., permissiveness in all of its definitions). Could this be because of a serious misreading and misinterpretation of a seemingly vulnerable Paul and his treatment of the Law of the Old Testament, vis-á-vis Christian freedom? The fact that the church has not clearly and forcefully spoken, more precisely, has not allowed Paul to be heard on the question at hand, could very well be the reason for the blatant misreading and misinterpretation and thus violation of Pauline ethics.

As has been alluded to, Paul was misread, misinterpreted, and misunderstood by those to whom he wrote, the Corinthians, among others. Such misreading and misinterpretation could be attributed to Paul's vulnerability. Because he had been misunderstood (deliberately so?), he was moved to write again several times to the Corinthians to make certain he was understood. The fact that the deutero-Pauline letters, or epistles from the Pauline school, address themselves more elaborately to many of the issues to which Paul addressed himself in his letters, viz., church structure, immorality, slavery, structure, and responsibility of the family, makes it apparent that related problems existed in the church and society long after Paul, and indications are that many had taken what Paul had said and twisted it to suit their own selfish purpose:

> So also our beloved brother Paul wrote to you according to the wisdom given him, speaking of this as he does in all his letters. There are some things in them hard to understand, which the ignorant and unstable twist to their own destruction, as they do the other scriptures (2 Peter 3:15-17).

There was, therefore, the need to make plain once again the position of Paul regarding those areas in which he seemed vulnerable and had deliberately been misunderstood. The twisting of what Paul has said regarding Christian freedom and ethical living has not ceased since the days of old. It now becomes the church's task, however, to try and set things right. It is an inescapable task and is what this present work is about.

Neglecting Service to the World

Finally, the last area, which we shall cite at this juncture, in which Paul seems vulnerable is his understanding of the resurrection, or his eschatology. Again the Corinthians defied and violated Paul's cross-resurrection theological continuum; i.e., they accepted for themselves only one side of Paul's theology, namely, his theology of the resurrection, and they accepted that according to their own understanding and liking. They carved out for themselves a "theology of glory," vis-á-vis a theology of the cross. In their minds, they had experienced the "already" of the resurrection. They were already perfect (cf. 1 Corinthians 4:8-10). There was, therefore, no reason for them to be concerned with the welfare of their brother or the conditions of the society about them.[16] Their enthusiasm for the resurrection made them believe that they had already overcome the world and therefore had no responsibility to do anything about the wrong that was yet in the world; they had the Spirit.

Already I have tipped my hand as to why the Corinthians were characterized by a theology of glory over against a theology of the cross; they made the deliberate choice of selecting the one while rejecting the other, an indication of Paul's vulnerability. A similar deliberate choice has been made by a large segment of the contemporary church. The 700 Club and the Praise The Lord Club (PTL) and many others in this vein have brushed aside Paul's theology of the cross and all of its rigors and responsibilities in this world and have hewn out for themselves a theology of glory. "Heaven" is the only thing in which they are interested. They build riches and kingdoms on earth while pointing people by means of the electronic media of television to the "rapture" of eternal life. There is no concern for the social vexations and political problems that shackle thousands in our society. Theirs is a kind of *de nova* religious opiate that lulls the people to sleep while the proverbial Rome burns.

To accept deliberately Paul's theology of the resurrection, or his eschatology, while rejecting his theology of the cross (a *theologia gloria* vis-á-vis a *theologia cruxis*) would be a grotesque violation altogether of Paul's theology. Moreover, to interpret Paul's theology of the resurrection, his eschatology, in such a way as to excuse people from responsible living in this world is even more a flagrant violation of the apostle's theology. To be sure, Paul is not the easiest to understand among the writers of the New Testament, and some of his statements on eschatology could easily be understood to mean resignation from social responsibility in the world. The following passage is a case in point.

> I mean, brethren, the appointed time has grown very short; from now on, let those who have wives live as though they had none, and those who mourn as though they were not mourning, and those who rejoice as though they were not rejoicing, and those who buy as though they had no goods, and those who deal with the world as though they had no dealings with it. For the form of this world is passing away (1 Corinthians 7:29-31).

This passage could very well be interpreted to mean resignation from social responsibility in the world. Such an interpretation could have been at work when Jim Jones led more than nine hundred members of his Peoples Temple Cult to commit suicide in the Guyanese commune of Jonestown in South America. But to read Paul in this way would be the result of a superficial understanding of his theology of the resurrection. One would be culpable of not wrestling with the man in order to grasp the deeper meaning of his eschatology.

One cannot read Paul's powerful statement, "What do I gain if, humanly speaking, I fought with beasts at Ephesus? If the dead are not raised. . . ." (1 Corinthians 15:32) without recognizing that the statement appears in his discussion of the resurrection of Jesus Christ and the resurrection of those who die in Christ, i.e., in the context of his eschatology. When one comes to understand the radicality of Paul's understanding of the resurrection and his eschatology, one is drawn away from resignation-in-waiting for another and nebulous world (the rapture of heaven) and is drawn to social responsibility and conflict with the evils of this world. This understanding of the resurrection and Pauline eschatology is powerfully expressed by Jürgen Moltmann:

> To believe means to cross in hope and anticipation the bounds that have been penetrated by the raising of the crucified. If we bear that in mind, then this faith can have nothing to do with fleeing the world, with resignation and with escapism.[17]

He continues:

> Peace with God means conflict with the world, for the goad of the promised future stabs inexorably into the flesh of every unfulfilled present.[18]

How Others Rediscover His Radicalism

It should be rather clear now that Paul provides for us a road map back to the landmark of freedom. History belies any notion that Paul has been ineffective for the cause of freedom. A careful perusal of history will disclose not only that Paul came through as a dynamic revolutionary for freedom in his own world but also that he has provided the theological matrix upon which the church through the centuries could build a dynamic revolutionary movement for freedom. The fact is, the greatest revolutionary moments in the history of the Christian church have been those moments when Paul's theology of freedom has been rediscovered and has been permitted to come alive. In his book *Paul* Günther Bornkamm makes what could be called a classic statement that lends itself to the point:

> It is . . . true . . . that the great moments in the church's history and the revolutions which have been of benefit to her have always taken place at times when Paul's gospel again burst forth like a supposedly extinct volcano. . . . The powerful, revolutionary influence of his person and theology can best be seen in their effects on other figures and movements in church history. One cannot conceive of Augustine's theology apart from his rediscovery of Paul, and the same is particularly true of the breakthrough to new insights on the part of Luther and Calvin at the Reformation and, centuries later, of John Wesley's movement in England. Finally, we have also to remember that the so-called dialectic theology, without which the church's struggle against the deranged heresies of national socialism is unthinkable, stemmed from Karl Barth's rousing new exposition of Romans.[19]

The thought Bornkamm sets forth here can be carried further. When one reads the *Ethics* of the German martyr Dietrich Bonhoeffer, the conclusion easily can be drawn that his influence came, to a large degree, from his understanding and use of Paul. Martin Luther King, Jr.'s fondness and use of letter writing (*Letter from the Birmingham Jail,* for example) and his keen insight and use of eschatology could very easily be traced to his appropriation of Paul. The rebellion of the sixties by angry blacks in this country produced more than smoke and flaming cities; it produced a revival of interest of cosmic dimensions in Pauline freedom by such theologians as Bornkamm, Käsemann, Moltmann, and others. These Continental theologians brought forth a theology that resonated with neo-Pauline understanding of terms such as freedom, love, peace, justice, and hope.

It is this same Paul, who is an enigma to some, an anathema to others, and vulnerable to still others, whom we are trying to rediscover as one to lead us back to the landmark of freedom. If it is true that, as Bornkamm has said, ". . . the great moments in the church's history" have been those moments when Paul's theology has "... burst forth like a supposedly extinct volcano," and if it is true that Karl Barth and, more recently, post-Bultmannian theologians, such as Käsemann, Bornkamm, Moltmann, have through the medium of serious biblical study found relevance in Pauline theology for such terms as freedom, love, peace, justice, and hope, why can we not find the same in Paul today for the sake of the freedom for which Christ has set us free? It is this rediscovery that this discussion is pursuing.

The following five chapters will enlarge upon the thesis that Paul provides the theological road map that could lead us back to the landmark of Christian freedom for which we are in passionate pursuit. The second chapter will deal with claiming the freedom for which Christ has set us free. The argument will emerge out of the matrix of my understanding of 1 Corinthians 7:20-24, an understanding shaped by the process of exegesis. The third chapter will deal with the great reversal from the freedom for which Christ has set us free. It will be a treatment of Galatians 1:6-7 and explore how the Galatians strayed from the freedom experienced in Christ. We will try to learn from this discussion how black people in particular (and where the opportunity presents itself, we will try to deal with how this reversal impinges on Americans in general) have wandered from the freedom for which Christ has set them free. The fourth chapter will discuss the discipline that is needed for the long road to freedom (an exegesis of 1 Corinthians 9:24-27). The fifth chapter will be devoted to the body of Christ and to its unity as a factor of Christian freedom. The focus will be an exegetical treatment of 1 Corinthians 12:14-26. The sixth chapter will ponder the importance of economic independence within the free Christian community as the idea comes to us from 1 Thessalonians 4:9-12. The final chapter will be a summary of all that has gone before with the intention of extrapolating the gleanings into broader areas of bondage and freedom in American culture.

As a black theologian, because I am approaching Paul from a black point of view with an interest in what he might say to the black situation in America, it is understandable that this work would appear more oriented to black people and black peoples' interest in liberation. But in addition to this, I feel that whatever Paul says regarding liberation, he says not only to blacks but to all who are wandering in the wilderness of bondage, e.g., women, homosexuals, Indians, Mexican Americans, Puerto Ricans, and poor whites.

Although I will not make extensive use of every letter of the Pauline corpus, I consider the corpus to consist of Romans, First and Second Corinthians, Galatians, Philippians, First Thessalonians, and Philemon.

2

Claim Your Freedom

To speak of freedom in today's society seems that one speaks of a given, of something that has been accomplished. The era of Martin Luther King, Jr., brought about great strides toward freedom. Black people in America now seem to be enjoying a liberty that is unprecedented in all the years of their sojourn in this country. The spirit of freedom pervades the land as a result of the civil rights era. Women are free. Gay people are free. Everyone is free.

The Illusion of Freedom

Is this freedom as real as it appears? This is a prevailing question of our day. Strong suspicions are that the answer to the question is less than affirmative.

Economic, educational, employment, and other disparities of life in America make it evident that blacks are a long way from the promised land of freedom of which Martin Luther King, Jr., dreamed. Increasing sexual exploitation marks the absence of freedom and the presence of bondage for women. Gay people still are aware that it is an anathema to announce their gayness publicly. Freedom in America is not as free as it appears. Even those who seem to be free are ensnared by a peculiar kind of bondage: bondage to narcissism, money, quest for power, fear of sickness, and fear of death. Cultists who have sought communes across America have discovered that their newfound freedom is really bondage to the will and whim of another. Bondage transcends national and continental boundaries. The blatant reality of this is demonstrated in South Africa, which employs the incarcerating system of apartheid; the Moslem world, which excludes women; India, which employs the caste system; Ireland and its religious oppression; and Russia with its political oppression.

Freedom is evasive; it is an illusion. There still stands before the children of bondage the pressing assignment to claim their freedom.

The exhortation for persons to claim their freedom is preponderant in the New Testament of the Judeo-Christian faith. Especially is it profoundly and provocatively set forth in the writings of the apostle Paul. Nestled within the corpus of his first letter to the Corinthians, as if it were an exploding bombshell, is the exhortation to the slave to claim freedom in Jesus Christ. First Corinthians 7:20-24 is the locus of this provocative and challenging passage, and it is the one with which we will shortly deal.

What was Paul's concern with freedom and slavery? And why was he so obssessed with the notion of freedom in Christ? Just a few years before Paul wrote First Corinthians, Caesar Augustus had instituted his Golden Age, the *pax romana*. For the mere investment of their allegiance to Caesar and the Roman state, every citizen and subject was guaranteed freedom. Each was guaranteed protection by the Roman army and the conveniences of the Roman state. So why was there a need for Paul to talk about freedom? Because the Roman guaranteed freedom was not as free as it appeared. In fact, there was a grave and insidious presence of human bondage in that society. Freedom á la the Roman Empire was, in a very real sense, bondage—bondage to the *kaiser kultus* (Caesar worship), social custom, racial and religious prejudice, and lust for luxury. Slavery was one of the sickening realities that stood in the midst of Caesar Augustus' Golden Age. It was a reality with which Paul had to deal. And deal with it he did.

Corinth: A City of Illusive Freedom

Corinth was a city in which the illusion of freedom was very present. The city was totally destroyed in 146 B.C. by the Roman general Mummius but was rebuilt by Julius Caesar in 44 B.C. as a Roman colony. Later, Emperor Augustus made it the capital of the great Roman province of Achaea. The geographical layout of Corinth made it one of the prominent trade centers of its time. It lay between the Aegean and the Adriatic Seas. Merchandise from distant lands came into its ports. The city also was a center of industry and banking. As a new and bustling city, it drew hundreds of thousands of tourists, and thousands settled there to make it their home. Romans, Jews, and freedmen went there to live. Also hundreds of thousands of slaves were carried there aboard the many slave ships that landed in its ports. It is estimated that there were as many as 500,000 slaves in Corinth during the time Paul was there. It is understandable that the problem of slavery was crucial in the Corinthian letter, for there was bondage of a very real sort in this thriving industrial port city.

In this thriving city, there were other kinds of bondage; there was bondage to idolatry, fun and games, and luxury. The Isthmian Games were extremely popular and were financed heavily from the city's treasury. These were held every two years in honor of Poseidon, the god of the sea. Every four years the Olympic Games were held in honor of Zeus. These games drew thousands of athletes, sportsmen, and musicians from Corinth and abroad. So in the name of fun and games, tens of thousands were unconsciously enslaved to idolatrous worship. Corinth was in bondage to profligacy. In the name of fun and games, tens of thousands gathered at the temple of the goddess Artemis where a brothel of one thousand prostitutes waited upon the pious worshipers of the goddess. In Corinth, profligacy was a way of life. For the worship of idols, the devotees were granted free license to live the lowest of moral life. "Religion" was a cryptic code word to bless the life of levity and miasmic profligacy that gripped Corinthian culture with enslaving proportions. "To live like a Corinthian" *(Korinthiazesthai)* was the description of the gross immorality that ensnared those who lived in and visited Corinth. The city was much like the port cities of our nation, Miami, New York, New Orleans, San Francisco, and others. It was a city in which freedom seemed real and vibrant but, in fact, was a myth; and, it was one of the cities into which Paul went with unbridled audacity, carrying the message of freedom in Christ and establishing a church.

Modern Mixed Reactions About Pauline Freedom

Bondage in its many varieties is the sickening reality that stands in the midst of the myth of freedom in America. Therefore, it would seem valuable for us to reexamine the early church's most articulate writer and his attitude toward bondage and the remedy of freedom in Christ as it is discussed in the First Letter of Paul to the Corinthians. Slavery in New Testament times could very well be a paradigm of the many and varied kinds of bondage faced by many in our society, especially blacks and other minorities. The apostle Paul's exhortation for the Christian to claim freedom in Christ could be the key that opens the door to our house of bondage and leads us to the broad land of freedom and the Promised Land for which especially the Ebony Children of thralldom and others have so long strived.

However, one is ever conscious of the risks that are taken when the thesis is posited that Paul the apostle is an advocate for freedom. Women and minorities have had serious problems with Paul. Especially has this been true of blacks. Albert B. Cleage, Jr., insisted that Paul's deemphasis of the nation concept, which was promulgated and propagated by the black nation Israel and Jesus the black messiah, and Paul's emphasis of individualism provided the theological matrix for white preachers to justify the enslavement of the native sons and daughters of Africa.[1] James H. Cone thought Paul to be so vulnerable on the subject of slavery that he advocated that the apostle to the Gentiles be avoided at all costs; after all, he stated, Paul did acquiesce to slavery by instructing slaves to be obedient to their masters.[2]

What black theologians, black people, women, and others have failed to realize, it seems, is that we are dealing with a Paul who has been misrepresented, corrupted, perverted, and misused by the white church of the pre-Civil War era in America and, to a large degree, by the white church of today. The white church took from the deutero-Pauline writings (i.e., those letters not in the corpus: Ephesians, Colossians, and the Pastoral Epistles) the quasi-proslavery statement "Slaves, be obedient to your masters" (or its variant) and gave religious sanction and political legitimation to the peculiar institution of slavery in the name of Paul, although he neither wrote nor spoke those words. Whether knowingly or unknowingly, white preachers and the white church took those statements relating to slavery—albeit, taken completely out of the context in which they appear in these deutero-Pauline writings—and proceeded to pour holy water on the process of incarcerating the bodies and souls of black folk. They made it religiously right to dehumanize, ostracize, castrate, and kill those pitiable Ebony Children of Africa in order to feed their philosophy of racial superiority and sate their hunger for economic opulence.

So what we have today is a Paul who is trapped. On the one hand he is misrepresented, perverted, corrupted, and misused by the white church to perpetuate institutional racism. On the other hand black theologians castigate and disparage Paul for his seeming proslavery position. Women dismiss him for his seeming position of consigning the female to silence in the church. Whites have yet to admit their sin of willful misinterpretation. Blacks and women have yet to liberate the liberator. They have yet to wrestle with the man to find in him strong themes of liberation; they simply think of him as an unfortunate incident in the course of theological history, an opprobrious odium that hangs about the neck of the church. I think, however, that Paul offers something viable and dynamic in his understanding of Christian freedom, something powerful enough to destroy the idea and institution of slavery and every vestige of bondage. In their place he offers freedom in Christ in all of its dimensions.

An Examination of Paul's Statement About Slavery

In order to try to prove such a hypothesis, I will proceed by seriously considering the statement Paul makes regarding slavery and freedom, which is found in 1 Corinthians 7:20-24. It is my hope that from inquiring into the passage at hand I will be able to present a perspective on Paul yet to be seen by most black theologians, many women, and minorities or admitted by many white theologians as it relates to Paul on slavery and freedom—a perspective that would show Paul to be a rather militant opponent of slavery and an aggressive advocate of freedom.

For the interpretation of 1 Corinthians 7:20-24, I have chosen the commentaries of Frederic Godet, C. K. Barrett, and Hans Conzelmann.[3] These three commentaries represent different points of view on the passage in question. Godet's commentary represents a conservative point of view of nineteenth-century Swiss Protestant theology; Barrett's work is representative of rather conservative British theology, while Conzelmann's commentary represents a rather liberal Bultmannian–post-Bultmannian Protestant theology from Germany. Whenever it is necessary and possible, we will utilize other New Testament commentaries and tools pertinent to the text so that we may gain a more lucid view of Paul's understanding of slavery and Christian freedom.

First Corinthians was written by Paul sometime during the first half of the fifties A.D. From the reference to Ephesus in 1 Corinthians 16:8, it has been suggested that the letter was written there during the so-called third missionary journey.[4] The authenticity of the letter is generally accepted by New Testament scholarship, although the integrity of First Corinthians has been called into question.[5] But with the postulation that First Corinthians contains at least two interpolations (viz., 1 Corinthians 1:2b and 14:33b-35), sudden transitions, and discontinuity of thought, it could be concluded that First Corinthians maintains its integrity as a genuine Pauline letter. Thematically, the letter addresses itself to the theological importance of Christian freedom and unity in the church.

Opinions on the divisions of the letter are somewhat mixed. There seems to be common agreement that 1 Corinthians 1:1-9 constitutes the preface to the letter (verses 1 to 3 give the opening address and verses 4 to 9 are the thanksgiving). I conclude that there are two main sections in the letter. The first is 1 Corinthians

1:10–6:20, which I suggest deals with crises and divisions within the church. The second section is 1 Corinthians 7:1–16:24, which, in a general sense, contains Paul's instructions to the church.

First Corinthians 7:20-24 falls within the categorical limits of the second main section of the letter. Actually, it is part and parcel of the block of material that runs from verse 17 to verse 24 in chapter 7. First Corinthians 7:17-24 has been categorically described as "The Life Which the Lord Has Assigned."[6] The prevailing theme conforms with that of the second main section of the letter, i.e., Christian freedom, though it could be said that this theme has no specific point of beginning or ending in the letter. (Other chapters could be said to touch on freedom in some way, e.g., chapter 5 deals with the misuse of Christian freedom and chapter 6 with the failure to perceive Christian freedom. Also, it could be argued that chapters 2 and 4 contain discussions of Christian freedom [e.g., 1 Corinthians 2:15; 4:3].)

The foregoing verses in chapter 7 are a discussion of sexual freedom (cf. 1 Corinthians 7:1-18). Verses 17 through 19 of the block of material with which we are interested deal with the discussion of circumcision; they are Paul's answer to the Corinthians' question of whether they should be circumcised or attempt to remove the marks of circumcision. But the discussion of circumcision breaks off at verse 19, and Paul takes up the subject of slavery and freedom in verses 20 to 23. The block of material closes with the paraenesis in verse 24: "So, brethren, in whatever state each was called, there let him remain with God." Chapter 7 closes (verses 25-40) with Paul's instructions to the unmarried and married constituents of the Corinthian church.

Before we go much further, there is a need to say a word about the general problem Paul faced in the Corinthian church, a church that he had established prior to writing this letter. The occasion for the First Letter of Paul to the Corinthians seems to be described in 1 Corinthians 1:10-11 (see also 1 Corinthians 11:18); there were dissensions and divisions. The problem, which seems to have been conveyed to Paul in several letters (cf. 1 Corinthians 1:11), may have been created by Gnostic elements within the Corinthian church. These were people who held that *gnosis*

(knowledge) was the highest of values and who claimed possession of the Spirit *(pneumatikoi);* from their belief that they possessed *gnosis* and the Spirit, the Gnostics concluded that they
were free to yield their bodies, albeit immorally, to anything they
wished without reprisal. They engaged in intercourse with prostitutes (1 Corinthians 6:13-20), took part in sacrificing offerings
to idols (1 Corinthians 8:1ff.; 10:23ff.), and even lived immorally
with relatives (cf. 1 Corinthians 5:1ff). Their possession of the
Spirit led them to deny the future resurrection (1 Corinthians 15).
The Jesus of history was to be cursed while a spiritual Christ
was the only significant thing for them (cf. 1 Corinthians 12:1ff.);
the cross was foolishness (1 Corinthians 1:18ff.). The Gnostics
at Corinth demonstrated their spiritual prowess by speaking in
tongues (1 Corinthians 14:1ff.), an act which proved their superiority over those who did not possess that kind of Spirit. In
the final analysis, the problem at Corinth was that of runaway
enthusiasm by Gnostic elements within the church at Corinth;
the problem was a misuse of and an abdication of Christian
freedom.

It was out of this historical, theological, and ecclesiastical
milieu that the question of slavery emerged. It is at this point
that contemporary black people, women, other minorities, and
middle-class white Americans find consonance with the people
of the Corinthian church. Thus it becomes more crucial that we
wrestle with our present-day pursuit for freedom in light of the
situation within the Corinthian church and how Paul dealt with
it. Hence it becomes our task to move ahead in pursuit of Paul's
understanding of what it meant for a slave to be a Christian in
the light of, or maybe in spite of, the existing problem in Roman
society and the city of Corinth itself.

It seems reasonable to conclude that 1 Corinthians 7:20-24 is
a definite unit of material that is intimately connected with what
goes before it and what comes after it. It serves the definite
purpose of providing insight into the question of Paul's understanding of slavery and Christian freedom. If this be the case,
we can proceed to answer this serious question. The result of
our efforts should give us a more lucid picture of Paul's under-

standing of slavery in the context of Christian freedom. If positive data can be extracted from the material at hand, that data can be used to exonerate Paul from the charge of being proslavery; but more than this, we will use that positive data to relate to the present condition of black and oppressed peoples in America in an attempt to provide a viable theological alternative for liberation.

A History of Misunderstanding and Misinterpretation

As was stated in chapter 1 of this book, Wayne A. Meeks has offered a dramatic description of the apostle Paul; he calls him "The Christian Proteus." By this it is meant that Paul has been so deceptive and elusive that he has escaped all attempts by theologians to categorize fully and systematize his thought.[7] While the soundness of this analogy might be questioned (namely because the apostle Paul is not deceptive nor does his thought and intention elude those who wrestle with him), it might be true to say that many theologians, in their attempt to categorize and systematize his thought, have not grasped all that the apostle was about, especially his position on slavery and freedom.

The problem with Paul and his writings started in the New Testament itself (cf. 2 Peter 3:15-16). The deutero-Pauline epistles of Ephesians and Colossians attempted to systematize Paul's theology (maybe the writers were Pauline students) but failed to grasp his understanding of slavery and freedom in 1 Corinthians 7:20-24. They understood Paul to be saying "Slaves, be obedient to those who are your earthly masters, with fear and trembling, in singleness of heart, as to Christ . . ." (Ephesians 6:5; cf. Colossians 3:22). In the Pastoral Epistles' attempt to systematize Pauline theology and ecclesiology (the Pastorals were written sometime during the first half of the second century A.D.), there also was a failure to grasp what the apostle to the Gentiles was saying in 1 Corinthians 7:20-24. They, too, understood Paul to be saying "Let all who are under the yoke of slavery regard their masters as worthy of all honor, so that the name of God and the teaching may not be defamed . . ." (1 Timothy 6:1-2; see also Titus 2:9-10). It is also important to note that the place of women in the church in the Pastoral Epistles is far removed from that of

Paul's understanding (cf. 1 Timothy 2:9-12, where women are relegated to silence in the church, vis-á-vis 1 Corinthians 11:5a where Paul makes a case for women prophets). The catholic epistle of First Peter reflects a similar failure to grasp Paul's understanding of slavery and Christian freedom (cf. 1 Peter 2:18ff.).

In the early history of Christian thought, the Apologists and Apostolic Fathers adopted a position on slavery that was far removed from the Pauline position and more akin to the deutero-Pauline, Pastoral, and catholic epistles schools. Clement of Alexandria, Ignatius, *The Didache,* and St. Augustine all religiously subscribed to the notion that slaves were divinely obligated to give obedience to their masters.[8] These ecclesiastical luminaries held that even if a slave held an office in the church of which his or her master was a part and the slave, while in the church, held authority over his or her master, once they were outside of the holy community, their relationship reverted back to that of master-slave. In such an arrangement, the slave was to be totally obedient to the master.

Although we run the risk of overgeneralizing and becoming utterly simplistic, it could be said that up to the time of the Reformation the church did not see the need to deal with, let alone grasp, Paul's understanding of slavery. Even when slavery was dealt with by the Reformers, the position of the deutero-Pauline epistles, the Pastorals, and the catholic epistles was amplified. John Calvin is a good example here.[9] The failure of the church to sort out Paul's genuine letters from those attributed to him caused the proslavery position of the deutero-Pauline epistles, the Pastorals, and the catholic epistles to become mixed with and attributed to be the same as the position of Paul, although Paul's position would be diametrically opposed to the subsequent positions. The result of this was the adoption of a formal position by the church that slavery enjoyed the sanction of Christianity and that becoming Christian did not alter the social status of the slave. A good example of this is the response that was given by the Anglican Bishop of London to the inquiry from American slaveholders as to the social status of the slave once he or she was baptized:

To which it may be very truly reply'd, That Christianity, and the embracing of the Gospel, does not make the least Alteration in Civil Property, or in any of the Duties which belong to Civil Relations; but in all these Respects, it continues persons just in the same State as it found them. The Freedom which Christianity gives, is a Freedom from the Bondage of Sin and Satan, and from the Dominion of Mens Lusts and Passions and inordinate Desires; but as to their *outward* Condition, whatever that was before, whether bond or free, their being baptized, and becoming Christians, makes no manner of Change in it.[10]

The deutero-Pauline position on slavery (namely that New Testament literature attributed to him, i.e., 2 Thessalonians, Ephesians, Colossians, and the Pastorals of 1 and 2 Timothy and Titus) became the biblical proof texts for white preachers and slaveholders in their interest of sanctioning slavery and holding black human flesh in perpetual thralldom.[11]

Modern biblical scholarship did little to grasp Paul's true understanding of slavery and Christian freedom and, therefore, get us back on track. For example, at the turn of the twentieth century, Albert Schweitzer could not see Paul's position on slavery in any other light than that of encouraging the slave to remain in servitude. In his interpretation of 1 Corinthians 7:20-24 (especially verse 21), Schweitzer asserts that "if . . . a slave became a believer he should not, . . . if he were afterwards offered freedom, accept it."[12] He further intimates,

If Paul is exposed to the reproach that he did not in the Spirit of Christ oppose slavery, and consequently for centuries lent the weight of his authority to those who regard it as compatible with Christianity, the blame rests on the theory of the *status quo*. His mysticism did not permit him to hold a different view. For what need has one who is already a free man in Christ Jesus, and momentarily expects to enter as such into the Messianic glory, to be concerned about release from slavery for the few moments that he has still to spend in the natural world? Accordingly Paul enjoins upon Onesimus, the escaped slave whom he had come to know during his imprisonment, that he should return to his master Philemon, and although as a believer he is now a freeman like his master, nevertheless to continue to serve him.[13]

There is still among more recent New Testament scholars the failure to grasp Paul's understanding of slavery in the light of Christian freedom. There is a strong penchant among many New Testament scholars today to adopt the more conservative (and maybe racist?) view of 1 Corinthians 7:20-24. For example,

Leander Keck,[14] Lucas Grollenberg,[15] and Rudolf Schnackenburg,[16] believe that becoming a member of the church did not alter the social status of the slave. A contemporary and intense scholar, Günther Bornkamm, insists that

> . . . the gospel [does not] call slaves and freemen to seek to change their existing social status, for "in Christ" the slave *has already become* a "freedman" of the Lord's, and the free man (in the social sense) a "slave of Christ's," both alike his property, body and soul (1 Cor. 7:17-24).[17]

It may not be fair to say that the history of failure to grasp Paul's understanding of slavery in light of Christian freedom on the part of the Christian church and its scholars is a racist proclivity (i.e., bent on keeping in subjection and even destroying a certain class or race of people), but it would be fair to say that there has not been a mad rush on the part of white theologians to the opinion that, for Paul, Jesus meant freedom for the slave in the church as well as in society. It has been because of this negatively skewed interpretation of Paul that the black church and black theologians have ignored the Apostle to the Gentiles and, in fact, have held him as an object of scorn. But I argued earlier that the culpability under which black theologians and the black church labor now is that of failing to investigate Paul's theology for themselves to see whether or not he was soft on slavery or had things to say on the question more revolutionary than they knew. Therefore, the immediate task for black theology, and all theology, is to try to get at Paul's actual position on slavery. This will be our task in the pages to follow.

A Close Look at a Controversial Passage

First Corinthians 7:20-24 is the locus of our concern. Paul's brief but powerful statement on slavery is introduced in verse 20: "Every one should remain in the state in which he was called." Conzelmann[18] and Barrett[19] are right in saying that this verse harks back to verse 17. There Paul instructs each Corinthian to ". . . lead the life which the Lord has assigned to him, and in which God has called him." In elucidating on the meaning of this for the Jewish and Gentile constituents of the Corinthian church, Paul says if the Jewish member of the congregation was

already circumcised when he was called, he should not attempt
to remove the marks of circumcision. Likewise, the Gentile
member of the congregation who has never been circumcised
should not seek to do so. It follows for Paul that neither circumcision nor uncircumcision counts for anything in the congregation
of God's people; the only thing that counts is keeping God's
commandments (cf. verse 19). The position Paul takes here is
understandable, for it is altogether rational that a woman who is
added to the church should not try to become a man, or a black
man attempt to become a white man or a white man attempt to
become a black man, and so on. Paul is correct; there is no need
for one to change identity once he or she enters the church.

Paul takes a similar position on marriage (1 Corinthians 7:1-
16, 25-40). He does not have any command from the Lord on
the subject (1 Corinthians 7:25), but in his opinion, the person
who is bound to a wife should not seek to get free; likewise, the
person who is free of a wife should not seek to get married.
There is no need to alter one's status as it relates to marriage
because, in Paul's opinion, "the form of this world is passing
away" (1 Corinthians 7:31).

If we were to extrapolate Paul's instructions to the circumcised
and uncircumcised and the married and unmarried to what he
says about slaves in verses 20 to 24, we would be forced to
conclude that if people were slaves when they were called, they
should not seek freedom afterwards. The same would apply to
persons already free. But the question becomes, should the meaning of verses 17 to 19, as it relates to circumcision and uncircumcision, and the meaning of verse 27, as it relates to marriage,
be applied to verses 20 to 24 and the question of slavery? Does
Paul instruct persons who were slaves at their call to remain
slaves after the call? This is the crucial question.

The answer to the question cannot be obtained by means of
facile fundamentalism, i.e., literal interpretation without historical examination. We must raise some basic literary and historical
questions and seek answers to those questions in order to answer
the central question. We might begin by raising the question,
What does Paul mean when he says, "Every one should remain
in the state in which he was called" (v. 20)?

Hans Conzelmann sees the answer to the question as already given in verse 17. He thinks there is no need for one to change social status in order to obtain salvation. In the eschatological community, i.e., the church, social status and differences are obliterated.[20] Thus, in the eschatological community, the slave is equal with constituents and free (i.e., the internal self, the soul is already in heaven) while his or her external social condition remains the same. "Remaining in one's own particular status is, like remaining in the world, not a concession to the facts, but a logical consequence of genuine theology."[21] C. K. Barrett takes a similar position: "A man is not called (so far as this passage is concerned) to a new occupation; his old occupation is given new significance."[22]

One would concede that there is nothing a person can do before the fact of salvation that can enhance his or her possibility of attaining that blessed state of eschatological existence; thus, Conzelmann is right to say that salvation is *sola gratia,* by grace alone. But this seems not to be the answer to the question. Paul seems not to be dealing with the question of whether or not a slave must remain a slave or seek freedom in order to be saved; he is dealing with the question of slavery itself. Moreover, Barrett's suggestion that the slave's erstwhile occupation becomes glorified after the fact of salvation seems to be far from the point of verse 20 but certainly in conformity with racially biased interpretations of Paul and slavery.

Vital Words: ". . . Remain in the State of His Calling"

The burden of Conzelmann's and Barrett's failure to grasp the intent of verse 20 rests on their emphasis of *en taute meneto,* i.e., "in this let him abide." But to accuse Conzelmann and Barrett of blurred perception that results in unbearable conclusions elicits the obvious question of where the emphasis in verse 20 should be placed. Godet gives us valuable assistance in addressing this matter. He places the emphasis in verse 20 on *te klesei,* "the call."[23] In treating the subject, he says, "The word *klesis,* call, vocation, . . . is applied here, as elsewhere, to the call to salvation."[24] But does Godet understand the meaning of salvation to be—as in the case of Conzelmann and Barrett—

primarily eschatological and not social? The answer is, surprisingly, no! ". . . The idea of the call must be taken to embrace all the external circumstances which furnish the occasion and determine the manner of it."[25] Thus, for Godet, the primal theological factor in verse 20 that opens up Paul's understanding of slavery is the "call," *klesis*. The call bears with it the determination of the slaves' external (social) circumstance as well as their internal (spiritual) circumstance.

It would not be justifiable to shunt off the interpretation of Conzelmann and Barrett onto a side road of insignificance and assume that Godet's interpretation of verse 20 is on track without investigating further the letter of First Corinthians and the entire Pauline corpus.

K. L. Schmidt's study of the use of *klesis* in the New Testament discloses that it appears eleven times in Pauline and deutero-Pauline literature as a technical theological term. In all instances, it is translated as "a call that goes out from God," cf. Romans 11:29.[26] The Corinthians are "called to be saints" in 1 Corinthians 1:2. They are exhorted to "consider your call" (1 Corinthians 1:26), which comes from God. The Romans are addressed by Paul as "the ones who are called of Jesus Christ" (Romans 1:6). Paul himself has received this call of God—which often appears as coming through Jesus Christ—"Paul, called by the will of God to be an apostle of Christ Jesus . . ." (1 Corinthians 1:1; see also Romans 1:1). It is the upward call of God in Christ Jesus to which Paul presses as his *telos* and prize (Philippians 3:14). Thus, in virtually every case, Paul uses *klesis*, "call," as a technical term in the theological sense, viz., the call from God. Hence it seems justifiable to conclude that in verse 20 of the text, slaves are enjoined by Paul to remain in the calling received from God to which or in which they have been called.

Some translators do not opt for this conclusion. For example, Walter Bauer translates *klesis* as "station in life, position," or "vocation." He further suggests that the term is used as such only by Paul in 1 Corinthians 7:20.[27] However, I conclude that it is erroneous to translate klesis as "state" (Revised Standard Version [RSV]), "station in life," "position," or "vocation" and permit that translation to stand. If this were permitted, an obvious interpretation of verse 20 would be that Paul instructs slaves to remain in slavery even after they receive the call. However, the appearance of *te klesei* and *he Eklethe* in verse 20 suggests that the verse should be translated thus: "each should remain in the state of the calling in which he was called" (see King James Version [KJV], Phillips, and Godet). If such a translation stands, the interpretation of verse 20 emerges as something different; it would take into account the change in religious and social status that comes as a result of the call and not assume the continuation of one's former social status though he or she has received the call. Therefore—contrary to those who, whether deliberately or inadvertently so, translate this verse to mean that slaves were to remain in their social condition of servitude even after they received the call—Paul seems to be instructing slaves to recognize the spiritual and social metamorphosis that comes about as a result of their call.

Our investigation of the importance of *klesis*, "call," in Paul's theology already opens up possibilities for seeing him in our text as an advocate of freedom and a liberator of slaves. But such a conclusion about Paul cannot be drawn until further questions are raised and answers found so that the following verses in the text can be further illuminated for the sake of liberation. The most preponderant question has to do with our continuing interest in Paul's understanding of "call," *klesis*. More precisely, to what were slaves called? If slaves were exhorted to remain in the state in which they had been called, it follows that there was some specific state of existence to which they were called and in which they were to remain. If this is true, it is imperative that we examine the matter further; such examination should broaden our horizon, sharpen our view, and provide important pieces to the puzzle of Paul's understanding of slavery and Christian freedom.

What was the specific state of existence to which slaves were called and in which they were to remain, according to Paul? The first possible answer that comes to us is the kingdom of God. In 1 Thessalonians 2:12, Paul states that the call that has gone out from God to the Thessalonians is that which beckons them into

God's kingdom and glory. However, the lack of Paul's use of the term "kingdom of God" indicates his preference for some other term to describe the state of existence into which slaves, or other believers, are called and in which they must remain.[28]

The most prominent term that Paul uses to describe slaves' specific existence after the call and an existence in which they must remain is *ekklesia,* i.e., the church. The word *ekklesia* comes from *ek,* meaning "out of," and *kalein,* meaning "to call." *Ekklesia* appears in First Corinthians alone some twenty-two times.[29] Paul's salutation to the Corinthians is cast in the language of *ekklesia:* "To the church of God which is at Corinth" (1 Corinthians 1:2). It becomes obvious that *ekklesia* bore with it some very important meaning and possibly theological, social, and political ramifications for Paul.

The Derivation and Meaning of *Ekklesia*

Before we proceed further with the question of what Paul interpreted *ekklesia* to mean, we must examine the meaning of the word as it developed historically. Barrett,[30] Conzelmann,[31] and Godet,[32] point out that *ekklesia* had its origin in Greek culture and politics. There the term was descriptive of the assembly of citizens that was called together in the *polis* (city) to deal with political matters. The term also could mean a general gathering of people to deal with any matter that arose in the *polis.*[33] The Septuagint used *ekklesia* almost one hundred times as the translation of the Hebrew term *gâhal* (congregation). The term described any gathering of people that had been assembled for any of many different reasons. Most significant among these gatherings in the Septuagint was the assembling of Israel before God to receive the Law (cf. Deuteronomy 4:10; 9:10; 10:4; and 18:16).[34] One could surmise that this gathering of Israel before God was significant politically as well as theologically. It was this Septuagint theological tradition, i.e., Israel as a people assembled before God or the people of God, that the early church (the Jerusalem church) and Hellenistic Christianity inherited.[35] Subsequently, by the time Paul adopted the term *ekklesia,* it had accumulated a rich tradition of meanings. On the one hand, its secular meaning was an assembly of citizens in the Greek *polis* that had gathered to deal with political matters; and on the other hand, its theological meaning was the assembly of Israel before God or, simply, the people of God.[36]

This investigation of the historical development of *ekklesia* fails to give us the most candid view of that theological entity into which Paul understood slaves to be called and in which they were to remain. Just what was Paul's interpretation of the *ekklesia* into which slaves were called and in which they were to remain? What was his conceptualization of its locus in the world? What was his understanding of its worldly nexus? What, if any, were the political and social ramifications of its existence in the Corinthian society in which it found itself?

Barrett and Godet do not help us answer these questions. Conzelmann gives a brief description of the Pauline understanding of *ekklesia* as "the assembly of the saints of the last days."[37] Rudolf Bultmann, writing before Conzelmann, took a similar position: "The preached word calls and gathers men into the *ecclesia*, the *Church*, the *Congregation* of those who are 'called' and 'saints'. . . . It is the eschatological Congregation, and hence its existing belongs to the eschatological salvation-occurrence."[38]

In Pauline literature, there is strong justification for the conclusion Bultmann and Conzelmann offer. Paul thinks the *ekklesia* already enjoys eschatological freedom because the form of this world is passing away (cf. 1 Corinthians 7:29-31; also Romans 13:11-13). The *ekklesia* that has been baptized into Jesus Christ now has been raised to walk in the newness of eschatological freedom—such an existence has been described by Albert Schweitzer as the "already-not-yet" (cf. Romans 6:1-2). The locus of the *ekklesia* in the world is any place where people have been called together by God through Jesus Christ. At times, individual *ekklesiai* are referred to specifically by the geographical area in which they are located, e.g., "To the church of God which is at Corinth" (1 Corinthians 1:2; cf. 1 Thessalonians 1:1). Wherever located, individually or collectively, unity is maintained as the "body of Christ" (cf. Romans 12:4-5ff.). Also, members of the body of Christ are referred to as "brothers," *adelphoi,* who are members of the "brotherhood," *tou adelphou*

(1 Corinthians 6:5-6). Though this is a truncated analysis, I think that it gives a fairly clear view of Paul's conception of the *ekklesia* in the world.

The Separation of Ekklesia and the World

We must move from this point and try to grasp Paul's understanding of the relationship of the church, *ekklesia,* to the world. Rudolf Bultmann has made a very interesting and important observation relative to Paul's understanding of the relationship of the *ekklesia* to the world. Bultmann suggests that in the *ekklesia* there was "*a consciousness of separateness and delimitation from the world.*"[39] He says further, "This separateness is first of all, of course, a self-exclusion from *non-Christian cults of every sort.* This is seldom mentioned in the text because it was taken for granted."[40] This statement from Bultmann is profoundly interesting and important, especially as it relates to the question of the *ekklesia* being that entity into which slaves were called and in which they must remain. For nowhere does Paul speak more about the separation of the *ekklesia* from the world than in his two letters to the Corinthians.

In the sixth chapter of the first letter, the Corinthians are caustically castigated for going before pagan courts with matters that should have been settled within the *ekklesia.* Paul chastens them because they dare go before an unrighteous judge in pagan courts rather than before the saints of the *ekklesia* to settle their disputes (1 Corinthians 6:1). In 1 Corinthians 10:20, Paul enjoins the Corinthians not to be partners with demons. Individual and collective members of the *ekklesia* are considered by Paul to be the *naos theou,* "temple of God," and are not to corrupt their bodies or spirits with vanity (e.g., chapters 5 and 6) or idolatry (e.g., chapters 8 and 10). The point of this complete separation from the world is made more poignantly in 2 Corinthians 6:14-18:

> Do not be mismated with unbelievers. For what partnership have righteousness and iniquity? Or what fellowship has light with darkness? What accord has Christ with Belial? or what has a believer in common with an unbeliever? What agreement has the temple of God with idols? For we are the temple of the living God; as God said,

> "I will live in them and move among them,
> and I will be their God,
> and they shall be my people.
> Therefore come out from them,
> and be separate from them, says the Lord,
> and touch nothing unclean;
> then I will welcome you,
> and I will be a father to you,
> and you shall be my sons and daughters,
> says the Lord Almighty."[41]

Bultmann's observation that the *ekklesia* bore a "consciousness of separation and delimitation from the world" has opened up an even wider panorama of possibilities as it relates to liberation, for Paul. The *ekklesia* was for Paul a self-contained entity: it was not to have religious intercourse with idolatry or idolatrous people; it was to have nothing to do with unbelievers; it was not to have social intercourse with the world; it was not to conform to the traditions of the world (Romans 12:2) for the form of this world was passing away (1 Corinthians 7:29-31); its citizenship was not in Corinth or the Roman Empire but in the heavens, *humon gar to politeuma en ouranois huparchei*, "our commonwealth is in heaven" (Philippians 3:20); political institutions had no jurisdiction over it (i.e., the Roman empire and the Corinthian municipal government), although there were times when its worldly engagements violated political conventions (for example, Paul's escape from the governor of Damascus in 2 Corinthians 11:32-33 had political overtones. It could be conjectured that his fight with the beasts at Ephesus was a battle with Roman soldiers, again reflecting political overtones. If Luke's account in Acts 17 bears any historical veracity, it details a most severe violation of political law by Paul. Acts 17:7 says of Paul and Silas, "they are all acting against the decrees of Caesar, saying that there is another king, Jesus"). Thus the *ekklesia*, the New Testament people of God, was called out of the world by God through Jesus Christ, called to be saints (1 Corinthians 1:2), sanctified, consecrated (set aside) to the worship of God and working God's purpose in the world (1 Corinthians 1:2 and Philippians 2:12-13).

The Ekklesia *as an Underground Movement*

In the final analysis, what we have in Paul's understanding of *ekklesia* is the concept of a religious secret society, an underground movement, that which was more popularly known in Roman culture as *collegia*. There were many *collegia* in the Roman Empire, although few of them had legal sanction from the Roman government.[42] As to their composition, *collegia* were something of a trade guild, a religious brotherhood, or a local association.[43] They were headed by a religious master.[44] Numbers of *collegia* began to increase as slaves and freedmen sought membership.[45] *Collegia* became the locus of ferment for freedom for slaves and freedmen; they often carried out the function of a mob or gang with military training, staging revolts and insurrections in an attempt to secure freedom for slaves and freedmen.[46] In 56 B.C., a provision was made for a law against membership in *collegia* in the *Lex Iulia*.[47]

Such was the *ekklesia*. It was an underground movement. It was an illegal entity within the Roman Empire.[48] During the time of Nero (ca. 54–68 A.D.), Tacitus described Christians and Christianity as "the pernicious superstition" and "disease."[49] Eventually, the *ekklesia* came under attack and suffered flagrant persecution because of its theological tenets that amounted to serious aberrations from conventional Roman religion and posed a threat to the common political good of the Empire.[50]

It was into such an entity that slaves were called by God through Jesus Christ and it was in this calling where they were to remain, according to Paul. They were called in the *ekklesia* of freedom or *eleutheria* (see Galatians 3:28; 5:1, 13; 2 Corinthians 3:17; 1 Corinthians 9:1; 4:3-4; 2:15). For the slaves, there was no longer to be intercourse between the *ekklesia* into which they had been called and the world from which they had been called; more precisely, the slaves' membership in the *ekklesia* guaranteed their freedom from their erstwhile state of servitude and therefore delivered them from the requirement of returning to their master and slavery. (Such a conclusion raises serious questions regarding the interpretation of Philemon; Paul is charged by black theologians with flagrantly sending Onesimus back to his master. This question will be dealt with in more detail later.)

If this is good reasoning, then we seem to have a clearer view and a more intelligible understanding of what verse 20 in the text meant for Paul. Our investigation seems to steer us away from an erroneous and racist interpretation of the verse, i.e., that of conventional white theology and the majority of New Testament translations of the verse that convey the notion that Paul is exhorting slaves to remain in their state of servitude even after they receive the call. Our investigation seems to disclose something altogether different. What is more, the foundation that we have laid as a result of our inquiry provides sounder footing on which a building of better understanding for what follows can be constructed. We have laid the foundation for showing Paul to be a theologian and preacher of liberation, in fact, the leader of an underground movement within an oppressive society, viz., the *ekklesia* within the Roman society and the Corinthian world. Now we must complete the structure.

Paul's Rhetorical Question to Slaves

"Were you a *slave* when called?" (italics mine) is the RSV's translation of *doulos eklethes* in verse 21. It is significant that the RSV translates *doulos* as "slave" because Edgar J. Goodspeed has noted, "slavery is so disagreeable a subject that it has been almost obliterated from the English New Testament."[51] An excellent example is the King James Version of the Bible, the version that dominated the English Bible-reading world and continues to be *the* Bible for many black people. The KJV never uses the word "slave" as the translation for *doulos;* its translation for *doulos* is "servant." In the KJV Paul's question in verse 21 reads, "Art thou called being a servant?" It is significant that the KJV, written at a time when slave traffic and bartering in cargoes of ebony flesh were beginning to flourish, mitigated the heinous force of such a sordid enterprise by rendering *doulos* "servant" instead of "slave." One is not sure whether this was done because the subject of slavery was so disagreeable, as Goodspeed suggests, or because it was a way of playing down its seriousness and importance. The fact is that by means of translation, the flagrance of slavery was played down by the KJV

Bible. It is also interesting to note that only in a most recent supplementary edition of the *Interpreter's Dictionary of the Bible* does there appear an article on slavery during New Testament times, viz., Greek and Roman slavery that provided the blueprint for the form of slavery utilized by America to enslave black people.[52]

Now as for Paul's rhetorical question, "Were you a slave when called?" Barrett and Conzelmann fail to grasp the import and impact of it. Robertson and Plummer ignore it altogether.[53] The point seems to be that just as questions had been raised with Paul as to matters of conduct within the *ekklesia* (cf. 1 Corinthians 5:11; 7:1), there had been questions raised with him about slavery.[54] Of the question itself, we are not certain, for it is not stated. However, it is doubtlessly clear that there was grave concern within the sector of slaves who now had become members in the *ekklesia*. What was that concern? It could not have been concern for admittance into the congregation in the slaves' struggle for freedom, for the slaves to whom Paul was addressing himself were already called into the *ekklesia*. However (without presupposing the meaning of verses 22 to 24), possibly there was concern on the part of the slaves as to their security in the church. It is unlikely that the slaves would become homesick for the slavemaster and wish to return once the exciting wine of freedom in the *ekklesia* had been tasted; but how could the slaves keep the slavemaster from coming to them? How could they avoid being forcibly dragged back into that dehumanizing existence of servitude in Corinth? If these are some of the possible problems that lay behind Paul's rhetorical question, we can suppose that the slaves of Corinth were suffering serious anxiety and psychological trauma. It would be an unsettling thought to have to return to slavery: slavery in Graeco-Roman culture was most flagrant.

Slavery's Degradation—What Paul Had to Address

Slavery, as it was practiced in the Roman Empire during Paul's era, was adequately defined some time before Caesar Augustus's Golden Age by Greek philosophers. Slaves were not to be a prominent part of the ideal state. Youths were to fear slavery more than death and were not to represent slaves or perform the offices of slaves.[55] Some three hundred and fifty years before Paul appeared in history, Aristotle posited the place of slaves in society as being part of the master's household, the master's possession, chattel property, his instrument of action. For Aristotle, society was neatly divided into two categories, the rulers and the ruled: "For that some should rule and others be ruled is a thing not only necessary, but expedient; from the hour of their birth, some are marked out for subjection, others for rule."[56]

From the philosophical theory of slavery, according to Aristotle's scheme, came its *praxis* in the republican era of the Roman Empire. The venality of slavery is reflected in the life of Cato the Elder. Cato, who had a penchant for luxury, as was the case of many Romans in his day, bought a large number of slaves for the sole purpose of profit.[57] For Cato, slaves were to be treated as animals and some were to be kept in chains.[58] It was his belief that slaves had to be either at work or asleep, at work in order to bring him profit, asleep to keep them docile.[59]

Slavery in the emerging Roman Empire became more vicious and venal. Quest for luxury led many Roman families to acquire and breed massive numbers of slaves. During the reign of Caesar Augustus, some slave owners had as many as four thousand slaves.[60] During the reign of Emperor Nero, the practice of Roman families accumulating slaves to insure luxurious living was probably at its highest level.[61] Although slaves facilitated luxury for Romans, they still were considered to be less than human. In the Roman Empire, slaves were designated as *res,* "a thing," *mancipium,* "chattel," and *res mortales,* "a mortal object to be bought or sold as property."[62] In Juvenal's *Satires* the Roman attitude toward slavery, that slaves were not human, is reflected:

"Crucify that slave!" "But what has he done to deserve it?
Who has witnessed against him? Who has informed on him? Listen—
No delay's ever too long in the death of a human being."
"A slave is a human being? You fool! All right, he's done nothing.
This is my wish, my command; my desire is good enough reason."[63]

No reason was ever needed to kill a slave; a whim, a wish, this was all that was needed. He could be poisoned.[64] He could be crucified[65] or tortured.[66] Slaves were not permitted legally to marry,[67] and if they had families, the families could be torn apart at will[68] and members given away as presents.[69] It must have been a thoroughly traumatic experience for slaves to think of the possibility of having to return to this form of brutal life after having been called into the *ekklesia* of freedom.[70]

The freedman was probably no less anxious about his freedom. He certainly must have been aware that according to Roman Law, he was obligated to show *obsequim* (respect), to perform *operae* (render service), and even give *munera* (gifts) to the erstwhile master.[71] Thus it was these kinds of prodigious problems that Paul was confronting when he addressed himself to the concerns of slaves and freedmen that had obviously been conveyed to him.

Paul's Answer to His Own Question

Paul's response to his rhetorical question follows in the remaining part of verse 21: *me soi meleto,* "never mind" (RSV, Moffatt), "Don't let that worry you" (Phillips), "Care not for it" (Godet), or "Let not that trouble you" (Barrett). Is Paul being facetious? Was this response a reflection of his indifference to slavery?[72] Or was this response Paul's way of mitigating the slaves' anxiety and alleviating their fear of being reenslaved or of falling back into the power of their patron?

Certainly Paul was not being facetious; only a few times did he resort to comedy and sarcasm, e.g., the times he berated the *Pneumatikoi,* "spiritual men" of the Corinthian congregation (cf. 1 Corinthians 4:6-13). It would seem correct to say that slavery was too serious for Paul to deal with it in lightness and levity. It was so awesome in its degradation of humanity that he could not ignore or be indifferent to it.[73]

The middle and ruling classes of the Roman Empire may have been indifferent to slavery, but not all were indifferent. The fact that flourishing *collegia* of slaves and freedmen were present in the Roman Empire, staging revolts for freedom and against the system of slavery, is indicative that the matter was not treated indifferently by all. The slave revolts of 61 A.D., during Nero's reign, and 100 A.D., during Trajan's reign, are reminders that there was disturbing discomfort with the system of slavery in those days. Most of all, the *ekklesia* did not treat slavery indifferently or ignore it. *Me soi meleto* was not Paul's way of treating slavery indifferently; it was his way of comforting the slaves,[74] of relieving their anxiety and removing their trauma.

A Choice of Two Contrary Translations

This cannot rightly be understood aside from what follows in the verse. Paul continues: *"all' ei kei dunasai eleutheros genesthai, mallon chresai."* The translation of this phrase is utterly difficult.[75] But the difficulty of Paul's instructions to slaves at this point seems not to be dependent on unraveling the difficulty of grammatical construction.[76] Obviously, something must be added to *mallon chresai* "avail yourself of the opportunity," so that it might be understood what Paul is saying at this point. Conzelmann suggests the alternatives are (1) *te douleia,* "slavery," and (2) *te eleutheria,* "freedom." It seems logical that these are the only two alternatives. However, Conzelmann concludes that because the matter at hand is that of comfort for the slaves, *te douleia,* "slavery," is the only logical addition.[77] Barrett insists that *te douleia,* "slavery," is the only logical alternative, in agreement with Conzelmann. He sees Paul's statement *all' ei kai dunasai eleutheros genesthai,* "but even though you should be able to become free" (Barrett's translation), to be a reference to seeking emancipation according to Roman law. Thus, it is Barrett's conclusion that Paul is suggesting to slaves, who might be faced with the possibility of obtaining emancipation, to "put up rather with your present status"; more precisely, be content as a slave.[78]

But is *te douleia,* "slavery," that which should be added to *mallon chresai,* as Conzelmann and Barrett suggest? One means of answering the question is to look at Conzelmann's and Barrett's conclusions in the light of what Paul would have to say about those conclusions. Conzelmann concludes that Paul would insist on slaves being content with servitude. Because of the function of eschatology in Paul's theology, according to Conzelmann, Paul would see civil freedom as a civil affair, an affair that was of no value in the church.[79]

The reasoning here is not logical; if civil freedom is a civil affair, as Conzelmann has said, what does Paul mean when he says, "For freedom Christ has set us free . . ." (Galatians 5:1)?

Was not "freedom" an ecclesiastical and social (or civil) matter for Paul? Did not "Jesus" mean "freedom" in the social (or civil) as well as ecclesiastical sense (cf. 2 Corinthians 3:17)? Further, if civil affairs had no value in the church, why would Paul recommend *te douleia,* "slavery," to those who were inquiring about their condition? If these slaves had tasted the eschatological freedom of the *ekklesia,* would Paul recommend that they continue in their social and civil servitude, making daily visits to their master and paying deference? If Paul were to suggest such, it would amount to double-talk in the most grandiose fashion. He had already said in verse 20 that all persons (slaves included) were to remain in the situation they were in when they were called by God, a calling that beckoned people to come out of the Corinthian world and into the *ekklesia.* It was without question that slaves were called out of the Corinthian world of sin into the *ekklesia* of righteousness; there was to be no passage back and forth between the latter and the former because the former no longer had jurisdiction over the latter.

In Romans 6 Paul addressed himself to the radical change or existence that comes about as a result of putting on Christ by baptism (cf. Galatians 3:27). Symbolically, the initiate who enters into the *ekklesia* dies with Christ in baptism (Romans 6:1-4) and rises to walk in a new life (cf. 6:4). The initiate's death is to sin; the initiate's resurrection is to righteousness.

In Romans 6:20-23, Paul says:

> When you were slaves of sin, you were free in regard to righteousness. But then what return did you get from the things of which you are now ashamed? The end of those things is death. But now that you have been set free from sin and have become slaves of God, the return you get is sanctification and its end, eternal life. For the wages of sin is death, but the free gift of God is eternal life in Christ Jesus our Lord.

If we interpreted this passage metaphorically, the following conclusion could be drawn: Earthly slavery, for Paul was sin (Paul defined sin as anything that does not proceed from faith [cf. Romans 14:23b]. Certainly slavery did not proceed from faith). The result of slavery was death; slaves had no rights of their own; they were not their own; they belonged to their dominus, their master; they were dead to themselves. On the other hand, when slaves were baptized into the *ekklesia,* they were freed from sin (or slavery) and became slaves of God, sanctified or set aside for God's purpose, with the assurance of the eschatological reward of eternal life. The point of this is that *te douleia,* "slavery," was not a continuing obligation for slaves once they had been called by God into the *ekklesia.* Thus the notion posited by Conzelmann that because of the function of eschatology in Paul's theology, slaves should choose "slavery" falls flat on its face.

Barrett's justification for choosing *te douleia* as the alternative for *mallon chresai* is tenuous at best and confusing altogether. He never tells us why he thinks Paul would have the slave "put up rather with your present status" (Barrett's translation of *all' ei kai dunasai eleutheros genesthai, mallon chresai*). As he rushes to verse 22, we are told that the freedom that Christ gives the slave is freedom from "bondage to sin and death, and to the evil powers of this age." There is no alteration in the slave's social status after the call.[80] In effect, slaves live in two worlds; on the one hand, they are a member of the *ekklesia;* on the other hand, they continue as slaves in the world. The slaves return to their master, in keeping with their obligation, to become totally subject to him as their *dominus,* lord, and master. They must participate in the family worship of images and celestial beings and hold the emperor to be divine. Then, when the church meeting is held, the slaves return to the congregation to worship Jesus the Savior of their souls, who only has fit them for heaven.

Ludicrous! Paul would have none of this fork-tongued religion. In the eschatological *ekklesia,* slaves now belong to God entirely (Romans 6:22); although "there are many 'gods' and many 'lords'" (1 Corinthians 8:5), for slaves in the eschatological *ekklesia,* "there is one God, the Father, from whom are all things and for whom we exist, and one Lord, Jesus Christ, through whom are all things and through whom we exist" (1 Corinthians 8:6). Barrett seems to fail to grasp in Paul's theology the inconsistency of being a part of the *ekklesia* while at the same time remaining in the world. Although for two different reasons, both Conzelmann and Barrett agree that, in Paul's theology, the slave could be both slave and Christian at the same time.

Of course, this has been the typical racist interpretation of Paul's understanding of the question of slavery and Christian freedom.[81] With what we have already seen in this discussion, the meaning of *klesis,* the importance of the *ekklesia,* and the function of eschatology in Paul's theology, it seems reasonable to say that such conclusions about his understanding of slavery and Christian freedom are absurd.

It becomes obvious now that the meaning of verse 21 cannot be obtained on the basis of grammar or personal prejudices. C. F. D. Moule seems to be correct when he says it is not only a matter of grammar that causes clearer visions to come for the translation and interpretation of verse 21, it is also a matter of context.[82] Moule suggests that *mallon chresai* should be understood in the light of *te eleutheria,* "freedom." Therefore, he suggests that the phrases should be translated to mean "but if you can gain your freedom, choose to use (the opportunity to do so).[83]

If we were to take this statement in the context in which it stands, we would take it to mean that Paul is reminding the slaves of the freedom they have at their disposal as a result of the call they had received from God to become a part of the eschatological *ekklesia;* thus, they are to make use of that freedom.[84] The slaves had been called into the community of freedom; it is in this community that they were to remain (7:20).

An All-Encompassing Freedom

What is this freedom that is to be enjoyed by the slave in the church into which he or she has been called? The word Paul uses for "freedom," *eleutheria,* is the same as that which is used by Aristotle and Plato in their discussion of freedom in the Greek society or *polis.* For Aristotle and Plato, "freedom" meant "to be at one's own disposal, to be independent of others." However, such freedom was experienced only in the context of the state *(polis)* and was guaranteed only under the aegis of the law *(romos).*[85] It is interesting that Paul makes use of the same term for freedom as Aristotle and Plato. However, contemporary theologians wish to allow the term for Paul to mean freedom only from sin, the Law, and death and not freedom in the social or political sense.[86] This seems to shield both the cryptic and candid political meaning of the term for Paul and his theology. Those slaves and others who became Christians at Corinth must have known this political meaning of freedom *(eleutheria)* when Paul used it.

It is even more interesting what Paul did with the term *eleutheria*. Although he used the same term as Aristotle and Plato when they spoke of political freedom in the state and under the law, his use of the term meant the freedom that was guaranteed to slaves and everyone united with the church and was given by Christ: "For freedom Christ has set us free . . ." (Galatians 5:1). It is freedom to which the slaves and everyone else were called (Galatians 5:13). The freedom that is promised to slaves was that which was promised to the citizen of the Greek city-state and to the citizen in the Roman Empire, but it was free from the encumbrance of political restraints of the city-state and the Roman Empire and the burden of Roman (and Jewish) law; it is freedom in Christ (the meaning of which we shall shortly discuss). Paul himself enjoyed this freedom (1 Corinthians 9:1). It was a freedom that exempted him from the judgment of any human court (1 Corinthians 4:3). Moreover, for the assembled congregation, freedom in Christ meant freedom anywhere and everywhere, for "where the Spirit of the Lord is, there is freedom" (2 Corinthians 3:17). So the Christian, whether former slave, man or woman, white or black, Jew or Gentile, was free wherever he or she went. So this is the freedom that is offered in the church, the *ekklesia,* the free community.

Verse 22 is explosive. It destroys any pseudo-interpretations that may have been drawn on what has been said before now. It is a commentary on verses 20 and 21: "For he who was called in the Lord as a slave is a freedman of the Lord. Likewise he who was free when called is a slave of Christ." Biblical translations of this verse generally concur with each other. (See KJV, *New English Bible,* Phillips, Moffatt, *The Jerusalem Bible, The Amplified New Testament;* see also, the nuance in the translations of *The Living Bible* and the *Good News Bible.*)

Conzelmann's interpretation of verse 22 is determined by his understanding of Pauline eschatology: the slave is free from sin.[87] In violation of all reason, Barrett argues that the slave's call into the *ekklesia* brings about no change in his or her social status but does bring about a change in spiritual status: "The slave who becomes a Christian, though he retains his social status, has been freed from bondage to sin and death, and to the evil powers of this age. . . ."[88] Godet's interpretation of this verse seems to be a transgression of what he already has said. Previously, Godet understood Paul's concern in verses 20 and 21 to be with the slave's external condition. But here he says, "The sentence of emancipation was pronounced by the Lord; by it He delivers this spiritual slave from the power and condemnation of sin; thenceforth this freedman belongs to Him as His servant."[89]

The reasoning here is inconsistent; the slave's deliverance is no longer linked with his external condition but with sin. We are not told what "sin" means. Thus, if we are dependent on the interpretations of Conzelmann, Barrett, and Godet for our understanding of what Paul is saying in verse 22, our conclusion would be that the slave's call into the *ekklesia* only assures freedom from the power of sin (whatever that means) and fits the soul for heaven. But is this really what Paul is saying? From the content of verse 22, the answer seems to be no.

The term *gar* seems to indicate that what follows is an elucidation on the point made in verse 21, i.e., make use of the freedom granted by the call into the *ekklesia*. Thus the slave who has been called in the Lord becomes the Lord's "freedman," *apeleutheros*. Walter Bauer[90] and Heinrich Schlier[91] spiritualize the meaning of *apeleutheros,* "freedman." They seem to see no connection, socially or politically, between the slave's former civil status and the new status in the *ekklesia*, viz., as the Lord's freedman. To be sure, Paul seems to be saying that a radical transition indeed has taken place, a transition that breaks the slave away from all social and political obligations. F. Lyall seems to be closer to the point of 1 Corinthians 7:22. He states:

The point Paul is making is clearly the fundamental equality and worth of the individual believer. The slave Christian is a *freedman,* a full human being yet not detached from his patron. Christ has freed him and will perform the duties of a patron toward him, summed up shortly in caring for him. The freedman owes reciprocal duties to Christ, *obsequim, operae* and *munera* in their fullest extent. The free Christian is to consider that he is the slave of Christ, that he owns nothing and is subject to the direction of his owner, yet knowing that his owner will look after his welfare.[92]

If we can assume that Lyall's assessment of the meaning of 1 Corinthians 7:22 is plausible, we can conclude that upon the call, slaves are extricated from their social and political servile condition and immediately become the possessions of Jesus Christ. Unlike the former condition of the slaves (but similar to that of Roman freedmen), the former slaves owe respect, works, and gifts entirely to Jesus the Liberator.

The situation is similar as it relates to free persons (free Roman citizens) who are called by the Lord. The free persons become the slaves *in toto* of the Lord. Roman citizenship is given up (or the concern for that citizenship) in favor of the citizenship guaranteed to all members of the eschatological *ekklesia* (cf. Philippians 3:20). Pagan worship is renounced, e.g., worship of the emperor as divine (the *kaiser kultus),* and the multiplicity of gods in the Roman pantheon. The free persons are now totally slaves of Christ.

It seems that what is being said in verse 22 by Paul is that liberation is a matter of social importance (contrary to Conzelmann, Barrett, and possibly Godet) as well as spiritual significance. Nowhere is this interpretation of verse 22 seen more clearly than in Paul's position on the question of slavery in his letter to Philemon. It may appear suicidal to turn to Philemon for corroborative evidence for Paul's antislavery position in 1 Corinthians 7:20-24; many black theologians believe Paul was terribly wrong for sending Onesimus the slave back to his master, Philemon. But is this a legitimate criticism of the contents of Paul's letter to Philemon? A brief analysis should prove otherwise.

Philemon Concurs with Corinthians

From the information provided in the letter, Philemon seems to have been a member of the *ekklesia;* he is referred to by Paul

as a "beloved fellow worker"; the *ekklesia* met in his house
(Philemon, v. 2). Paul addresses Philemon as "my brother" (v.
7).[93] He declines the use of apostolic authority as a basis for his
directive to Philemon (v. 8) but places his appeal in the context
of love ("for love's sake," v. 9).[94] Thus the foundation is laid;
the message to be heard by Philemon is that the community of
believers, *he ekklesia,* is comprised of *adelphoi,* "brothers,"
who relate to each other as equals (cf. 1 Corinthians 6:5, 8).

Paul uses the term for "brother" some one hundred and thirty
times in his writings; his understanding of the term he learned
from Judaism, viz., that Christians are "physical brothers" in
the strict sense and "spiritual brothers" in the more general
sense.[95] Regardless of the previous state of individuals, once they
are converted by the Christ and added to the church, they are
called to treat each other as brothers (and sisters) (cf. Acts 9:17).

The prevailing ethic within the Christian community of brothers
is "love," *agape* (cf. 2 Corinthians 5:14). It is a God-like, all-
giving love that is to prevail in the church. This kind of love
places one at the service of a brother or sister (cf. Galatians
5:13).[96] This is precisely what Paul is saying that Philemon is to
do for Onesimus.

Now Paul assaults the central problem. His aim is to inform
Philemon in no uncertain language that there is neither master
nor slave in the *ekklesia.* Onesimus, who has become a convert
to the faith as a result of Paul's preaching, is to be accepted now
as a member of the brotherhood. Paul informs Philemon that he
is sending Onesimus back to him "no longer as a slave but more
than a slave, as a beloved brother, especially to me but how
much more to you, both in the flesh and in the Lord" (v. 16).
As a result of his call, Onesimus is now a brother with Philemon,
both physically and spiritually. As one who has been called in
the Lord, Onesimus no longer belongs to Philemon but belongs
entirely to the Lord as his freedman.

In a most insightful essay on the social ethics in Paul's letter
to Philemon, Theo Preiss says:

> If Paul had wished to reinstate Onesimus in a social order which must not
> be changed, if he had juxtaposed life in Christ to an order of creation,

and love to civil justice, he would have written something like, 'my dear Philemon, in the Lord, you are brothers and one; in the life of the world you remain each in his place socially.' Above all Paul would have respected the master's right of ownership over his slave. In actual fact Paul does no such thing: fraternity, unity in Christ, seizes upon the relation of slave and master, shatters it and fulfils it upon quite another plane. Onesimus will be considered not merely as an equal, another member of the Church, he will be a member of Philemon's family, a full brother. Thus there remains no margin of paternalism, what we have is a total fraternity.[97]

Preiss seems to have captured the full force of Paul's intention. He understands Paul to be instructing Philemon to accept Onesimus on a fraternal level, as a Christian brother, both in the spiritual and physical (social) sense.

This discussion does at least three things: (1) it negates the erroneous conclusion by black theologians (because of the misrepresentation of Paul by white theologians) that the letter to Philemon represents Paul at his proslavery best; (2) it points up Paul's consistency in his concept of Christian freedom (e.g., the harmony between Philemon and Galatians 3:28); and (3) it negates the conclusion of conventional white New Testament scholarship that Paul's understanding of freedom for the slave was spiritual and internal, a matter of freedom from sin. It confirms the fact that the slave who was called in the Lord is liberated from civil and social servitude and becomes the Lord's freedman.

A Final Word About Resistance

Paul seems to presuppose possible misunderstanding of what he has already said as it relates to slaves and Christian freedom. He proceeds to drop his final bombshell that, on the one hand, clears the air for the inquiring slaves as to the security of their newfound freedom in the *ekklesia* and, on the other hand, provides a challenge for them to defend their freedom at all costs. Verse 23 reads: *Times egorasthete. Me ginesthe douloi anthropon*, "You were bought with a price; do not become slaves of men."

The focus in this verse, as far as conventional theologians are concerned, is on *times egorasthete*, "you were bought with a price." Barrett considers this to be a reference back to verse 21b where, he thinks, Paul instructs slaves to remain in their servitude. He thinks this phrase could be an echo of concern for Christian slaves who were seeking to sell themselves back into slavery.[98] The problem with this conclusion is that there is neither a direct nor indirect allusion from Paul regarding self-sale of freed slaves back into slavery. Further, self-sale of former slaves back into slavery seemed to be a rarity at best in the Roman Empire.[99]

Conzelmann's comments on *times egorasthete* are devoted to refuting Deissmann's theory that there is similarity between the position conveyed here by Paul and the pagan practice of slaves being liberated by being sold to the gods.[100] Godet's comments on verse 23 are confusing and his intention escapes me.[101]

Contrary to the interests of Barrett and to Conzelmann and Godet's uncertainty, it would seem plausible to argue that 1 Corinthians 7:23a is a resonant reminder to the slaves that Jesus purchased their freedom on the cross. Not to remember this basic fact of liberation would cause a breach in the marching phalanx of Christian soldiers; it would empty the cross of its power (cf. 1 Corinthians 1:17). Paul's fear was that if former slave owners and men stealers were permitted to enter the *ekklesia* and seize their own or other former slaves, what would the world think of the power of Jesus' death on the cross to claim and sustain the freedom of slaves? Paul's concern seems to parallel that of Moses when he shouted in the wilderness to Yahweh, "Now if thou dost kill this people as one man, then the nations who have heard thy fame will say, 'Because the Lord was not able to bring this people into the land which he swore to give to them, therefore he has slain them in the wilderness'" (Numbers 14:15-16). If the slaves failed to remember that their liberation was claimed by the death and resurrection of Jesus and were returned, of their own volition or involuntarily, to slavery, the world would consider that death and resurrection to be of no effect. They would say of this Jesus, the Jew who was hanged on an ignoble gibbet, "He was able to bring the slaves out of the bondage of slavery but was not able to deliver them into the Promised Land of freedom." Paul was concerned that the cross not be emptied of its power, for the kingdom of God was to be known for its power (cf. 1 Corinthians 4:20).

Therefore, Paul's emphatic exhortation to the slave is "Do not become slaves of men," *me ginesthe douloi anthropon*. He does not say, "Do not become slaves of sin [*hamartia*]"; nor does he say, "Do not become slaves of another brother [*adelphos*]"; for these would be inconsistent with the principles of the *ekklesia*. He emphatically says, "Do not become slaves of men [*anthropon*]"—any men; more precisely, "Do not allow slave masters, former slave masters, men stealers, or any man to make you a slave once you have gained your freedom in Jesus who now has become your Lord." Essentially, Paul is exhorting the slaves to claim their freedom in Jesus Christ. The emphatic tone of *me ginesthe,* "do not become," bears the thought of resistance, resistance to any forceful attempt to reenslave a former slave. This seems not to be an illogical rationalization if we see Paul himself as an example *par excellence* for the slave.

Paul's life in Christ was one of incessant attempts to claim his freedom, of perpetual resistance and nonconformity against the norms and conventions of this world (cf. Romans 12:2). His mind-set was that of radical freedom; he was such a spiritual man that he could judge all things, but he was to be judged by no man (cf. 1 Corinthians 2:15). He counted it insignificant to be judged by any human court (or as Rudolf Bultmann put it, "dependent on the value judgements of men"[102]); it was the Lord who judged him (cf. 1 Corinthians 4:35). Paul was convinced he had the Spirit of God (1 Corinthians 7:40); therefore, he was free (cf. 1 Corinthians 9:1 and 2 Corinthians 3:17). It was this psychological mind-set, grounded in the theology of the cross and the call of God, that convinced Paul that no man had power over him, either physically or spiritually.[103]

For Paul the matter of psychological freedom that came as a result of Jesus' death on the cross and the call of God must inevitably be tested by physiological acts *(praxis)*. Thus he takes great liberty, even to the point of boasting, to delineate his physical encounters for the cause of preaching the gospel *(euaggelion)* of freedom (cf. 2 Corinthians 11:23-33). Determined to defend the gospel of freedom from the oppression of the law,

Paul physically opposed Cephas, face to face, when he came to Antioch (cf. Galatians 2:11). God only knows why Paul fought with the beasts (Roman soldiers?) at Ephesus; but we know that because Paul was assured of his eschatological reward in heaven, he dared to engage in physical fisticuffs with soldiers on earth (cf. 1 Corinthians 15:32). Because Paul was of Christ, he felt compelled to reflect his psychological mind-set of freedom in the physiological act of resistance to any attempt to negate that freedom. Of such activity, Paul urges the Corinthians, and especially the erstwhile slave membership of the eschatological community, to "be imitators of me" (cf. 1 Corinthians 4:16; 11:1). Thus we conclude that, in verse 23, Paul is giving fighting orders to an army; he is instructing slaves to resist any attempt to make them once again slaves of men; he is urging them to claim the freedom for which Christ has set them free.

Verse 24 provides a powerful climax for all Paul has said. He winds up his argument for freedom by insisting "in whatever state each was called [the call being that which brought the slave into the *ekklesia*], there let him remain with God."

We All Can Claim Our Freedom

In summary, we have attempted to contest the long-held presupposition of many black theologians—a presupposition held primarily by Albert B. Cleage, Jr., and James H. Cone—that Paul was proslavery and on the side of the slave system. I have attempted to remove the stigma that has been imposed upon the apostle by those white theologians and churchmen who, for centuries, have misrepresented the apostle's theology of freedom as we hear it coming to us from Holy Scripture. In my attempt to perform this most difficult task, I chose to deal with 1 Corinthians 7:20-24. My investigation disclosed that the slaves of the Corinthian church were probably concerned with the security of the freedom they had found in the *ekklesia*.

I concluded that Paul's instructions to the slave inquirers were that they were to remain in the calling into which they had been called, viz., the church, *ekklesia*. It did not matter that they were slaves when they were called, in the *ekklesia* they had the opportunity for freedom. Therefore, they were to claim that freedom, for in the *ekklesia* there is neither slave nor master; the slave who was called in the Lord became the Lord's freedman and was totally indebted to God in every respect. Likewise, the free person who was called in the Lord became the possession, a slave, of the Lord. Paul reminded the slaves that their freedom had been obtained through the death of Jesus on the cross; therefore, Paul urges them not to become slaves to men. In fact, I concluded that the text of verse 23 suggested strongly that slaves were to resist any attempt to be made slaves once again. I concluded that Paul instructed the slaves, in verse 24, to remain in the calling to which they had been called, viz., the *ekklesia*, the church, and to claim freedom.

If the foregoing argument is in any way sound, the question becomes, how does the Pauline understanding of church, *ekklesia*, relate to the Western and American understanding of church? Further, if we assume there still are vestiges of bondage in society, how can Paul's understanding of freedom in the context of *ekklesia* assist in liberating those who are bound—black people, Indians, Mexican Americans, women, homosexuals, and the white middle class?

From what I have presented, the understanding of "church" in Western and American cultures is far removed from that of Paul and the early church of the first century. To speak of the church today is to speak of an entity that generally worships God, believes in the death and resurrection of Jesus Christ, and is guided by the Holy Spirit. However, it is for the most part very rich and well organized into denominations, conventions, dioceses, districts, and the like and is divided into two distinct segments, one white and the other black. Although the church in America exists in a nation that is predominantly Christian, or quasi-Christian, the political arrangement within the nation is contradistinctively different. Although this is glaringly true, the church seems to be assimilated and at once consonant with the politics of the nation. If my understanding of Paul's view of the church hangs together, then there seems to be a serious need to rethink the meaning of "church" in the light of his understanding.

Wherever there is an entity that calls itself a church in the sense of the Pauline *ekklesia,* freedom in Christ is to be a reality; and it is this freedom that believers must claim. According to Paul's understanding of "church," *ekklesia,* black people who are a part have only to claim their freedom. This freedom, freedom in the fullest sense of the word, has been achieved in the cross-resurrection event of Jesus who is the Christ, and it does not have to be regained; it only has to be claimed by the believer.

Therefore, the challenge is set before black people and other minorities who are a part of the church and are in a quest for freedom. There is no need for blacks to whimper and whine and beg for their freedom in the church; all they need do is claim it! It is already guaranteed and is there for the taking! Equality, acceptance, and access to the economic resources of the *ekklesia* are guaranteed to the Ebony Children of America. They are not to be bargained for; they are to be claimed. The same freedom is guaranteed for the multitude of minorities in American culture; the native American, i.e., the Indians, whether located in their enclaves in Florida or the reservations in Minnesota and the Northwest and far West; Mexican Americans in the Southwest and western part of the nation; or Latin Americans in the Southeast and Northeast sectors of the country. If people of these minorities have been called into the *ekklesia,* they have access to freedom in its fullest meaning merely by claiming it.

In the *ekklesia,* no one is enslaved to another because of color or ethnic origin. In the *ekklesia* "There is neither Jew nor Greek, there is neither slave nor free, there is neither male nor female; for you are all one in Christ Jesus" (Galatians 3:28). For Paul, this is what it means to enjoy freedom in Christ in the *ekklesia.* People have only to claim it.

Just as Paul exhorts slaves to claim freedom from masters, so he exhorts women to claim their freedom from male dominance and second-class standing in the church. For Paul, women are free! If they have been called by God, they are free to prophesy

(1 Corinthians 11:5). Women held prominent and authoritative positions within the church of Paul's day. Euodia and Syntyche of the church at Philippi worked side by side with Paul in the work of the gospel (Philippians 4:2-3). Phoebe, a deaconess of the church at Cenchreae, is sent to the church at Rome, and the Romans are told by Paul to receive her "as befits the saints" (Romans 16:1-2). In the greetings of Paul's letter to the Romans (chapter 16), women are widely mentioned. It is likely that they held prominent positions in the church. Thus nowhere else in the New Testament are women elevated and venerated in the church as they are in Paul's writings. Women, in Paul's understanding of the church, not only are valuable but also are totally free (Galatians 3:28). Therefore, it would be an error of no small proportion for the contemporary church to make use of Paul's writings fallaciously (e.g., 1 Corinthians 14:33b-35) in order to consign women to silence. (Some churches and sects are known for this more than others.) Likewise, it would be a grave error of equal proportions for women to accept the church's consignment to silence. As a prominent representative of the New Testament's understanding of the church, Paul insists that women are free. They must claim this freedom!

For the homosexual, there is freedom within the context of the church that he or she is challenged to claim; it is freedom from promiscuity and inordinate sexual weakness. Within the context of the *ekklesia* it does not matter that a person once was a homosexual, the death and resurrection of Jesus Christ has "washed" and "sanctified" one and set one free from past captivity (cf. 1 Corinthians 6:9-11). There were homosexuals in the church at Corinth (1 Corinthians 6:9). But Paul said, ". . . such *were* some of you" (1 Corinthians 6:11). It does not matter in the church that a person once lived such a life. Now that one is in Christ, that person is a new creation; the old has passed away (2 Corinthians 5:17). There is freedom in the *ekklesia* for the homosexual; claim it!

In the *ekklesia* of Paul's understanding there is freedom from bigotry and racial prejudice. Paul challenges contemporary white

Americans, and anyone who is infested with the dreaded disease of bigotry and racial prejudice, to claim freedom from that sickness, a freedom that is offered in the *ekklesia* through the death and resurrection of Jesus Christ. It is a freedom that opens one's eyes to the height, depth, and breadth of the church and lets one see that it is comprised of more than oneself or one's ethnic group (cf. Acts 13:1; Romans 16; 1 Corinthians 11:17-22). It is a freedom that brings about the awareness of the mutuality of the Christian experience, i.e., that one not only is free from fellow humans but is free for them or is bound to them for each other's mutual good (cf. 1 Corinthians 9:19-23). It is a freedom that gives clearer perception of the end *(telos)* of the work of Christ at Calvary, e.g., that at the foot of the cross all men are equal (cf. Galatians 3:28).

It is this kind of freedom, which Paul describes, that stands in condemnation of the contemporary church which, because of racial prejudice and bigotry, has become divided into a church that is white and a church that is black. This kind of freedom stands in judgment on those church groups and organizations that claim racial equality but, in truth, reflect a preponderance of white rule and authority. It speaks against religious groups and church organizations that, in the name of Christianity, reprehensibly denounce the equality of all people and consign them to inferiority while the groups establish and maintain private schools of religious and secular learning to perpetuate racial separation in the church. But this freedom, freedom from the dreaded disease of bigotry and racial prejudice, according to Paul, is available to any and to all who need it today. It has only to be claimed!

Finally, the *ekklesia* offers freedom for those bound by greed for money and material wealth. Paul's life in the church is a shining example of the truth of Jesus' words that ". . . a man's life does not consist in the abundance of his possessions" (Luke 12:15). Paul's calling into the church liberated him from the greed and the need for the abundance of possessions. He had the right to financial support from the church, but his freedom in Christ and his love for the gospel relieved him of the need and the greed for financial security (cf. 1 Corinthians 9:8-18). Deep roots in history and a rich heritage belonged to Paul, all of which guaranteed economic security for him, but he said, "I count everything as loss because of the surpassing worth of knowing Christ Jesus my Lord. For his sake I have suffered the loss of all things, and count them as refuse, in order that I may gain Christ and be found in him, not having a righteousness of my own, based on law, but that which is through faith in Christ . . ." (Philippians 3:8-9). Paul's freedom to count all things as loss for the sake of Christ was far greater than any need for economic security and greed for financial gain. The proof that Paul made the right choice in accepting the freedom offered in the *ekklesia* is borne out in the facts that his name has dominated the conversation of the church through the centuries and his writings have influenced hundreds of millions for good. It is this freedom from need and greed, freedom to accept real security, that Paul offers to those who are bound. It merely has to be claimed.

So for Paul, "Jesus" means "freedom." The *ekklesia* is the community in which this freedom is experienced. It is a freedom that is to be guarded at all costs against the encroachments of the world, the people and customs of it. Whether Jew or Gentile, slave or free, male or female, black or white, rich or poor, freedom and equality are available in the *ekklesia*. Claim it!

3

The Great Reversal

If, according to Paul's exhortation to the Corinthians, the Christian claims freedom in Jesus Christ, then it stands to reason that there must be a vigorous effort to maintain that freedom. Freedom must be maintained by the Christian by means of faithfulness to Jesus Christ and the sustaining power of the Holy Spirit. To violate this Christian freedom is to commit a flagrant error, viz., apostasy, a reversal of direction, an about-face from that which has been obtained by the Christ on the cross and, at one point in time, claimed by the Christian through acceptance of Jesus as Savior and Lord.

Such was the situation among the churches of Galatia. Paul labored among the Galatians, delivering them from their servitude to idolatry and barbarism and their slavery to the fickle and capricious ways of their former life. But as soon as he had passed on to another field of labor and the *euangelion* of freedom in the Spirit of Christ had cooled in the Galatians' hearts, they reversed their course and found solace in another kind of bondage, bondage to the Jewish law and to their former pagan practices.

In our continuing study of Paul's strategies for freedom, his experiences with the churches of Galatia may disclose to us that it is not enough to make the breakthrough to Christ and claim the freedom that has been obtained at Calvary. There must be a successful follow-through to maintain that freedom. There must be a vigilance in the faith, an intransigent obstinacy in righteousness and a militant opposition against attempts to eat away that freedom in the Spirit that might cause one to reverse field and again embrace bondage to the unspiritual. If such is not the case, the inevitable ensues—what I call the great "reversal."

The ever-present challenge that Paul sets before each generation is that freedom claimed in Jesus Christ must also be freedom maintained in Jesus Christ. But Paul's haunting criticism for all generations and centuries since his time is that Christian communities have over and over again failed in their efforts to maintain in the Spirit the freedom, obtained in and by means of Jesus Christ, the cross-resurrection event, and the Holy Spirit.

In the previous chapter, I utilized a more technical approach to Paul's writings to the Corinthians in order to get at the deeper meaning of his statements on slavery and freedom. Literary criticism, form criticism to some extent, and exegesis were used to facilitate this effort. In this chapter and the chapters to follow, there will be no wide use of these techniques. I will depend primarily on the Revised Standard Version (RSV) of the Bible; however, other translations will be called upon as the need arises. A variety of commentaries will be utilized in my attempt to arrive at a more lucid view of Paul's challenge to the Galatians and to our age. At the bottom of all the efforts will be the attempt to allow Paul's hermeneutical message to speak to the question of apostasy, turning away from the faith and from freedom in the Spirit.

In focusing on the Galatian letter, we find ourselves dealing with Paul's classic treatise on Christian freedom. We also discover that this is the primary work in which he attacks head-on the serious problem of the great reversal in faith of the Galatian Christians. Galatians is, according to Hans Deiter Betz, Paul's apology, his defense, as it were, of the Christian faith as well as of himself.[1] It is possibly the one book in the New Testament in which apostasy is so forthrightly dealt with with such volatile reprehension.

And so using Galatians as the point of departure, I expect to draw from it Paul's caustic criticism of not only the Galatians but also the ill-practice of Christianity by Americans, viz., our own return to forms of bondage. I hope to show the resemblance among the reversals of the Galatians of antiquity, the Puritans of American infancy, and black people in their emergence from American slavery. My suspicion is that Paul still stands before us as our arch critic of bondage, the champion defender of Christian freedom, a voice out of ancient Christian history, calling us to cease our wanderings from the foundational moorings of Christian freedom and to return to the rock on which our faith is based.

The Origin of the Galatians

The focal passage in the Galatian letter will be Galatians 1:6-7. However, a cursory look at the entire letter itself will be necessary in order to experience the full impact of Paul's frontal attack against Galatian apostasy and his defense of Christian freedom. In order to understand the dynamics of the Galatians' reversal of direction and departure from the faith, we must look at their history, origin, religious practice, and social behavior prior to Paul's appearance. It will be important also to examine briefly Paul's message of Christian freedom, the message that liberated the Galatians from their past bondage. We then will determine how the Galatians gravely erred and fell back into the throes of bondage.

Who were these Galatians of antiquity? Where did they come from? What was their life-style? What were the circumstances of Paul's advent in Galatia, and what were the results? What was the cause of the Galatians' great reversal? What was Paul's response? These are some of the questions with which we must immediately deal.

Ancient Galatia was located in Asia Minor in approximately

the location of modern Turkey. The area originally contained a mixture of peoples: Bithynians, Phrygians, Lycaonians, Pamphylians, and the like. The chief city came to be Ancyra (modern-day Ankara). The development of the Galatians, as such, occurred hundreds of years prior to the time of Paul. They originated in the area now known as France, Germany, Britain, and Ireland and were known by the name of Celts or Gauls. Hordes of these barbarian Celts, or Gauls, swept down from northern Europe into Italy about 390 B.C. When they had satisfactorily whipped Rome and extorted indemnity from the Romans, they withdrew. About one hundred years later they unsuccessfully attacked Greece only to retreat in defeat. But the Celtic wave kept moving.

In about 239 B.C., they overran Asia Minor but were defeated by Attalus I, king of Pergamum, and were relegated to a territory that was bordered by Bithynia on the north, Pontus on the east, Cappadocia and Lycaonia on the south, and Phrygia on the west. The land was parceled out to the three tribes of the Gauls: (1) The Trocmi settled in the land that was easternmost, bordered by Cappadocia and Pontus, and took Tavium or Tavia as the chief city; (2) the Tolistobogii took up residence on the westernmost frontier of Bithynia and Phrygia with Pessinus as the capital; and (3) the Techtosages settled in the center of the land and took Ancyra as their seat of government.[2] Though now settled in their own land, the Gauls or Celts were unable to withstand Roman dominance. The country became a dependent kingdom under Roman rule. Eventually the land became a Roman province, all the while accumulating additional nations that were contiguous with it, e.g. Pisidia and Phrygia. This was the land that came to be known as Galatia.

The predecessors of the Galatians—the Gauls, or Celts, of Europe, Britain, and Ireland—were fiery barbarians. Julius Caesar described them as warlike. However, their frequent incursions into Italy and Greece often resulted in humiliating defeat, so that eventually there developed within the race a kind of self-effacement, a penchant to national inferiority.[3] J. B. Lightfoot seems to think that the social intercourse of the Gauls with the Greeks and especially the Phrygians of Asia Minor, whom he called the most effeminate and worthless of Asiatics, caused further deterioration and degeneration of the character of the Gauls.[4] Epictetus, the Stoic philosopher of New Testament times, viewed the Gauls as people driven to deterioration and degeneration of character by "madness and wine."[5] In addition, much of the degeneration of character of the Gauls seems to have come from their insatiable greed for wealth and luxury.

Possibly the two most salient characteristics of Gauls were their fickleness and their leaning toward dark religious superstition. Of their fickleness, J. B. Lightfoot says that they were "inconstant and quarrelsome, treacherous in their dealings, incapable of sustained effort, easily disheartened by failure."[6] The Galatians of Asia Minor, Lightfoot suggests, brought with them from Britain and Europe their proclivity for fickleness.[7] Julius Caesar referred to the earlier European Gauls or Celts as having a "sheer instability of temperament."[8] He held them in utter suspicion because of their whimsical, vacillating tendencies. He said of them,

> . . . they are capricious in choosing a course and prone to revolution. It is characteristic of them that they force travelers to stop, even when they are unwilling, and question them on any news or rumors they may have heard, and in the towns the crowd surrounds traders and forces them to say where they have come from and what they heard there. On the basis of such hearsay they enter upon grandiose plans which they inevitably regret, for they credit rumor unquestioningly and their informants lie to please them.[9]

The religious life of the Gauls was just as fickle, unsettled, and ephemeral. Following the religious erudition of the priestly Druids, the European Gauls were driven by dark superstition and an obsession with death.[10] Again, Julius Caesar describes their grotesque religious practice:

> The whole Gallic race is addicted to religious ritual; consequently, those suffering from serious maladies or subject to the perils of battle sacrifice human victims or vow to do so. The officiants they employ are Druids. It is their belief that human life must be rendered for human life if the divinity of the immortal gods is to be appeased. There are regular public sacrifices of the same character. Some weave huge figures of wicker, and fill their limbs with live humans, who are then burned to death when the

figures are set afire. They suppose that the gods prefer this execution to be applied to thieves, robbers, or other malefactors taken in the act; but in default of such they resort to the execution of the innocent.[11]

Later on, during the latter part of the first century A.D., Epictetus alluded to the Galatians as having a fondness for the cult of Cybele.[12]

These were the people Paul encountered when he dared to enter the land of Galatia and carry the message of Christ into Lycaonia, Pisidia, Perga, Phrygia, and all the region of Galatia. (See Acts 14; 16:1-6; 18:23. Citing these passages raises the question of the South Galatian and North Galatian controversy, a matter that is far beyond my present intent and purpose. In essence, however, the question is whether Paul wrote to the churches of the southern sector of Galatia—of which we have record of his travels, viz., the cities of Lystra, Iconium, and others—or to the entire Galatian region, which includes the area to the north.) They were the kind of religiously superstitious, barbaric, unstable, and fickle people about whom history had spoken.

Paul's Relationship to Them

When Paul entered Galatia, he met those whom J. B. Lightfoot suggests brought with them from Ireland, Britain, France, and Germany a capriciousness and unstable character.[13] They were worshipers of and in bondage to "beings that by nature are no gods . . ." (Galatians 4:8). In Gerhard Herm's study of the Celts, it is confirmed that the Celts set aside days of the month for special observance and sacrifice[14] (see 4:10). To confirm further Paul's discovery of mysterious religious practices among the Galatians, Herm refers to the discovery of a maze of early Celtic deities, 374 in number, that claimed allegiance[15] (see 4:8-9).

In keeping with their barbaric nature of old, the Galatians' socially masochistic behavior (it was discovered by Paul) led them to a pastime of biting and devouring one another (cf. 5:15). Their inclination to be guided by the promptings of the flesh led them to perform a catena of degenerative practices such as "fornication, impurity, licentiousness, idolatry, sorcery, enmity, strife, jealousy, anger, selfishness, dissension, party strife, envy, drunkenness, carousing, and the like'' (5:19-21). These were the volatile and venal characteristics of the Galatians spoken of by Julius Caesar, Epictetus, and Paul when he met them. But somehow Paul's message of one God and freedom in Christ was met with heartening acceptance, and it served as a corrective for the Galatians' capriciousness and dark superstition.

When Paul first came upon the Galatians, he had been smitten with a fierce physical ailment (4:13). However, Paul's malady gave them an opportunity to show unusual hospitality: ''you would have plucked out your eyes and given them to me'' (4:15). It seems as though they anticipated his coming and were waiting for the message he brought: ''you did not scorn or despise me, but received me as an angel of God, as Christ Jesus'' (4:14). But more than this—they received not only Paul but also the message he brought. As though wearied from the confusing pantheon of gods and the need for many sacrificial appeasements, the Galatians readily received Paul's message of one God (3:20). They accepted through faith that Christ had been crucified so that they might be justified before God (3:1; 6:14). Through faith they received the Spirit of freedom and observed the miracles of God in their midst (3:3-5). They had accepted Paul's good news of Christian freedom and were running well in that freedom (5:7).

But then something happened about which we learn only in Paul's letter to the Galatians, for in Luke's account of Paul's travels in the region of Galatia, there is no indication of trouble. On Paul's first missionary journey, Luke's account says that in the Galatian region he ''appointed elders for them in every church, with prayers and fasting, they committed them to the Lord in whom they believed'' (Acts 14:23). On the second missionary journey, according to Luke, Paul went again through the region of Galatia, strengthening the churches in the faith, their numbers increasing daily (16:5). On the third missionary journey, Paul went back through the region of Galatia again, strengthening the disciples (18:23). There is no indication of trouble from within or without. But trouble there was. Somewhere during Paul's travels to Ephesus or maybe once he had arrived in Galatia, he received news of the Galatians' great reversal from the faith. It was then that he wrote his letter and expressed his shock and called them to return to the right path.[16]

Indications of a Turnaround from Faith

Paul's letter to the Galatians is smartly written. It hints at the sophistication of the Roman letter. The first section (Galatians 1:10–2:21) is devoted to Paul's apostolate, which he says is from God. The second main section (3:1–5:12) contains Paul's emphasis of faith over against the law. The third main section (5:13–6:10) is devoted to ethics. Galatians 1:9 is an introduction that contains an anathema, and 6:11-18 is his conclusion, which contains the last outburst against circumcision.

The letter is caustically written because something terrible had happened in the churches in Galatia: "I am astonished that you are so quickly deserting him who called you in the grace of Christ and turning to a different gospel . . ."(1:6). What were the indications of the Galatians' reversal and their desertion of the God who had called them in the grace of Christ? What caused them to turn to another gospel?

A Questioning of True Apostleship

The first indication of their reversal was their questioning of Paul's legitimacy as an apostle. In spite of the fact that the Galatians received Paul as an angel from God and as Jesus Christ himself (4:14), they came to the point of questioning the legitimacy of his apostleship.

Paul responded to this questioning of his apostleship by brushing aside his usual congenial introduction (like the one in 1 Thessalonians 1:2-10) and angrily plunging into a vindication of his calling, which he insisted was from God: "Paul an apostle— not from men nor through man, but through Jesus Christ and God the Father, who raised him from the dead . . ." (1:1). He underscored the initial vindication of his divine apostleship by providing an elaborate commentary on it, explaining that it issued forth from a call from and commission by God rather than from man (see 1:13–2:10). Moreover, he argued the authenticity of his apostleship time and again by asserting that his was the only authentic gospel (1:8), reminding the Galatians of their earlier acceptance of him as a true apostle (4:12-20), and audaciously giving them exhortations and prohibitions, e.g., "But I say," "I warn you" (see 5:16, 21, *passim*). He let no one doubt the fact that he had been authentically called to be an apostle of Jesus Christ. In fact, as he closed the letter, he reminded them, "I bear on my body the marks of Jesus" (6:17).

A Rejecting of the True Gospel

The second indication that the Galatians had reversed field and had become apostates was their rejection of the gospel message that Jesus had been crucified for their redemption and justification, a message that had been received by them through faith. The first hint of this rejection is Galatians 2:21. Paul goes on to remind them that Christ was publicly portrayed before their eyes "as crucified" (3:1). Paul further countered the Galatians' rejection of the crucifixion of Jesus by providing a midrash on the extent Jesus went to redeem humankind from the curse of the law (3:10-14). Paul's explanation of Jesus' crucifixion on the cross was that it was Jesus' way of taking upon himself the curse of humanity, according to Deuteronomy 21:23.

The Galatians' rejection of Jesus was also rejection of their justification before God. Paul countered this rejection by reminding them that justification before God was not required by works of the law (cf. 2:15-21). Painfully, Paul once again postulated that God did not provide them with the Spirit nor work miracles among them through the works of the law but did this by "hearing of faith" (3:5). Here Paul made use of a midrashic interpretation of Abraham of the Old Testament as a classic example of how one is justified by faith (cf. 3:6-9).

Inasmuch as the Galatians had reverted to another gospel, viz., the law of the Old Testament, Paul took this opportunity to elucidate on Jesus as the fulfillment of the law. According to Paul, the law was given four hundred and thirty years after God's covenant with Abraham and his offspring (i.e., Jesus). Because of human transgressions, the law was given by God, not as a promise or inheritance, and ordained by angels through an intermediary (3:19-20) to consign all to sin and to keep humanity under constraint. It served as a custodian, a *pedagogos,* a schoolmaster, a harsh instructor, until Christ should come. Now that Christ had come, people were no longer under the custody of the law but were justified before God as sons and daughters through faith in Christ; they now were free in the Spirit. The Galatians had abruptly rejected this message, but Paul took great pains to remind them of it. Horrors, that such a thing had to be done! But it was necessary because the Galatians were subscribing to a gospel that said the law of circumcision was that which justified them before God (cf. 5:3-12; 6:13).

A Reverting to Superstition

A third indication of the Galatians' reversal from the faith was their resumption of practices of former idolatries. Formerly, the Galatians were in bondage to beings and idols that they had accepted as gods. They were enthralled to "weak and beggarly elemental spirits" (4:9). They were enslaved to the observance of "days, and months, and seasons, and years" (4:10). According to Paul's discussion about this in the letter, the Galatians had gone back to such superstitious practices in spite of their tremendous beginning in the faith.

A Deserting of the New Ethic

A fourth indication of the Galatians' reversal from the faith was their abandonment of personal and community ethic. Somehow the new gospel they had adopted afforded the Galatians the delusive privilege of satisfying desires of the flesh. In a state of total confusion, adopting a strange amalgam of freedom in the Spirit and the law of the Jews, the Galatians thought they could do violence to each other (5:13-15), look upon the fallen and the weak with arrogant indignation (6:1-5), practice the enslavement of human beings and discrimination between Jews and Greeks and male and female (3:28), and abandon all personal ethical restraints (5:16-24). The result of the Galatians' abandonment of

the message of the crucified Christ and of their practicing the
ethics brought about by an irresponsible freedom in the Spirit
was like that of a river swollen by precipitous rains that had
overrun its banks and had flooded the valley and plains. The
waters now lay still and polluted, destroying land and vegetation.

The Reversal's Perpetrators and Victims

Such were the glaring indications of the Galatians' reversal of
direction from the faith in Jesus in which they had so great a
beginning. But what was it or who was it that caused this tragic
and colossal turnabout among the churches of Galatia? And how
did Paul deal with the phenomenon, trying to get the Galatians
back on track?

Of course, Paul was incensed and utterly enraged. Waiving
his usual glowing accolades seen at the beginning of much of
his other correspondence, Paul released his rage upon the Galatians and centered on what many have thought was the problem
in Galatia and the cause of Galatian apostasy. In the first chapter
he said,

> I am astonished that you are so quickly deserting him who called you
> in the grace of Christ and turning to a different gospel—not that there is
> another gospel, but there are some who trouble you and want to pervert
> the gospel of Christ. But even if we, or an angel from heaven, should
> preach to you a gospel contrary to that which we preached to you, let him
> be accursed. As we have said before, so now I say again, If any one is
> preaching to you a gospel contrary to that which you received, let him be
> accursed (1:6-9).

It seems that someone had taken advantage of the Galatians, had
crept in surreptitiously, and had deposited in their minds another
gospel that was contrary to that which Paul had earlier preached.

But was Paul's concern with certain people who had come
into the Galatian camp and unsettled the faith, causing the Galatians to commit apostasy? Hardly so! A closer look at the letter
may prove that Paul had no real problem with the opponents, as
some have called them, but did have a problem with the Galatians
themselves. At the outset of the letter, Paul says, "I am astonished
that *you* are so quickly deserting him . . . and turning to a different
gospel" (1:6, italics mine). His ensuing torrent is not against

anonymous opponents who had peddled a perverted gospel but against the Galatians who should have been convinced that the gospel Paul had preached to them was the real thing. Paul's continuing attack against the Galatians in chapters 1 and 2 is a painful reminder of his credentials as the authentic, God-ordained bearer of the genuine message of Good News to the Gentiles and of the fact that at the beginning of his first visit, the Galatians had received him as an angel of God, as Jesus Christ himself. They even would have plucked out their eyes and given them to him (4:15).

Paul's wrathful astonishment and anger in chapter 3 is not vented against some unknown opposition but against the Galatians: "O foolish Galatians! Who has bewitched *you,* before whose eyes Jesus Christ was publicly portrayed as crucified?" (3:1). Paul had demonstrably and convincingly preached, and they had believed that Christ had been crucified. Paul had taught that baptism in Christ brought about oneness in the believing community and not division (3:28). Paul had unrestrainedly planted the seed of the message, and the Galatians had tucked that germinating seed into their hearts. How was it possible that even the most beguiling knave could come along and pluck from their hearts a message so firmly rooted therein?

Further, through Jesus Christ the Galatians had become one. Their new identity counted it a violation of the Spirit of Christ to allow social, sexual, or religious distinctions (3:28). In Christ, they were heirs, offspring of Abraham, and sons and daughters of God. This being true, Paul wanted to know how they could once again want to be subject to the weak and beggarly elemental spirits of their former pagan worship (4:9). More than this, in the Galatians' inability to withstand opposition forcefully and, in fact, in their submission to it, they evidenced a new desire to be under the law (4:21). Paul rushed to apostasy's altar upon which they had allowed themselves to be sacrificed and snatched them from it with a father's complaint: "*You* are severed from Christ, *you* who would be justified by the law; you have fallen away from grace" (5:4, italics mine).

Like a hammer that drives nails into hardened oak, making its former disarray into a house for one's abode, Paul drives home his point that *"you,"* i.e., the Galatians, "are the culpable ones whose lives need to be set back in order. *You* were running well; who hindered *you* from obeying the truth?" *"You,"* the Galatians—not the opponents—are the ones against whom Paul directs his tirade in his attempt to correct their misguided trajectory and reshape their disheveled lives. *"You"* were running well; *you* disobeyed the truth!" (5:7). Soaring to one of the zeniths of his argument, Paul delivers what could be described as the coup de grace: "This persuasion is not from him who calls *you"* (5:8, italics mine). The belief and conviction that the law was important for the guidance of life, the observance of days and months, and the worship of weak and beggarly elemental spirits, all of which were inherent in their former life as pagans, were not from him who *called* them. Paul emphatically reminds the Galatians, ". . . *you* were called to freedom" (5:13, italics mine), but not to freedom that could be used for an opportunity for the flesh.

So, in fact, what we have come upon here is a treasonous act by the Galatians. They had forsaken the *call* that had gone to them from God through Jesus Christ through the preaching of Paul. It is of no small importance that Paul refers to the Galatians in his introduction as ". . . the churches of Galatia" (1:2b). The Galatians, as all others who had accepted Paul's message, had been called by God to be the New Israel, the people of God, a new nation, the body of Christ, the *ekklesia* in which persons individually and churches collectively were sanctified, set aside, to do the will and purpose of God on earth. Being called by God through Christ, they were no longer to hold slaves (3:28) nor were they slaves themselves, whether of men (cf. 1 Corinthians 7:23) or the ideologies of their former lives. They were free (cf. Galatians 4:31). Under this new arrangement, the Galatians were obligated to accept no other view than that of Paul, God's ordained spokesman. Anyone who tried to undermine his teaching would have to "bear his own judgment," but the Galatians themselves were obligated to stand firm therein (5:10).

So here, for Paul, is where the crux of the problem was: the Galatians had faltered, failing to hold fast to what it meant for them to be *called* by God through Jesus Christ, what it meant to be *called out* to be the church (*ekklesia*), and what it meant to experience and enjoy freedom as children of God. In the previous chapter where I discussed the Pauline meaning of "freedom" (*eleutheria*), I indicated that "freedom" for Paul meant that blessed existence enjoyed by the believer and made possible by Jesus' cross-resurrection event, in which the believer was released from bondage to another individual, family or group, political structure, idolatries, and human weakness. The believer was called out of the world by God through Jesus Christ into the church, the *ekklesia,* where he or she became a slave to Christ, bestowing all allegiance upon him as Lord. It was this entire process that had been violated by the Galatians. In this rested the apostasy of the Galatians.

Of course there have been and are contradicting opinions as to what the problem was in Galatia. Modern theologians have flirted with every theory and notion as to who it was that caused the problem in Galatia, i.e., the Galatians' renunciation of their call by God. For example, Ferdinand Christian Baur set forth one of the earlier arguments that the troublemakers in Galatia were Jews of the genuine old stamp or Jewish Christians who were not in agreement with liberal Pauline Christianity.[17] A. Lukyn Williams, following the line of thought of the earlier Baur, argued similarly that the problem in Galatia was caused by Jewish Christians who taught a false Christianity, viz., that the acceptance of Jesus as Messiah also included the acceptance of the law of Moses and its exhortations to observe seasons and circumcision.[18] Herman N. Ridderbos[19] and Werner Georg Kümmel[20] also argued that the troublemakers were Jewish Christians who taught that true Christianity was inclusive of circumcision and fulfillment of the law.

Building on the Tübingen position of Jewish Christian opposition in Galatia were those who sharpened this formulation to focus on Simon Peter and Barnabas. Eduard Meyer has drawn the conclusion that Paul's reference in Galatians 5:10 is to none other than Simon Peter.[21] The implication is that Simon had gone into Galatia after Paul left and had taught a view of circumcision contrary to Paul's, thus confusing the Galatians. Hans Lietzmann argued that the true opponent of Paul in Galatia was Barnabas.[22] James Hardy Ropes insisted that there were two opposing forces at work in Galatia. On the one hand, there were the Judaists who precipitated the teaching of circumcision; while on the other hand there were the libertinists who advocated freedom to satisfy the yearning of the flesh.[23]

And still another postulation of the cause of the great reversal in the churches in Galatia is given by Walter Schmithals. He thinks the opponents were Jewish-Christian Gnostics. He draws this conclusion from what he thinks are, anti-Gnostic strata that he finds in the letter.[24] Willi Marxsen takes a similar position, concluding that the problems in Galatia were caused by Christian-Jewish-Gnostic syncretists.[25]

These conclusions, however, do not bring us any closer to settling the question of who the opponents in Galatia were. We are left merely to draw straws to make the determination. The suggestions of Jewish Christians, Jewish-Christian Gnostics, or Christian-Jewish-Gnostic syncretists as posited by Baur, Williams, Kümmel, Schmithals, and Marxsen, respectively, are not altogether helpful. The Jewish and Gnostic tenor of the letter discloses to us that the opponents had to be of that persuasion. However, we still do not know who they were.

Contrary to Meyer, it seems unlikely that Simon Peter would be the culprit. Paul's discussion in 2:11-15 discloses no indication that Simon Peter is charged as the guilty one. Paul really does not know who the guilty one is; his reference "whoever he is" in 5:10 is indicative of this. Paul's warm references to Barnabas in 2:9 and 13 do not indicate that Barnabas could have been the varmint in the barnyard scattering the chickens. So we really do not get a clear picture of who Paul's opponents were in Galatia.

The fact is that Paul was not concerned in the least with who the opponents were in Galatia. In contrast to what seems to be a large majority of New Testament theologians, the cause of *the great reversal* in Galatia was not a group of opponents who clandestinely crept in behind Paul and undid what he had done there. After Paul had gone, the Galatians themselves allowed their fickle nature and capricious character, about which Julius Caesar had written, to surface and overcome their new beliefs. They yielded to their penchant for new tales and theological ideas that seemed so intriguing. The Galatians abandoned the spiritual route of freedom charted by Paul and, enchanted and overwhelmed, willingly adopted the way of bondage to the law introduced to them by Paul's opponents, whoever they were. The Galatians were like little children who, though taught by a parent the ways of right and wrong in life, so easily are led astray by the winking eye of a stranger seducer. One cannot expect any other behavior from a stranger seducer than to be about the business of seducing; but one expects a well-taught child to avoid and resist the seducer. This was not so with the churches of Galatia. They behaved as children who had never been taught, in whom Christ had not become real.

This seems to be the reason Paul gave his attention not to the opponents—he was not concerned about them—rather, he was troubled over his children whom he had taught with much pain but who had flunked the test of perseverance in the faith, a test that inevitably would come. He was concerned about his children whom he had set on the road and who had been running well but who had then allowed themselves to be lured from the path (5:7). His anguish was over those at Galatia who had developed a case of tired spiritual blood and had so soon become weary from the journey (6:9). So Paul laments, "My little children, with whom I am again in travail until Christ be formed in you! I could wish to be present with you now and to change my tone, for I am perplexed about *you*" (4:19-20, italics mine).

The strategy for freedom that seems to explode before us in Paul's letter to the Galatians is that once one claims freedom in

Jesus Christ, it is incumbent upon the claimer to maintain that freedom at all cost, to persevere in that freedom that was secured through a response in faith to the call of God through Jesus Christ. The irony of the Galatian situation is that although the Galatians had such a great and noble beginning, they failed to follow through to the logical end and, therefore, prove faithful to the strategy. Their whimsical nature and capricious character caused them to be lured from a course clearly charted by the apostle. Hence, Paul's excoriating letter, styled as his classic treatise on freedom, was sent as his corrective measure. The Galatians' great reversal caused Paul to write his most caustic and volatile letter. Paul was angry, and his letter to the Galatians seethes with anger and righteous indignation.

The Galatians' Bequest to America's Founders

Paul's letter to the Galatians continues to be relevant, and his anger is still painfully felt when it is considered that Americans, the offspring of the Galatians, have yet to correct their sin of retrogression. For this reason, Paul's theology of freedom continues to condemn and challenge the brand of Christianity that is practiced by whites and blacks and others who have subscribed to a perversion of the Christian faith. In spite of a great and noble beginning in founding a nation in which Christian freedom would delineate the nation's character, Americans made a great reversal and virtually abandoned that freedom as their highest objective. If we Americans are to redeem the Christian faith of the New Testament from the pit of contemporary perversion, it may be good for us to begin by reconsidering Paul's criticism of and corrective to the Galatians and allow such to address us and call us back to the high road of Christian freedom.

It is not fantasy to speak of American people as the offspring of the Galatians of the New Testament. The fact is that America was founded by sons and daughters of the Galatians to whom Paul wrote. Early English settlers in America, the Puritans, were descendents of the Galatians and when the Puritans landed in America, they brought with them not only lofty desires and noble beginnings to found a Christian nation but also an innate tendency to fickleness and the inability to follow through on a mission nobly begun, characteristics of their Galatian predecessors.

The seventeenth-century Puritan founders of America were, for the most part, from England. Though they separated themselves from the mainstream of English religion and culture, they could not separate themselves from their English heritage. Their English heritage was Celtic. The Celtic predecessors of the Puritans were inhabitants not only of England but Scotland, Ireland, Brittany, France, and other nations on the European Continent. The Celtics were interchangeably called Gauls; especially was this true of the invading Romans, as it is seen in the writings of Julius Caesar (see "The Origin of the Galatians" at the beginning of this chapter). These somewhat amorphous, heterogeneous people, of whom the Puritans were offsprings, were the ones who inhabited Galatia in Paul's day. In a study of the Celtic people and their religion, J. A. MacCulloch says, "In 279 B.C. some of the Celts had advanced into Greece and pillaged Delphi, Galatia was also occupied by them."[26] In an earlier study of the Celtic people, MacCulloch refers to the people in Galatia as "Galatian Celts." He says,

> Successive bands of Celts went forth from this comparatively restricted territory, (meaning the territory of Gaul, the territory to which the Romans confined the Celts) until the Celtic 'empire' for some centuries before 300 B.C. included the British Isles, parts of the Iberian peninsula, Gaul, North Italy, Belgium, Holland, great part of Germany, and Austria. When the German tribes revolted, Celtic bands appeared in Asia Minor, and remained there as the *Galatian Celts*[27] (emphasis mine).

These are the people who gave birth to the people called Puritans who founded America.

The Celtics bequeathed to the Puritans a propensity to fickleness. In a list of characteristics of the earlier Celtics, MacCulloch includes fickleness as one of their peculiarities:

> The folk of a Celtic type, whether pre-Celtic, Celtic, or Norse, have all spoken a Celtic language and exhibit the same old Celtic characteristics—vanity, loquacity, excitability, *fickleness*, imagination, love of the romantic, fidelity, attachment to family ties, sentimental love of their country, religiosity passing over easily to superstition, and a comparatively high degree of sexual morality[28] (italics mine).

Just as the Puritans could not sever themselves from the genetic connection with their Celtic progenitors, so they could not sever themselves from the Celtic characteristics that were bequeathed to them. They brought these characteristics, including fickleness, to the new land. This I will try to show briefly.

Wearied from the oppression of the Roman Catholic Church and dissatisfied with the corruption of the nascent Anglican church, the Puritans separated themselves from both churches and withdrew to Holland. After spending a brief time there and then drifting slowly back into their homeland, Britain, they set sail for a new land, America. Imbued with the Spirit of freedom in the Christian faith, much of which was of the Pauline strain á la Calvin, the Puritans pondered the kind of world that would emerge in the new country. While sailing west over the turbulent Atlantic on the ship *Arbella,* the leader of the new community, John Winthrop, preached a sermon to his shipmates that adequately described the venture: "Wee shall be . . . as a Citty upon a Hill, the eies of all people are uppon us; soe that if wee shall deale falsely with our god in this worke wee have undertaken and soe cause him to withdrawe his present help from us, wee shall be made a story and a by-word through the world."[29] So the destiny of these righteous separatists was set; they were to establish "a Citty upon a Hill." Their new world was to be that of a theocracy; the reign of God would be preeminent and the rule of the land would be the Word of God, the Bible. Freedom under God was their quest.

Perry Miller's and Thomas H. Johnson's pensive, prolific, and apologetic writings about the Puritans take us deep into the thinking of those who were founders of this country. Miller and Johnson corroborate the fact that the Puritans established in their new country a theocracy in a religious (supposedly Christian) context: "The Puritan state was thus from one point of view purely and simply a 'theocracy'; God was sovereign, His fiats were law and His wishes took precedence over all other considerations; the magistrates and ministers were his viceroys."[30] The Christian faith thoroughly permeated the life of the Puritans, both

ecclesiastical and civil. The Christian faith, as the Puritans understood it, governed every move of the New England citizen,
whether in the realm of politics or piety. Because this religion
was so cogent to the civil and ecclesiastical life of New England
Puritanism, the Puritans set forth stringent requirements for their
clergy who were responsible for the interpretation of Scripture
in light of their theocratic objectives. Miller and Johnson say that
"Puritans considered religion a very complex, subtle, and highly
intellectualized affair, and they trained their experts in theology
with all the care we would lavish upon preparing men to be
engineers or chemists."[31] The thinking that the Christian faith
was complex and that Puritan clergymen needed careful and
rigorous religious training was the reason for the founding of
schools such as Harvard and Yale universities.

The Failure to Build "a Citty upon a Hill"

So the Puritans began well what was at first a noble and appeared
to be a God-ordained venture. They came to this country to
establish a "Citty upon a Hill," a nation established under the
reign and rule of God. They were running well! But something
happened! Something prevented them from following through on
a venture they had so nobly begun. Indeed the Puritans helped
to lay the foundation for what is now America, the richest and
most powerful nation upon the face of the earth. But they were
not successful in establishing a "Citty upon a Hill," a theocratic
koinonia that conformed to the organization and ethic of Paul's
theology as expressed in his letter to the Galatians.

Human-Ordained Clergy

When we lay the measuring rod of Paul's theology and ethic
beside the Puritan effort, there are at least four areas in which
the Puritan effort failed to measure up to the requirements laid
down by the apostle. The first area in which there was failure
was the Puritans' acceptance of men entering the profession of
clergy on terms other than being called by God. Puritan literature
and literature written about Puritans do not disclose that men
assumed the responsibility to be clergymen on the basis of a call

from God. Puritan clergymen came to be such on the basis of their personal decision or the decision of the religious group itself. A thorough religious education rather than a call from God was the qualification for the ministry. Puritan preachers did not have to be formally ordained, as was the case with John Winthrop; they could be laymen. This approach to the ministry of the gospel was quite contrary to that of Paul. For Paul, the minister of the gospel and the apostle had to be called by God through Jesus Christ; hence, "Paul an apostle—not from men nor through man, but through Jesus Christ and God the Father, who raised him from the dead . . ." (Galatians 1:1). For Paul, there was no such thing as becoming an apostle through the ecclesiastical mandate of people or a church or by a personal decision; such a decision was strictly God's and God's alone.

Stringent Scriptural Interpretation

The second area of failure for the Puritans, probably a derivative of the first area of failure, was their return to the utilization of Scripture as law. The Puritans believed that if they were to establish an orderly society in their new land, there had to be some way to control both the civil and the ecclesiastical behavior of its citizens. Hence, the Bible was resorted to as the medium that provided the laws of life. The law, therefore, became the means of justification for the Puritans and their cause, rather than the grace of God through faith in Jesus Christ being that medium. Such a position was in diametrical opposition to Paul's theological ethic for the *koinonia* of the called of God.

Paul never approached the question of the ethical behavior of Christians living together from the "negative" point of view of the law. The law was good (Romans 7:12) and was in effect until Christ came (Galatians 3:24); but when Christ came, the law was nullified by the Spirit. When Paul spoke of the regulatory guidelines of the *koinonia,* he spoke in terms of walking by the Spirit, which produced that which he called the "fruit of the Spirit" (5:22-23). To conduct the business of the *koinonia* in terms of the law would mean to be engaged in the "works of the flesh" (5:19-21), which were opposed to the fruit of the Spirit. Regressing to the utilization of the law of the Jews as the regulatory agent for community behavior was the thing that raised the ire of Paul toward the Galatians of the New Testament.

In spite of Paul's painful condemnation of the Galatians for their reversion to the law and in spite of the Puritans' theological erudition, which surely apprised them of what the apostle had said to their biblical predecessors, the Puritans committed the same mistake by making use of the Old Testament Scripture, instead of the Spirit, as law for their justification and the regulation of behavior in their nascent society. Paul's judgment upon the Galatians seems to be quite appropriate here: "Now I, Paul, say to you that if you receive circumcision, Christ will be of no advantage to you. I testify again to every man who receives circumcision that he is bound to keep the whole law. You are severed from Christ, you who would be justified by the law; you have fallen away from grace" (5:2-4). For Paul, community behavior was not regulated by the law but by living in the Spirit and walking with the Spirit (5:25).

But reversion to the law was not the only sin of the Puritans; worse yet was their determination that as viceroys of God, they were the authority and arbiters of the Word of God. As did the scribes and Pharisees of the Gospels, the Puritans thought they were divinely ordained to have the final word on the meaning and application of the teachings of the Scripture. The matter is stated clearly by Miller and Johnson:

> The Puritans were assured that they alone knew the exact truth, as it was contained in the written word of God, and they were fighting to enthrone it in England and to extirpate utterly and mercilessly all other pretended versions of Christianity. When they could not succeed at home, they came to America, where they could establish a society in which the one and only truth should reign for ever.[32]

Having the absolute and exact truth of the written Word of God, the Puritans allowed no dissent from their understanding and application of it, for as Miller and Johnson say, "To allow no dissent from the truth was exactly the reason they had come to America."[33] So then when it became a matter of law, for example, that all Puritans attend worship services on the sabbath and pay tithes into the ecclesiastical coffers for the operation of the church and government, all transgressors were punished in accordance with the law as the Puritans had prescribed. The situation became an exercise in authoritarian enforcement of the law as the Puritans understood it.

And to exacerbate the situation, the Puritan subscription to law was not to the pure Jewish law. They took the Jewish law of the Old Testament, the theology of the New Testament, both of which were corrupted by them, and infused this combination with the philosophies of Aristotle, Plato, and other Greek philosophers, the philosophies of Thomas Hobbes, Sir Francis Bacon, and Petrus Ramus, and the theology of John Calvin. They made use of the Roman law as well. In doing so, they plunged themselves into further contradiction with Paul's theology and ethic for the Christian *koinonia*. In contrast, while Paul seems arrogantly to portray himself as the only one with the authentic gospel (cf. Galatians 1:8-9), he quickly reminds the Galatians that his knowledge of Jesus the Christ came from God (1:11-12); he had no counsel from man, not even the apostles in Jerusalem (cf. 1:15ff).

So, in the Puritan camp, instead of setting up a society characterized by Christian freedom, the people, in effect, became enthralled to law hewn out of Scripture according to their understanding, an understanding entangled with a varied assortment of philosophies and theologies. All of this they set in an arbitrary, authoritarian mold. Thus, they proceeded to retreat into an entangled field of unrighteousness.

A Propensity for Witchcraft

A third area of failure for the Puritans was their penchant for witches and witchcraft, a return to a peculiar characteristic of their Galatian forebears. The Celtic predecessors in England, Europe, and Galatia were superstitious among other things; and so were the Puritans. In Massachusetts in 1692, the Puritans, as did Don Quixote of Cervantes's novel who mistook windmills for giants and flocks of sheep for armies, mistook human beings and dogs for witches. In that year, an old woman was accused of bewitching four children, and before the event was over in

Salem, twenty people and two dogs had been executed for being witches while one hundred and fifty people similarly charged waited in prison and still hundreds of others stood so accused.[34] All of this transpired with the sanction of both the civil and ecclesiastical authorities. Horrors, that such a thing could happen among Puritans of such educational and theological erudition!

Paul said to the Galatians, "Formerly, when you did not know God, you were in bondage to beings that by nature are no gods; but now that you have come to know God, or rather to be known by God, how can you turn back again to the weak and beggarly elemental spirits, whose slaves you want to be once more?" (4:8-9). His question could have been addressed to the Puritans, offspring of the Galatians, with equal severity and power, for they, like their predecessors, had committed a great reversal in turning to spirits and witches.

Participation in the African Slave Trade

Possibly the worst failure of the Puritans was their allowance and rationalization of and participation in the African slave trade. It is a fact that the Puritans shared in the responsibility for institutionalizing slavery in America.

In the region of Galatia, obviously the theory existed that there were differences between Jews and Greeks, slaves and freemen, men and women, and obviously these differences were institutionalized. The Celts who settled in Galatia had a history of division and strife among themselves and with others. But when Paul took the gospel of Jesus Christ to them, he said, "For as many of you as were baptized into Christ have put on Christ. There is neither Jew nor Greek, there is neither slave nor free, there is neither male nor female; for you are all one in Christ Jesus" (3:27-28). So the Galatians had been well informed by the apostle of the unity brought about when people are baptized into Christ and that their racial and genetic background made no difference in their oneness in Christ. In spite of this, cleavages between Jews and Greeks, categorizations of slave and free, and discrimination between male and female obviously developed. Paul was enraged that such was the case and wrote to remind the

Galatians that those baptized in Christ, regardless of their ethnic, racial, or social background, had become one in Christ.

Paul's cutting anger and painful disappointment are still felt today when we see history's disclosures that the Puritans permitted and committed similar discrimination, yea, enslavement, of a people they considered inferior when they founded Massachusetts. The Puritans knew better than to allow slavery to take place in their newfound land, but worse yet, they provided religious and scriptural rationalization for such a sordid enterprise.

Puritan clergymen were well educated in secular things and especially in sacred things. One learned Puritan clergyman in England read the Scripture voraciously, reading fifteen chapters from the Bible each day: five in the morning, five at midday, and five just before going to bed. Benjamin Brook said, in his book *The Lives of the Puritans,*[35] that virtually every Puritan minister attended a school of learning, such as Cambridge and Oxford in England. Of course when they came to America, the Puritans educated their clergy well to the extent of establishing Harvard and Yale universities at which they could study. The Puritan clergyman, therefore, was a well-educated individual, knowing the Bible and its teachings well. Hardly could he miss the dictum of Paul that "there is neither Jew nor Greek, there is neither slave nor free, there is neither male nor female; for you are all one in Christ Jesus" (3:28).

Sure enough, however, not long after their feet had touched America's shore, the Puritans permitted and praised the introduction of slavery into Massachusetts. They executed this incredibly reversionary feat, not by following Paul's theology and ethic that is so clearly laid out in the Galatian letter. They followed, for the most part, the theology of predestination as it was spun out by John Calvin and infused with the classic philosophy of Aristotle and Plato and the philosophies of Thomas Hobbes, Sir Thomas Bacon, Petrus Ramus, and others. The Puritans adopted as a law of life, as Miller and Johnson put it, their version of the Aristotelian notion that ". . . some men are born rich and some poor, some intelligent and some stupid, some are lucky and others unfortunate, some are happy and some melancholy, some are saved and some are not. There is no reason but that God so ordained it.''[36]

So while enslavement of any person is unilaterally in opposition to Paul's prescription of human and brotherly relations in a Christian community, the enslavement of black Africans was very much in keeping with the spiritual and social architecture of Puritan Massachusetts in New England. Cotton Mather, a most prominent Puritan minister of his day, sanctioned and encouraged the enslavement of black Africans, generously saying that the Christianization of blacks made them more docile and manageable slaves:

> And suppose it were so, that *Baptism* gave a legal Title to *Freedom*. Is there no guarding against this Inconvenience? You may by sufficient *Indentures,* keep off the things, which you reckon so Inconvenient. But it is all a Mistake. There is no such thing. What *Law* is it, that Sets the *Baptised Slave* at *Liberty?* Not the *Law of Christianity:* that allows of *Slavery*; Only it wonderfully Dulcifies, and Mollifies, and Moderates the Circumstances of it. *Christianity* directs a *Slave,* upon his embracing the *Law of the Redeemer,* to satisfy himself, *That he is the Lords free-man,* tho' he continues a *Slave.* It supposes, That there are *Bond* as well as *Free,* among those that have been *Renewed in the Knowledge and Image of Jesus Christ.* . . . The Baptised then are not thereby entitled unto their Liberties.[37]

The fickleness of the Puritans, their failure to implement faithfully pristine Pauline theology and ethic in the establishment of their new society, caused a rupture in the nascent national fabric, a rot and rip that widened so that the country called America would eventually be rent in twain. Had the errant trajectory been checked at the beginning and the miniscule tear mended at the start, the national tragedy of white against black and a national mindset of black inferiority and white superiority and civil wars and civil strife for civil rights might have been avoided.

But the die had been cast, and every offspring of the Celts—Galatians and Puritans—was fickle in dealing with the question of slavery. This is no more clearly seen than in the case of Thomas Jefferson. Jefferson was a well-trained, articulate, and able lawyer who became founder of the University of Virginia, governor of Virginia, and president of America. He was astoundingly intelligent in law. It is little wonder that his peers looked to him when it came to penning the desire of the nation for liberty and independence. Thus he became the chief engineer of the Declaration of Independence. The irony is that although Thomas Jefferson was extremely intelligent and well trained and wrote the Declaration of Independence, in which he stated that "all men are created equal," and opposed slavery his entire life, he always believed in the inferiority of black Africans vis-á-vis white people and never freed the slaves he owned at Monticello.[38] The same Celtic fickleness is seen in Patrick Henry who, while exclaiming ". . . give me liberty or give me death," held slaves in Virginia.

Current Expressions of Fickleness

As it regards the freedom quest by blacks in America, the fatal flaw of fickleness has and still holds control over the offspring of the Puritans and the Celtics. Marcus G. Raskin, quoting the political scientist Alan Wolfe, wrote,

"There is a systematic campaign to reverse the 1960s, to roll back, one by one, every single gain made by progressive and minority groups of that period and to re-establish to status quo ante of 1952 in the United States. Some do not even seem satisfied with this, preferring a more golden age like 1927. Rip Van Winkle woke up to find himself in the future. In the aftermath of Vietnam and Watergate, America is waking up to find itself in the past."[39]

This is a classic description of the result of the fatal flaw of fickleness that still finds residence in the psychology of Caucasian Americans, descendants of Puritans and British, European, and Galatian Celtics.

During the celebration of the two hundredth anniversary of the birth of America in 1976, much was said about the virtue of our beloved country. Worthy it is of such praise, for the nation has emerged as the most rich and powerful in the world. But amid the panegyrics of 1976, one person raised a reminder that there remained in the psychology of Caucasian Americans the fatal flaw of fickleness, especially in attitudes toward black people. Gardner Taylor, pastor of the Concord Baptist Church of Christ of Brooklyn, New York, painfully remarked that after two hundred years as a nation and more than three hundred years after the landing of the Puritans in Massachusetts, America still is unable to fulfill the objective of freedom for all people which was set forth at its beginning. The reason, he insisted, is the nation's fickleness, its inability to practice what it has preached, to place into deed what it adopted as creed.

> There is one great weakness in the American temper which is revealed from a reading of our past. It is the inability of the nation to sustain its energies and resources in the pursuit of a goal when that goal proves elusive and difficult to attain and when great cost, financial or psychological, is required and when prolonged individual sacrifice is demanded. . . .
> There was a fitful start toward wiping out differences between Americans based on the accidents of birth, but the nation's moral energies were soon spent and found wanting in the chance to make a deal and to get ahead. Still again in May, 1954, the nation came to another great junction. The last sanctuary of American jurisprudence, the Supreme Court, said that segregation was, of itself, unjust. The nation made another start and seemed to surge forward until the late nineteen sixties. Then, the price seemed too high and the time demand too long in prospect. Now, so much of that is gone. It has been lost in the nation's inability to make long and sustained sacrifices in the cause of truth and of God.[40]

So then, more than three hundred and fifty years have passed since the Puritans landed and since John Winthrop preached his sermon saying that they were to be as a "City upon a Hill." In one sense, the Puritans were successful in establishing that city, for truly the eyes of the world are upon America. But in a most profound way, they failed to establish a city in which the full force of Christian freedom could be felt and enjoyed by all peoples who stepped upon its shores. The Puritans had the best intention and were off to a great start in that direction, but they were overcome by their fickleness. It may be at the very moment that John Winthrop spoke the words on the ship *Arbella* saying they were about to establish a "City upon a Hill," he knew the Puritan-Celtic tendency was not to follow through on an enterprise to its fullest extent. If such lay in the back of his mind at the moment, it could have been the reason for his deep and searching concern over the possibility of the Puritans dealing falsely with God in the work they had undertaken. Perhaps they were starting out for a goal they were unwilling or unable to reach. Then God would withdraw from them and their work, and they would become a story and byword through the world.

It could be that we live in a time when the thing Winthrop greatly feared is upon us. One is driven to wonder if God has withdrawn from our nation. The Vietnam fiasco, the Watergate tragedy, the recession that strangles us, the inflation that eats us up, and the holding of American hostages by Iran, a´ nation of lesser power, seem to be indications that God has absconded from our midst. In Iran and other nations of its kind, America has become a story and a byword. In addition to this, in every municipal precinct, virtually every city in America, there is a seething cauldron of racial unrest that threatens to explode at any moment: Liberty City in Miami, Watts in Los Angeles, and Roxbury in Boston are only a few. It seems that our nation's government is powerless to do anything about them. If this is true, it is true because the founding fathers of this nation failed to be truthful with God in setting forth a true Christian nation with freedom for every person as its hallmark and in working to make it happen.

In spite of the Puritans' vision of an ideal theocratic society and in spite of their intentions, they were unable to implement what they had perceived with their heads. They fell victim to their innate tendencies. While making a great start, they could not complete what they began; they committed the sin of the great reversal, reverting to bondage to guilt and immorality and enslaving a nation of people. This was the beginning of the irony of American history.[41]

Across the ages, Paul the apostle speaks a caustic and condemning word to the Puritans of past centuries and American Caucasians of today: "O foolish Galatians! Who has bewitched you . . .?" (Galatians 3:1). "You were running well; who hindered you from obeying the truth?" (5:7). Again, Paul is not concerned with who it might have been (the Calvinists, the philosophers, or others) that caused the Puritans and American Caucasians to swerve from the path of right; he is concerned about them: "I am perplexed about you" (4:20b).

The great reversal in modern times in America is not limited to the Puritans and their Caucasian offspring; the sin has been committed by black people as well. It is not wrong to conclude that the freedom obtained by black people in America came as a result of their passionate pursuit for freedom in Christ. Freedom for black people in this country did not come by fiat, i.e., from the Emancipation Proclamation of Abraham Lincoln. It came from their determination to be free in Jesus Christ. From their crude knowledge of the gospel of Jesus Christ emerged a message of freedom for black people that their captors failed to disclose. Black people vowed never to rest until that freedom was realized.

The enslavement of black African people is an incredible story, a tale of horror. Lerone Bennett[42] and John Hope Franklin[43] tell us that before being brought to America as slaves, black African people were great and noble in character. They were people of knowledge and had institutions of learning. They revered truth and respected morals. Families, father-centered and tightly structured, were the norm of their social life. They were intensely religious and judiciously ethical. They earned their living by industrious labor and creative ability. Perversity and immorality had no place in their scheme of living. But when they were brought to America as slaves, all of this changed.

Introduction into America meant for black Africans an introduction to slavery and a reduction to the status of less-than-human. It meant a characterization of black Africans as ignorant and immoral. Families were divided and dislocated. Men were dehumanized before their women; children were separated from their mothers and fathers. Women were sexually abused and made to bear children for their masters and a variety of men as an animal would give birth to a litter. Black men were used as studs and made to labor under the lash for the luxury of others. It was a horrible scene. None can tell the story more graphically than Frederick Douglass[44] and Booker T. Washington,[45] who themselves endured the slings and arrows of that peculiar institution.

In spite of the feverish effort by Puritans and subsequent captors of black folk in both the North and South to use the Bible to make certain their bondage was the will of God, black African slaves discovered in the Bible something specifically addressed to them, a message of freedom. From the Bible handed to them by their captors, the black African slaves hewed out for themselves a Christian theology of freedom—an ingenious feat. This theology leaped forth from the songs they sang:

> My Lawd delivered Daniel.
> My Lawd delivered Daniel.
> My Lawd delivered Daniel.
> He sho' can deliver me.
>
> O freedom, O freedom,
> O freedom, over me;
> And before I be a slave
> I'll be buried in my grave
> And go home to my Lord and be free.

The message of Christian freedom sprang from the lips of self-taught and unlettered black preachers such as Henry Highland Garnett, Frederick Douglass, Richard Allen, Nat Turner, Gabriel Prosser, and Denmark Vesey. So there moved in the slave camp a mood that raced like a tidal wave, relentlessly lashing against the shores of bondage until the quest for freedom would be secured. Just as Emperor Constantine acquiesced to the force of the Christian movement to declare that the Christian faith was the religion of the Roman Empire, so Abraham Lincoln acquiesced to the quest for freedom in the context of the Christian faith that had been launched by black slaves.

The years subsequent to the Emancipation Proclamation were tremendous indeed for the black sons and daughters of slavery. Freedom meant black men marrying the women they loved and establishing families; it meant securing land and beginning a farm; it meant earning a living for oneself and one's family by industry and ingenuity; it meant becoming a part of the federal and state political apparatus in order to participate in the process of regulating the lives of black people and assuring freedom's continuance; it meant the establishing of churches, associations, conventions, and organizations to perpetuate the religious unity of the people; it meant the establishment of schools for the religious and secular education of black people; it meant the establishment of businesses, insurance companies, banks, and publishing houses to assure the economic security of black people; it meant a return to the high ethics and morals known to blacks before they were forcibly made slaves and participants in a perverted and promiscuous culture.

Yet at the beginning of the twentieth century, something happened to black people in their determination to be truly free. The flaw of fickleness emerged in the fibre of black people's personality and blurred their vision and prevented them more and more from keeping their eyes on the bright and morning star of freedom in Jesus Christ. And today black people have committed the sin of the great reversal, born out of the fickleness they encountered at the turn of the century.

The Turnaround for Black People

There are at least four areas in which black people's great reversal from freedom in the Christian faith is evident: (1) abandonment of the Christian faith as the primary religion by which freedom is to be acquired; (2) abandonment of morals; (3) reversion to the mammon of materialism; and (4) contempt for labor.

Abandoning the Faith as the Way to Freedom

It is without question that the Christian faith provided the spirit and power by which black people in this country claimed their freedom. The only religious expression allowed on the plantation was Christian, albeit the perverted version introduced to the slaves by the plantation preacher. The practice of native African religions was prohibited on the plantation. Yet out of the perverted version of the Christian faith came the keen feeling by black people that Jesus meant freedom for them as he did for white people.

At the turn of the century, however, a turn, a reversal, in the religious trajectory of black people developed. Many black people resorted to a varied assortment of religions; such were the Falashas and the Black Jews of Harlem and a hybrid version of the Muslim religion called the Black Muslims in which the honorable Elijah Muhammad was worshiped as god. Cults with leaders such as Father Divine and Sweet Daddy Grace, men who elevated themselves to deity, proliferated in ghettos and black communities across the nation. Astrology became prominent as a form of religion among blacks; a sign observed in the Watts section of Los Angeles, California, read "God is the sun." Aberrant religious expressions among blacks reached its height, or its depth, in the late 1970s when more than seven hundred black people followed a deified Jim Jones, a white cult leader, to a sweltering jungle in Guayana and died at his feet from drinking at his command a concoction of poison and Kool-Aid.

The irony of black people's quest for freedom in America is that the Christian faith provided the spirit and power to move them from slavery to freedom, but they failed to follow its trail to the end. They made a tremendous beginning in that direction, but they fell to the fatal flaw of fickleness. In the first quarter of the twentieth century, James Weldon Johnson, the son of a black preacher of the Christian gospel, wrote the song *Lift Every Voice and Sing* in an attempt to check this great reversal. One verse in particular called black people to remain faithful to the God who brought them through slavery:

God of our weary years, God of our silent tears,
Thou who hast brought us thus far on the way;
Thou who hast by Thy might, led us into the light
Keep us forever in the path we pray.
Lest our feet, stray from the places, our God, where we
     met Thee,
Lest our heart, drunk with the wine of the world we forget
     Thee.
Shadowed beneath Thy hand, may we forever stand,
True to our God, true to our native land.

Yet the great reversal continued. The Martin Luther King, Jr., era of civil rights came, and once again the Christian faith proved to be the religion to provide the spirit and power to end segregation and dehumanization for black people. The Christian gospel and its morals and ethics, and the black church and its enthusiasm and songs were all a part of Dr. King's spiritual arsenal that blasted the lingering bastions of bondage and segregation for black people. When Dr. King was assassinated in 1968, civil rights laws had been passed, voting rights had been secured, and economic gains for black people had made great strides. Much of that which gave strength and substance to Dr. King's sermons and civil rights demands were the theology and ethic of the apostle Paul. But though Dr. King made a breakthrough to secure freedom in America for black people, after his assassination black people failed to follow through by taking that same Christian gospel as the arsenal with which to continue their battle for freedom.

The apostle Paul has not been the favorite writer in the Bible for black people—Dr. Martin Luther King, Jr., and Dr. Joseph Johnson are possibly the only two black theologians who unashamedly made use of his theology. Paul now speaks in derision of black people's inability to follow through on a quest for freedom in Christ so nobly begun. "O foolish Black People! Who has bewitched you, before whose eyes Jesus Christ was publicly portrayed as crucified? Let me ask you only this: Did you receive the Spirit of freedom by works of the law of Judaism or another religion, or by hearing with faith? Are you so foolish? Having begun with the Spirit, are you now ending with the flesh? Did you experience so many things in vain?—if it really is in vain" (cf. Galatians 3:1-4).

Paul continues to speak a caustically critical word about black people's reversion to the religious panacea of superstition, astrology, and making gods of men: "Formerly, when you did not know God, you were in bondage to beings that by nature are no gods; but now that you have come to know God or rather to be known by God, how can you turn back again to the weak and beggarly elemental spirits, whose slaves you want to be once more?" (4:8-9). Black people have not had the greatest respect for Paul; yet Paul steps forth now as the one who painfully derides their reversed religious trajectory. If blacks had studied the apostle's theology of freedom more carefully rather than developing an antipathy for him because of the manner he was introduced to them by plantation preachers, maybe they could have avoided the grand travesty of reversing their course away from the Christian faith.

Forsaking Morals

The second area in which reversal from the Christian faith is evident in black people's quest for freedom is their abandonment of morals. When a people's religious faith is shattered and shaken into confusion, they lose sight of the moral imperatives in life. This happened to black people. At the turn of the twentieth century an increase in aberrant religious expressions arose. Concomitant with this was a decrease in morals among people.

Native African people were highly moral prior to their introduction into American slavery. They knew nothing of untruthfulness, drunkenness, or sexual immorality or perversity. Immorality was introduced to black Africans by their captors who forced them into civilization's most immoral denigration of human beings, American slavery; by their religious overseers who introduced them to a perverted version of the Christian faith; by their plantation overseers who delighted in forcibly pitting black man against black man to see who could outdrink the other; and by slave owners who denied marriage between black men and women while forcing them to produce children to people the plantation and who made use of black women for their own sexual gratification and never recognized as their own the resulting children. So immorality among black people is a child of American slavery. Yet black people never allowed such immorality to deter their quest for freedom, a freedom they had been assured was theirs by the gospel of Jesus Christ. As they broke their chains of human bondage, simultaneously they flung from themselves the yoke of immorality. Freedom for black people also meant marriage and moral decency.

Yet, again, at the turn of the twentieth century, something happened to reverse black people's strivings to return to morality.

Freedom came to mean indulgence in drink and drugs and living for the weekend party. Marriage was no longer passionately sought by black men; black women became mere sex objects to be lived with and laid with. It has come to be that black women live to give birth to a child; marriage can come later, if at all. The fashionable thing now is for young people to listen to lewd music that blasts loudly in their ears, luring them into a life of sex and irresponsible love. Respect for another is a rare item among black people; the result is a variety of violent acts perpetrated against one another. There exists a thrill for thraldom, a dreadful drifting back to the regions of bondage.

The apostle Paul again has a word of criticism to speak against black people in their reversal from moral decency to moral decadence. His criticism entails a call to freedom in Jesus Christ or a threat to be forever bound by the works of the flesh:

> For you were called to freedom, brethren; only do not use your freedom as an opportunity for the flesh, but through love be servants of one another. For the whole law is fulfilled in one word, "You shall love your neighbor as yourself." But if you bite and devour one another take heed that you are not consumed by one another. . . . Now the works of the flesh are plain: fornication, impurity, licentiousness, idolatry, sorcery, enmity, strife, jealousy, anger, selfishness, dissension, party spirit, envy, drunkenness, carousing, and the like. I warn you, as I warned you before, that those who do such things shall not inherit the kingdom of God (5:13-20).

Paul challenges black people to return to and live up to their call to freedom that is in Jesus Christ, a call to which they once faithfully responded. To be sure, if black people continue to enjoy the thraldom that has come from their great reversal into immoral ways, then they not only will fail to inherit the kingdom of God but will also fail to obtain true freedom and will continue in bondage to immorality.

Relying on Materialism

A third area in which reversal from the Christian faith is evident in black people's quest for freedom is the development of a mentality of materialism. This phenomenon began to raise its head at the turn of the twentieth century, as in the case of the first two areas of reversal. Possession of material things—houses, clothes, rings, watches, and so on—was not in evidence among blacks in American slavery; if blacks did have material things, it was not in abundance. What was in abundance was a healthy and vigorous spirit of freedom born out of the Christian faith. Materialism as a priority was strongly resisted by blacks before the twentieth century; they sang, "You can have this world, but give me Jesus."

Less than fifty years after black people had gained freedom from bondage, fickleness overtook them. Like a weary antelope plodding through a sun-parched wilderness and suddenly coming upon a body of water, black people came out of slavery and happened upon the lake of materialism, knelt down, and lapped its addictive liquid until their minds became numbed in drunkenness and their eyes became blinded to the road that lay before them. Materialism quickly became the end sought by black people rather than freedom in Jesus Christ.

Early in the 1900s, W. E. B. DuBois prophetically observed the ominous cloud of materialism creeping upon the horizon of black culture. Passionately he pleaded that black folk not take refuge in its delusive shade. He saw materialism's coming creating a moment of decision when sons and daughters of slavery would have to choose which road to take in their pursuit for freedom; he begged that they not take the route of materialism, stating it was a road that would end in futility and failure, a cul-de-sac.

In the Black World, the Preacher and Teacher embodied once the ideals of this people—the strife for another and a juster world, the vague dream of righteousness, the mystery of knowing; but to-day the danger is that these ideals, with their simple beauty and weird inspiration, will suddenly sink to a question of cash and a lust for gold. Here stands this black young Atalanta, girding herself for the race that must be run; and if her eyes be still toward the hills and sky as in the days of old, then we may look for noble running; but what if some ruthless or wily or even thoughtless Hippomenes lay golden apples before her? What if the Negro people be wooed from a strife for righteousness, from a love of knowing, to regard dollars as the be-all and end-all of life? What if to the Mammonism of America be added the rising Mammonism of the re-born South, and the Mammonism of this South be reinforced by the budding Mammonism of its half-wakened black millions? Whither, then, is the new-world quest of Goodness and Beauty and Truth gone glimmering? Must this, and that fair flower of Freedom which, despite the jeers of latter-day striplings, sprung from our fathers' blood, must that too degenerate into a dusty quest of gold—into lawless lust with Hippomenes.[46]

DuBois's was a noble plea; it was passionately writ large on a scroll for coming generations to see and heed. But there were not very many takers. The farther black people proceeded along the raceway to freedom, the more they noticed and considered the golden apples of materialism that lay appealingly along the roadside.

Now almost *en masse*, black people have leaped for the lure, fallen for the fake, and dived for the deceptive apples of materialism. While blacks coming out of slavery accumulated houses and land, blacks today are accumulating clothes and cars. The desire for ownership of land has eroded among blacks. What black people like is to drive, not necessarily own, cars: big cars, little cars, any kind of car as long as it is a car. The first thing a young black boy wants is a car; he longs for this more than anything else. There is an obsession among black people for clothes, television sets, radios, stereo consoles, and other material things that wear out, rot, and decay.

Materialism being the end many black people seek, the acquisition of material things is achieved by any means possible. One of the surest ways to acquire material things is by lifting them from the possession of others without asking, viz., stealing. That sometimes is accompanied by murder. Theft of money and material things has come to be commonplace in black communities across the nation. Consequently, the black community in America finds itself in bondage to insatiable materialism and fear of losing that which has been acquired by theft. Houses with burglar alarm systems, barred windows and doors and businesses with iron gates to protect their plate glass window displays (as was observed on the main business thoroughfare in a major city in Indiana, a gruesome sight) are essential in some areas where there is a concentration of black people, a people who have become captive to the spirit of materialism.

Obsession with material possessions has often been a deterrent and diversion for people in quest for freedom. This is true of black people at the moment. It was true for some within the churches to which Paul preached, and he addressed himself to the issue, for materialism had become a diversion from true freedom in Christ: "Brethren, join in imitating me, and mark those who so live as you have an example in us. For many of whom I have often told you and now tell you even with tears, live as enemies of the cross of Christ. Their end is destruction, their god is the belly, and they glory in their shame, with minds set on earthly things" (Philippians 3:17-19). These seem to be words most cogent to the situation in which black people in America find themselves.

Paul has exciting exhortations to check black people's reversal into materialism: "Rejoice in the Lord always; again I will say, Rejoice. Let all men know your forbearance. The Lord is at hand. Have no anxiety about anything, but in everything by prayer and supplication with thanksgiving let your requests be made known to God. And the peace of God, which passes all understanding, will keep your hearts and your minds in Christ Jesus" (4:4-7). It is not a facile, half-baked formula that Paul offers black people as a cure for materialism; it is a sure remedy in that it calls for people to cast themselves completely upon the mercy and care of God through Jesus Christ, who will supply all needs (4:19) as well as contentment with whatever possessions they have.

"Not that I complain of want; for I have learned, in whatever state I am, to be content. I know how to be abased, and I know how to abound; in any and all circumstances I have learned the secret of facing plenty and hunger, abundance and want. I can do all things in him who strengthens me" (4:11-13). The aid Paul offers black people here is strength to be content in whatever material state they find themselves. Paul urges that the strength for contentment in plenty or want is in Christ, in the knowledge that he will supply whatever is needed. This is true freedom and a corrective for reversal into materialism.

Having Contempt for Work

The final area in which reversal from the Christian faith is evident in black people's quest for freedom is their failure to follow through in the development of business and industry. This enigmatic and disturbing development has been caused by an emerging contempt for labor.

It is too often an untold story that black Africans in American slavery were quite creative and innovative in providing for themselves. Slavery provided few, if any, comforts of life for black people; they taught themselves the way of survival and relative comfort. The need for shoes motivated Jan Matzeliger to develop the shoe machine. The need to tell the time of day and understand the changing of the seasons encouraged Benjamin Banneker to create the first American clock and produce an almanac; he also was responsible for laying the design for the nation's capital city, Washington, D.C. With the coming of the steam locomotive came the need for a system of communication for trains traveling the same tracks. There was also the need to develop a braking system strong enough to halt that hulk of moving steel. Another black man, Granville T. Wood, was responsible for developing a communication system through which two engineers could talk with each other, determining their location and preventing accidents. He also was responsible for the air-brake system that adequately stops trains.

Examples of creativity and innovativeness in business and industry among black people as a whole exceed that of other individuals. Especially toward the end of the 1800s and the beginning of the 1900s, black people surged forward in these two areas. For example, there were no provisions to care for the sick and to bury the dead on slave plantations; so black people developed their sick and burial societies, some of which evolved into insurance companies and funeral homes. Education was a commodity hungrily sought by blacks coming out of slavery. The result of this great need was that churches and associations spawned a flurry of schools that gave religious and secular education to both young and old. Some of these schools, begun with meager substance, developed into major colleges that still exist today. To aid in the provision of literature for their people, church denominations established publishing houses to produce such literature. These provided literature for their constituents and jobs for the people. Toward the end of the 1800s and the beginning of the 1900s, financial frugality was stringently observed. Thus banks were established to facilitate the saving of people's money and make it available to those who required a loan. Innately skilled as artisans and craftsmen, black people naturally provided the skill and labor to build the capitol buildings of many states in the nation, the railroad stations, buildings, and homes. Following the years of slavery, many of these black people formed their own companies to engage in the architecture and construction of buildings.

On and on go the citations of a people coming out of slavery, fiercely engaged in the labor of business and industry as they strove on their way to freedom. But in the past thirty years, something has happened to turn around the surge in business and industry among black people. Here, too, a great reversal has occurred. Industry among black people, i.e., the development of commodities out of raw materials, is virtually extinct. Businesses begun toward the end of the 1800s and the beginning of the 1900s have either disappeared or are just holding onto survival by a thread. There is little effort to harness and control the skills unique to black people and develop the skills into corporate efforts that would yield jobs and financial security and independence for the people. This truly is a great reversal, for it has thrown black people once again upon white people for security, the provision of jobs, and money. It is a new kind of slavery; but it has been caused by black people's failure to follow through on what had been begun by their forebears.

The apostle Paul has another word of advice for black people in this respect. It is not certain what he had heard about things in Thessalonica, but it could have been that a tendency to be slothful in business and industry was developing. So he wrote to the Thessalonians saying,

> But concerning love of the brethren you have no need to have any one write to you, for you yourselves have been taught by God to love one another; and indeed you do love all the brethren throughout Macedonia. But we exhort you brethren, to do so more and more, to aspire to live

quietly, to mind your own affairs, and to work with your hands, as we
charged you; so that you may command the respect of outsiders, and be
dependent on nobody (1 Thessalonians 4:9-12).

Paul admonishes the church at Thessalonica to engage itself
in productive work of its own (assuming that this means work
that provides the membership with jobs and income). By doing
this the church would command the respect of those outside the
church and would be independent of them for provision of jobs
and financial security, thus preventing the church from becoming
vulnerable to outsiders. The early church was independent and
self-supporting; it was not dependent on Roman philanthropists
for its financial support. Had the latter been the case, the early
church could not have demanded the respect of outsiders, and
its nascent movement would have died in the womb.

This advice Paul offers to black people in America as well.
Almost on every hand, blacks must turn to outsiders—white
people who control business and industry—for jobs and financial
security. As a result, black people find themselves obligated to
and dependent on white people for life's existence (for example,
the NAACP could fold if it had not the support of the Jewish
community and labor unions); and they fail to elicit the respect
of those to whom they are obligated. So Paul's advice is a viable
option for black people; return to the attitude of independence in
labor, business, and industry that characterized the early church
and their forebears. He urges them to shun contempt for labor
and return to love for labor and independence; this is the way to
freedom in Christ, according to Paul.

Follow Freedom's Prescribed Route

In conclusion, it is not easy when a people have made an about-
face to turn about and get back on the road that leads to freedom
in Christ. It will not be easy for America, nor will it be easy for
black people in America. There is always the deterrent of self-
doubt. Often it is easier to resign oneself to the situation because
of what someone else has done. Thomas Jefferson resigned himself to American slavery by insisting that King George of England
was responsible for slavery because he permitted ship lines to

engage in transporting African slaves. Black people in America have spent a great deal of time pointing out how white people have been responsible for blacks being the way they are; thus developing independence in business, industry, and jobs is thwarted. So it will not be easy for America or black people to make the turnabout, for these and other kinds of impediments and obstacles will be in the way. But if Christian freedom is to be realized, the effort must be made.

The apostle Paul lends encouragement and assistance in making that effort. He not only chides us, as he did the Galatians, for what we have done to reverse ourselves, but he also cheers us to get back to the road that leads to ultimate freedom and to stay on that road. He encourages the traveler to stay on freedom's road regardless of how weakened is the traveler's will or how strongly the traveler is wooed by the crouching seducer to leave it. Stay on the road! Paul is helpful in reminding the traveler that it is not by one's self or one's power and ingenuity that the traveler is kept on the road to freedom; "God is at work in you, both to will and to work for his good pleasure" (Philippians 2:13). If the Christian traveler ceases and desists from traveling the road to freedom and turns back to a previous state of bondage, that person is saying that God was unable to give the strength and will to complete the race. Such is not the case. The resurrection of Jesus Christ, the Son of God, is proof enough that God will not ordain and initiate anything he is not willing or able to see through. Thus if the Christian traveler starts out on the journey to freedom, convinced that it is the will of God, that person believes that God will give grace and power to complete the race. And having made such a decision, the Christian traveler stays on the road.

This was Paul's personal strategy, one he slavishly followed to the end. He did so because he had found freedom in Christ, and having done so, he vowed to stay on the road until ultimate freedom could be achieved. It was not easy for him, but he stayed on the road. There is none among mortals within the etchings of the Holy Record who was so burdened and crushed by life's oppressive circumstances (e.g., 2 Corinthians 4:8-12), but who could still say, "So we do not lose heart" (4:16) as Paul. Though intimidated and attacked from without and torn with strivings and contradictions from within, the prize of ultimate freedom ever eluding his grasp, Paul let nothing separate him from the love of freedom (cf. Romans 8:35-39). He stayed on the road; he pressed toward the mark till he made it his own (Philippians 3:12-14). For the Galatians his lesson was a hard one to learn and his model a difficult one to follow. Following Paul's pre-scribed route to Christian freedom has been problematic not only for the Galatians and other early Christian communities but also for Christians down through the centuries. Attempting to follow the apostle is cogently described by Günther Bornkamm: ". . . not a few who yield themselves to his gospel are left feeling like a traveler overcome by vertigo in an Alpine region surrounded by steep, cloud-covered peaks, who often does not know how to follow on and how he is going to last the journey." [47] But as Paul urged the Galatians (cf. Galatians 4:12), follow the apostle we must if we are to return to the road and continue on toward an existence in which we truly can be free.

4

Discipline: The Long Road to Freedom

If the Christian is to claim his or her freedom and is to avoid the dreaded sin of reversal, there must be some means by which freedom can be maintained. Paul's theory is that it is discipline by which freedom is maintained. For Paul, Christian freedom is not something that is obtained once and for all; it is a long journey that requires the tedium of discipline.

Of the many Pauline passages that set out the strategy of discipline for the long road to Christian freedom, there is none more powerful and persuasive than that found in 1 Corinthians 9:24-27. It is here that Paul details how the Christian traveler maintains the freedom that has been given by the Christ at Calvary and claimed by the believer in faith.

A serious reading of all of Paul's letters discloses that one of the grave problems with which he wrestled was the lack of discipline within the communities of faith to which he had introduced the gospel of freedom. As we saw in the previous chapter, the Galatians seemed to have all but abandoned the route of righteousness on which they had so nobly begun. The Corinthians were now this way and now that way, dissipating their energies in division, internal squabbles, lawsuits, drunkenness, and the popular religions and philosophies that crept into their camp. The blurry-eyed Thessalonians nearly lost view of the road because of their hesitance and uncertainty over the resurrection of themselves and their loved ones. The beloved Philippians, maybe the ones most dear to Paul, were stymied on the trail due to quarrels among the saintly women of the church and the joy that others found in debauchery. The Romans could make little progress because of their fog-enshrouded desire to continue in sin so that grace might abound. Last of all, Philemon, a high-standing official in the church, tripped over his obsession to lord it over the once-slave-now-Christian, Onesimus. Discipline, or the lack of it, was more than a problem in the churches; it not only impeded their stride toward ultimate Christian freedom but threatened to make a mockery of the faith as well.

Really the entire New Testament, from Matthew to Revelation, reveals that discipline for the long road to ultimate Christian freedom is indispensible, and the lack of it is reason for expulsion from or loss of the race, as Paul describes it. In the Gospels, Jesus exhorted the believer to discipline: "he who endures to the end will be saved" (Matthew 24:13). He also warned that lack of discipline resulted in unfitness for the kingdom: "No one who puts his hand to the plow and looks back is fit for the kingdom of God" (Luke 9:62). The letter to the Hebrews is composed of pages weighted heavily with hints of apostasy. In Ernst Käsemann's powerful little book *Jesus Means Freedom*, he observes that the church of the Hebrew epistle suffered from tired spiritual blood and stood every moment on the verge of recanting. However, the writer of the Letter to the Hebrews counters this tendency and says, ". . . let us also lay aside every weight, and sin which clings so closely, and let us run with perseverance the race that is set before us, ... It is for discipline that you have to endure" (Hebrews 12:1b-7). In the Revelation to John, the church at Ephesus is cautioned, ". . . I have this against you, that you have abandoned the love you had at first. Remember then from

what you have fallen, repent and do the works you did at first''
(Revelation 2:4-5).

So it was discipline that was needed in the early church—in
all of its manifestations—in order for it to complete the long road
to ultimate Christian freedom. The road would have tests and
temptation, pain and persecution, trials and tribulations, and
disappointment and even death; but discipline for the journey
would be sufficient to enable persons and churches to endure all.

The church—in all of its manifestations in America—is faced
as pressingly today as ever before with the challenge of discipline
for the long road to ultimate Christian freedom. Heresies are
flourishing within the church; social pressures to conform to the
norms of the day are closing in; government repression is slowly
eroding the church's strength; the clamor for ethnic purity, of
racial ruptures and cultural cleavages is dissecting the body of
Christ; insatiable greed holds captive the mind and might of not
too few in the believing community while suffering and want
hold captive far too many. Religion as a mode of escape and
means for personal aggrandizement has ascended to the throne
of ultimate concern while pursuit of Christian freedom enjoys
the ignoble seat of low esteem, and infidelity on the part of the
bride of Christ raises questions as to the continuation of the union
between Christ and his church. With all of these conditions both
within and without, the once galloping strides of the contemporary
American church have been reduced to a stall. The road to
ultimate Christian freedom seems to be too long and protracted.
Weariness has set in, and even apostasy looms as a dangerous
possibility. But in spite of the petty and pompous protrusions
that impede the church's trek along the long road to ultimate
Christian freedom, there is something it can and must do to finish
faithfully the course: it must commit itself to discipline, the
strategy employed by the apostle Paul and shared with those who
would dare follow behind him.

Seeing the Faith as a Race

We are not unfamiliar with the Corinthian church. We discussed
the church, the people in it, and the many problems it faced in

the second chapter of this book. There is no need to do a replay of the setting of the church at Corinth, only to say that it was mired in the quagmire of division within; caught up in court fights; inflated with arrogance; gripped by greed, debauchery, and chicanery; and warped by theological views that tripped its people up on trivia. There is little wonder why Paul was concerned that the Corinthians would get bogged down in their buffoonery or even retrace their steps from the road to ultimate Christian freedom and fail to make a run of it. His grave concern drove him to seal the ninth chapter of this first letter to the Corinthians with the powerful statement that serves as the locus of our concern for this chapter and the strategy for the long road to ultimate Christian freedom.

The strategy that Paul offers for the Christian traveler on this long road is something that he contends should be known already. "Do you not know . . ." is the manner in which he begins to explain his strategy in 1 Corinthians 9:24. It is a diatribe of which he makes copious use (see 3:16; 5:6; 6:2, 3, 9, 15, 16, 19; 9:13; 11:14, 22; *passim.*). Paul's use of the diatribe reveals his familiarity with the contemporary linguistic tools utilized outside the church by others, e.g., Stoics such as Zeno, Cleanthes, and Epictetus. They used the diatribe in an argumentative, rhetorical manner to prove their points. Paul's use of it here is the same; he raises a rhetorical question to which the Corinthians' only answer could be that they know the answer. He then lunges into his argument: "Do you not know that in a race all the runners compete, but only one receives the prize? So run that you may obtain it" (9:24).

Notice that here Paul profusely makes use of pagan imagery, e.g., *stadio trechontes,* "the ones 'running a racecourse.'" People run to receive a *brabeion,* a "prize." His use of the diatribe of Stoic notoriety and the racecourse and prize images strongly indicates his familiarity with pagan life-styles. Arnold Ehrhardt tussles with the question of whether Paul used certain unknown Orphic writings, maybe a similar statement from a neo-Pythagorean saying, to make this analogy in 1 Corinthians 9:24.[1] He concludes, however, that the sayings only show a similarity to Orphic writings and Paul's knowledge of the language of the pagan world. Paul was adept at expropriating pagan language and imagery, baptizing it and utilizing it for Christian purpose. So then, when Paul made use of such language as *hoi en stadio trechontes,* he was certain that the Corinthians were acquainted with his manner of conversation.

Corinth was the site of the Isthmian Games that were held every two years, the second and fourth years of the Olympiad.[2] The games were played in an elaborate stadium and were linked to the fortune of the city of Corinth itself; they were quite a religious affair.[3] The prize was a crown of pine, or, as was the case during Paul's time, a crown of celery.[4] The winner won immortality in the mind of the people and even became as one of the gods.[5]

Paul's concern with the Christians in the Corinthian church is not, however, that of their engagement in a secular race held in a stadium for the appeasement of and identification with the gods and the pleasure and honor of people; rather, he has in mind something altogether different. His objective is to make clear to them their engagement in the Christian race. In such a race, it is not that one among the many who compete wins the prize; rather, all have the possibility of claiming it.

Being Aware of the Pursuit and the Prize

Here then is the first piece of Paul's strategy for the Corinthians' engagement in the race along the long road to ultimate Christian freedom; it is their need to compete in the race in pursuit of the prize, the goal. Paul's concern was that the Corinthians become aware of the goal, the prize, and pursue it. It was a logical concern for Paul, for indeed the Corinthians had lost sight of the goal. Their once fleet feet had become moored by the shackles of self-interests, immorality, heretical hegemony, and twisted ideologies. If the Corinthians were to achieve the venerable goal of ultimate freedom in Christ that lay at the end of the long, long road, they had to keep that goal in sight and pursue it.

Paul's goal-oriented strategy for beginning the long, long road to ultimate Christian freedom is as cogent today as it was for the floundering Corinthians of his day. For today there is in our society a dreadful lack of awareness of the goal of ultimate Christian freedom and of the will to pursue it.

The womb of deep and dark social and religious dissatisfaction has borne noble visions of a new world of freedom grounded in religious faith. Such dissatisfaction with social conditions likely began in Great Britain when the pompous profligacy of King Henry caused Sir Thomas More to write *Utopia* as his response to it all. It was the result of his mental musings of a different and better kind of world. The craving for a different and better world became an obsession of Puritans such as John Bunyan. His idyllic *Pilgrim's Progress* was his response to the world about him, a world that was effete in its efficacy and whose morality was dying. Another Puritan, John Winthrop, while sailing toward a newly discovered land of freedom, stated the venerable goal of establishing a nation that would be as a "Citty upon a Hill," whose only king would be God, whose only rule would be the Bible. Even as the early founders of this nation made their way into the wilderness, visions of a utopian goal loomed large on the horizon.

Ralph Waldo Emerson groped for a national castle that could be built by self-reliance, and Henry David Thoreau mused of a society that could enjoy the placid peace and rustic restfulness of Walden. Even in the shaping of America's political future, there was a sensational utopian symmetry. While envisioning the noble destiny of his still-forming nation, Thomas Jefferson built into the Declaration of Independence the goal of an ideal world in which all people would be considered created equal and endowed by their Creator with certain inalienable rights, the right to pursue life, liberty, and happiness. What a world this was to be! Peering out of the desolate dungeon of their house of bondage, black Africans of American slavery saw and sought the loftier world of freedom. They sang of it in their spirituals: "Trampin', trampin', tryin' to make heaven my home"; "Walk together, chillun; there's a great camp meeting in the Promise Land."

These people—some preachers, some who were theologically astute, some who were deeply religious politicians and statesmen, and some who were slaves—lifted their sights out of an entangled social and political quagmire to see a world that would be a better place in which all people could live in freedom. They gave nascent America the vision of egalitarian Christian freedom, freedom that would appease the thirst of the oppressed and poor, freedom that would sate the hunger of the neglected, freedom that would extend welcome to that vast array of huddled masses yearning to be free. These, to name a few, pursued this vision of freedom that was alluringly emblazoned on America's horizon.

Losing Sight of the Goal of Freedom

But that vision now has become dim and the goal unsure. In the latter third of the twentieth century, America has all but lost sight of the goal of freedom that beckoned the religious visionaries and castle-building statesmen of its infancy. Robert Nisbet, in his *History of the Idea of Progress,* cites America's revolt against rationalism and science, i.e., the cultivation of irrationalism in a variety of forms and the growth of subjectivism in the form of preoccupation with one's self and one's pleasures, as different from anything the West has ever known. Having stated this, he raises the question: "Will the historic idea of progress be driven entirely from the intellectual field by the massed forces of pessimism: belief in cycles of civilization, with our own Western civilization even now hastening toward the bottom of the downswing?"[6] Subjectivism and pessimism pervade the character of America. This is the case because the nation has lost its grip on the future and its goal has disappeared from view. This has resulted in, as is indicated in Nisbet's question, a "hastening toward the bottom of the downswing."

The truth of Nisbet's observation is borne out in a mass of writings that cite the obliteration of ultimate Christian freedom in America and the advent of a contrived future for which no one is prepared. These writings detail the demeanor of a people whose economic and political future has spoiled before their eyes, and, who, in the face of such horrid realities, have recoiled into a protective cocoon of self and self-fulfillment.

A possible source of the beginning of the downward spiral of our society, the plummet toward the bottom of the downswing that has blocked from our view the vision of ultimate freedom, could be our growing concern with the technological developments that are rapidly emerging as our promised future. In their article "A Framework for Speculation," Herman Kahn and Anthony J. Wiener have cited developments, such as improved metals and materials, use of nuclear and radioactive power, use of automation and cybernation in management and production, experimentation in determining the sex of unborn children and in changing sex organs for adults, sophisticated spying networks, elaborate use of computers for home and business, long-range weather forecasts, and broadcasts from satellites to home receivers,[7] among many other innovations in technology, as the expected goals of society as it moves toward the year 2000. But in spite of such a gleaming future contrived by technologists, Kahn and Wiener surmise that ". . . the year 2000 will find a rather large island of wealth surrounded by 'misery,'"[8] This future for America and Western society was projected by these two men in 1967.

The emergence of such a future has been swift. This future, compared to the future spoken of by the apostle Paul and envisioned by the castle builders of pre-American and early American history, has brought about a terrible dilemma in our society. The arrival of such a future, described by Kahn and Wiener, has caused a dissembling of the social, ethical, religious, and political norms previously known.

The nation has begun to suffer from what Alvin Toffler termed future shock: ". . . the dizzying disorientation brought on by the premature arrival of the future."[9] Toffler cites the emerging lifestyles of people—inundated with information, nomadic in nature, not living in one place very long, living at an extremely fast pace, living in a world of throwaways, bottles, clothes, cars, and other expendables—as the way of life in the future. Traditional families, he says, will become fractured only to come together in other forms, i.e., professional parents will take on the child-rearing responsibilities of others, or homosexuals will marry each other and adopt children. The society that Toffler sees converging upon America is also characterized by a "surfeit of subcults," a proliferation of old and new groups of people with religiously and socially aberrational life-styles. Acceleration of the pace of life such as the integration of the races in America, minority demands on the social and political structures, world travel, and so on, has brought into conflict blacks and whites, men and women, foreigners and Americans (e.g., Iranians and Americans). All this, Toffler argues, has swept in upon American life and has thrown it into a state of shock. The shock has been caused by the advent of a disconcerting future for which American life is not prepared.

The prognostication of Kahn and Wiener, i.e., ". . . the year 2000 will find a rather large island of wealth surrounded by 'misery,'" seems to have come about some twenty years before its time. Already the economic resources of our nation are fast coming under the control of a few rich and super-rich corporations while the masses flounder in a sea of enveloping poverty. Inflation, a shrinking dollar, rising prices, soaring interest rates, increasing strictures on credit, and other financial woes are creating an economic situation that John Kenneth Galbraith calls the Age of Uncertainty.[10]

Black people in America have not been excused from the ravages of the encroaching future that is unpleasantly settling in upon American life. Integration that has come to mean annihilation, rising unemployment, removal of educational institutions from black communities and control, erosion of social progress and social programs gained in the sixties, mounting cases of injustice in the courts of the land, and a sweeping mood of conservatism in the likes of the Moral Majority movement and the reappearance of the Ku Klux Klan—all have thrown black people into a state of shock, disbelief, and disorientation. The vision of the Promised Land that Martin Luther King, Jr., saw, toward which black feet invincibly marched, has suddenly vanished. Speaking at the October 1980 Founders' Day observance at Westwood Baptist Church, University Center in Nashville, Tennessee, Dr. Frederick Humphries, president of Tennessee State University, said, ". . . Since the Martin Luther King era, black people have lost sight of the goal. There now needs to be a new set of principles, a new set of goals for black people."

So the future that has been hewn out by our society is a disconcerting imbroglio at worst and an uncertain enigma at best. There is no national spirit, no definite goal for the people. This being true, what then is our manner of running? For what are we searching? Ourselves, our individual satisfaction and survival!

The Reaction of Narcissism

In the face of the complexities of the emerging future that we have contrived, America has turned into what Christopher Lasch calls the culture of narcissism. In his telling tale of the obfuscation of the future, Christopher Lasch writes of ". . . a way of life that is dying." The American life-style now is a ". . . culture of competitive individualism, which in its decadence has carried the logic of individualism to the extreme of a war of all against all, the pursuit of happiness to the dead end of a narcissistic preoccupation with the self."[11] In the American's relationship with business, industry, education, the family and individual encounter, the objective is personal satisfaction. The eclipse of America's future has given birth to a people, who, as Daniel Yankelovich says, have discarded many of the traditional rules and standards that once characterized American life.

> They encourage greater tolerance, permit more sexual freedom, and put less emphasis on sacrifice for its own sake. In their extreme form, the new meanings simply turn the old ones on their head, and in place of the self-denial ethic that once ruled American life, we now find people who refuse to deny themselves *anything*—not out of bottomless appetite, but on the strange moral principle that "I have a duty to myself."[12]

Because of the debilitation of our economic institutions and the rapid approach of the age of uncertainty, in the words of John Kenneth Galbraith, economists and financial advisors are advocating that individuals get all they can while they can. Howard J. Ruff, for example, paints a horrid picture of the financial future for America. The American financial institution is in a state of imminent collapse. He arouses fear and selfish interests when he says,

> The purpose of this book is to persuade *you* that the United States is about to enter its greatest test period since the Civil War—an inflationary spiral leading to a depression that will be remembered with a shudder for generations. . . .
>
> So what is *your* future? A grisly list of unpleasant events—exploding inflation, price controls, erosion of *your* savings (eventually to nothing), a collapse of private as well as government pension programs (including Social Security), vastly more government regulation to control *your* life, and eventually an international monetary holocaust which will sweep all paper currencies down the drain and turn the world upside down. Paper fortunes based on lending will be destroyed and a new kind of investment and financial planning morality will put some very unlikely people on the top of the heap. And *you* can join them there, if *you* know what *you* are doing when the heap turns over.[13] (Emphasis added)

Ruff's idea that the financial future of America will be rough leads him to recommend that people concerned about themselves sell any property they might have in the cities and move to a rural, small-town community, invest in gold and silver, and store up food for at least one year. For Ruff and company, selfish hoarding of money and materials is the response to a diminishing future, if there is a future.

It would seem that in such a time as this, the conventional church would have some word of hope and some suggestions of how to cope with the times. But the conventional church itself is preoccupied with its own security and survival. High-powered television programs, which make passionate appeals for funds, sophisticated public relations campaigns in newspapers and other printed matter, energetic programs to evangelize minorities, and massive busing programs to transport inner-city black children to suburban churches are all means to achieve financial security, to sustain the gargantuan empires churches have built against an uncertain financial future. As for a word of hope and ways to cope with the hell of a threatening future, the conventional church has only mouthings about eschatology and musings about the rapture that is to come in the sweet bye-and-bye.

The black church has not given itself to the task of preparing its people for the future that is at hand. It is overly engaged in eschatological emotionalism that has little to do with space and time. Its members, congregations, associations, conventions, conferences, and so on, have not escaped the national mood of individualism and selfishness. In all too many cases, the future of the black church and the members in it is that of the survival of self.

Recall to the Race

All this is a radical departure from the shining future envisioned by the founders of our nation, the shapers of the constitution, black folk of American slavery, and certainly Paul the apostle of the New Testament. For the apostle Paul, the Christians in the Corinthian church should have known that they were in a race, not like a race on a racecourse, but another kind of race. It was a race that held a certain prize, Christian freedom. The race was such that to obtain the prize, the Corinthians must "run." Paul's position was that the Corinthians could not recant in fear because of what the future might hold. They could not draw back into their cocoon of selfish interests; they had to pursue the prize: "So run that you may obtain it" (1 Corinthians 9:24b). Here, then, is Paul's reminder to America, the contemporary church, and the black church in their pursuit for freedom. If white people and black people are truly Christian, if Jewish people are believers in the kingdom of God, if our nation still operates on the constitutional premise that all people are created equal and endowed by their Creator with certain inalienable rights (life, liberty, and the pursuit of happiness), then the goal still is before us in spite of the grim future we have created for ourselves. Paul's strategy is "So run that you may obtain it."

The Necessity of Discipline

A second and most important strategy that Paul offers is that discipline is utterly necessary in order to follow the long, long road that leads to ultimate Christian freedom. The strategy is found in verse 25: "Every athlete exercises self-control in all things." Essentially what Paul is saying is that the Christians at Corinth, if they were to make a successful run for ultimate Christian freedom, had to exercise discipline, self-control, in order to endure the long, long road.

Paul makes this point by continuing with his analogy. The word that is translated "athlete" is *agonizomenos*. It connotes one who is engaged in a contest, a fight, a struggle of some sort. It is the same word that, when transliterated, means one who "agonizes" in some activity. The other word of importance that Paul uses in his analogy is the word *egkrateuetai,* which bears the meaning "to exercise self-control."

The concept of self-control is not very popular in the New Testament. In fact, the only other place it appears in the New Testament is in 1 Corinthians 7:9a where Paul uses the term in relation to marriage. Maybe the absence of the term in the New Testament is due to its close identification with asceticism. But when Paul makes use of the term, he elicits the Corinthians' awareness of its meaning in athletic circles. Self-control was a fundamental requirement of the athletes who participated in the Isthmian Games that were held in Corinth as well as the Olympic Games held in cities of the Greek world. As athletes engaged in strenuous training and exercised self-control in order to participate in athletic events, so Christians at Corinth were to engage in their own strenuous training and self-control in order to run their peculiar Christian race.

An Athlete's Self-Discipline

Athletes who participated in the Isthmian, Olympic, or other games in Greek and Hellenistic cultures were obligated to train for at least ten months.[14] According to Nicolaos Yalouris, the period of training conceivably could be longer.[15] In sports, the self-discipline of training began very early and gradually for young boys and girls; for example, Plato states that boys training to be archers or heavy-armed runners would run only half the racecourse of that of adults.[16] The older the youth became, the more intense the training. In fact, all youth in Greek and Hellenistic cultures were provided with trainers, *gymnastes,* who monitored and assisted in their development and technique.[17] Training for the athlete covered the gamut—diet, physical exercises, and abstinence from excesses of all sorts. In Lucian's *Anarcharsis,* a rather lengthy discussion is held on the extent of preparation the athlete made for a contest.[18] In describing the extent of training engaged in by the athletes, Solon the Greek tells Anarcharsis the Scythian of how participants greased themselves with oils to make their bodies more pliable, how they developed their muscles and trained in all kinds of weather (both heat and cold), how they ran in sand rather than on solid ground and battered each other to the point of shedding blood—all this in preparation for the athletic contests to come. Plato's theory of self-discipline in training also included the athlete's abstinence from sexual involvement the full time he or she was engaged in intensive training for the contest.[19]

Thus went the training in self-control which was engaged in by the athlete who participated in the Isthmian, Olympic, and other games. When Paul made use of the terms *agonizomenos* and *egkrateuetai,* terms which were familiar to him, he was sure that the Corinthians could relate to them as well. Inasmuch as he was sure the Corinthians could relate to the image of athletic self-control ("Do you know . . . ?" v. 24), he was certain that they could make the application to the Christian race in which they were engaged.

An Ancient Church's Self-Indulgence

All too often either Paul called the Corinthians to self-control as they attempted to make their trek along the long road to ultimate Christian freedom, or he condemned them for the lack of it. In the other verse (7:9a) where he makes use of the term *egkrateuetai* or, in that instance, *egkrateuontai,* he makes reference to the Corinthians' need to exercise self-control in marriage. In 1 Corinthians 6:12ff., Paul calls to the attention of the Corinthians that although all things were lawful for them, not all things were helpful. He enjoins them, therefore, to avoid over-indulgence in food consumption and to avoid erotic activity with prostitutes.

The problem that led Paul to his classic statement on the Lord's Supper in chapter 11 of First Corinthians was that of gluttony and drunkenness around the Lord's Table (11:20-22). His concern with division within the church at Corinth (e.g., 1:10-13 and 11:18-19), arrogance and impenitence (4:6-7 and 5:2), lawsuits among the members (6:1-8), disrespect for Paul's apostleship (9:1-27 and 2 Corinthians 10:7-11:33), mismating with unbelievers (2 Corinthians 6:14–7:1), and hesitance at sharing resources with other saints of the church (1 Corinthians 16:1-4 and 2 Corinthians 8:10-15), existed because of the Corinthians' lack of self-control. And so, although Paul alluded to the fact that athletes exercise self-control in all things, Paul really was calling the Corinthians into account for not exercising self-control as a church. In essence the church's job was that of preserving and perpetuating the faith as it moved on its way toward ultimate Christian freedom. If the church at Corinth was to reach its goal successfully and receive the prize of ultimate Christian freedom, it had to exercise self-control in all things.

Modern-Day Self-Indulgence and Lethargy

Although Paul's analogy of athletic self-control was not used by most New Testament writers, for whatever reason, it certainly was cogent and to the point in the circles in which he preached. Like his Lord, Jesus the Christ, Paul always used metaphors and analogies with which the people to whom he preached could relate. So it was then; so it is now. The nation of America and the church itself, both black and white, can certainly relate to the analogy of athletic self-control made popular by the apostle Paul. Americans know of the rigorous self-discipline engaged by its sports heroes in boxing, football, baseball, basketball, swimming, and the like. Lucian's and Plato's descriptions of the training and self-control of the Greek and Hellenistic athlete are very familiar to us all. But the nation of America and the American church, both black and white, have the same problem as did the church at Corinth; they lack discipline, self-control, for the long road that leads to ultimate Christian freedom; this lack contributes to the weakening and erosion of Christian faith in the land.

Having lost sight of the goal of ultimate Christian freedom, which was viewed clearly by the founders of the nation—churchmen and statesmen alike—Americans have opted for opulence rather than abstinence. While a large part of the global community is suffering from famine, Americans are overweight. Americans are probably the only people in the world who are diet-crazed in search of ways to lose fat that has come from inordinate eating habits—clearly a lack of self-control.

Alcohol and drug consumption has reached unprecedented heights as a result of lack of self-control. A surfeit of court fights and lawsuits has inundated the halls of justice so that courts are hopelessly backlogged and beleaguered and have not enough lawyers and judges to see themselves clear. Barriers of division—racial, social, religious, and political—are growing higher, stronger, and more impregnable. The institution of the family is disappearing because of a rate of divorce in which one out of every two marriages ends. Inflation is galloping out of control because the government continues to print paper money without adequate amounts of gold and silver to back it. This occurs in order to sate the lust and glut of a people who wish to maintain a life-style of luxury and comfort. Crime is on the increase because crumbs, credit, and credibility are on the decrease. Crime is thriving because greed is raging and need is reeling. Governments would rather incarcerate than educate their children. Money is in the hands of a few while madness is in the minds of many. All of this exists because there is no national commitment to self-control.

Black people in America are no better than the nation in their lack of self-control. Black people have allowed the affliction of the nation's lack of self-control to infect themselves. The litany of ills is lengthy: selfishness, drug addiction, alcoholism, promiscuity and inordinate sexual behavior, marital breakdowns and family breakups, uninhibited anger and violence, economic erosion, political impotence, and spiritual anemia. All are part of the long list of afflictions that characterize a people who lack self-control.

Black people in America seem to be smitten with a sprint mentality, the inability to make the long haul to ultimate Christian freedom. The emancipation of black slaves following the Civil War in this country was a great and promising time for the Ebony Children of the sun. The reconstruction era saw black people elected to state legislatures, appointed to federal positions, obtaining land and beginning farms, and founding schools and hospitals to educate their children and heal their sick. But the tests of freedom and the post-reconstruction era dissipated much of the zeal and zest that characterized those times. Much of what was gained has been lost.

The turn of the twentieth century and the coming of the Harlem renaissance saw a new surge of activity among black people. Businesses and industries were begun, and black people moved from the South to the North where they found relatively good paying jobs in factories and industries. But somehow black people in the North could not cultivate their businesses and industries and build them into corporations strong enough to cope with the fierce competition of a competitive economy. The Harlem renaissance spawned a flurry of activity in culture and arts. Black writers prolifically produced writings in virtually every field of endeavor. Black artists, dancers, and musical virtuosos literally transformed the nation with their tap dancing, their version of the charleston, the blues, big bands, poetry, and piety. But this, too, dissipated with the winds of change and the industry's inability to cope with the havoc of hegemony and the chaos of co-optation of the competing culture.

The celebrated civil rights era of Dr. Martin Luther King, Jr., is one that thrills even those in opposition to the idea of granting full rights to black people. For thirteen years, Martin Luther King, Jr., made a breakthrough for the acquisition of civil rights for his people, but black people today have failed to follow through. In every major era that has been cited, black people have failed to build a momentum and exercise self-control for the long, long road that leads to ultimate Christian freedom in this land.

Paul's analogy of the race is certainly cogent for black people in America; but alas, they are weighed in the balance and found wanting. Black athletes train and discipline themselves long and hard for various athletic events, but even here there is evidence of the sprint mentality. Jesse Owens and Wilma Rudolph are two of the greatest runners the world has ever seen, but both of them have majored in sprints. Hardly any of the black runners have completed or even competed in the mile run or cross-country jaunts. These events are for those who have given themselves to strenuous training and self-control.

Considering the notions that black people have not been able to follow through in most of the history of freedom in this country and that even on the racetrack there are only those who have majored in sprints, the question must be asked: Are black people plagued with a sprint mentality? Yes! In addition, black people are plagued with the self-imposed inability to exercise self-control via serious training. In the latter part of the twentieth century, the myth of Atalanta that was proffered by W. E. B. DuBois in the first part of the twentieth century, has come to haunt them again. Like faltering Atalanta, black people have not controlled themselves enough to avoid the shining apples of temptation planted adroitly alongside life's raceway by a pursuing Hippomenes. Ignoring the goal at the end of the raceway, black people have fallen for the fake, dived for the dollar, bitten the bait, and gone for the golden apple that lies alongside the raceway. Blacks have little aspiration for education, a modicum of motivation for salvation, and a minimum of zest for the quest of a higher, better, nobler world in which they can live now and to which they can go after this life. The problem has come about because of a lethargy, a sprint mentality, and a woeful lack of self-control necessary for the long, long road to ultimate Christian freedom.

The Present-Day Church's Failure

The contemporary church, both black and white, has failed in its effort to exercise self-control, like its Corinthian counterpart of the New Testament. Coming off the starting blocks, leading this nascent nation, the white church lunged forward at neck-breaking speed. Though it ran, its running was uncertain, for it did not know what to do about the slavery of black Africans. It miserably faltered along the way when, before the Civil War, virtually every denomination split over the slave question. Although during the reconstruction era the white church aided black congregations, associations, conventions, conferences, and districts in their organizational efforts, in the latter part of the nineteenth century white preachers and churches led the fight against accepting black people as fully human. During the Martin Luther King, Jr., civil rights era, the organized white church was either conspicuously silent or incredibly active in opposing Dr. King's efforts to end the dreaded evil of racial segregation in America. Even today, in spite of its mouthings of a nebulous message of brotherhood among white and black people, the missionary and evangelistic efforts of the white church are geared for nothing more than social, political, and ecclesiastical control and economic security against an uncertain future. And so the history of the white church in this country has been that of running an uncertain race, a race that has been bogged down in bigotry, hindered by hypocrisy, restrained by racism, hampered by half-heartedness, entangled in the webbing of a twisted theology, and inhibited by so many other factors that the church has been prevented from running a creditable Christian race. Like the Corinthian church, its problem has been lack of self-control and loss of sight of the ultimate goal of Christian freedom.

The black church does not escape the indictment of the apostle Paul; it, too, has suffered from lack of self-control and loss of sight of the goal of ultimate Christian freedom. Clarence M. Wagner's book *Profiles of Black Georgia Baptists*[20] is a bristling reminder that every black Baptist Association in Georgia during the latter slavery and reconstruction eras birthed schools of learning that provided the only opportunities for the religious and secular education of black people in Georgia. Such noble achievements were duplicated across many of the states of the South. But today, in spite of the opulent economic circumstances of black people, churches, associations, conventions, and the like, it is difficult if not impossible to maintain, build upon, or improve on what their forebears out of their penury began. With only a strong will and a modicum of wealth, black churchmen and churchwomen founded banks, hospitals, burial societies, and publishing houses to build economic strength, to give medical attention in sickness, dignity in death, and literature for learning. Theirs was the noble beginning of a race. But keenness of competition, machinations of the marketplace, and complexities of an ever-changing economy have all wearied the running of those who have followed.

One final area to be considered as one in which lack of training and self-control is evident in the black church is the development and perpetuation of the theology hewn out by the founders and forebears of the black church. It is obvious and lamentable that the black church today espouses the theologies born out of the white theological communities in America, England, and Germany—and that, after the fact. But more lamentable than this is the failure of the black church to develop and perpetuate the unusual theologies dug out by its forebears from the freight and flowing froth of deceptive theologies mouthed by the white church. The black church's failure has been that of allowing itself to be sidetracked from the raceway by following deceptive theological "jargon" such as discussions on the origin of man, designed to substantiate the inhumanity of black people; theological determinings of whether or not God is dead, contrived by those who do not know him or who doubt his existence; and, a theological obsession with the rapture, an inordinate concern with a nebulous heaven after a person dies, while neglecting the vexations of the hell in which people must live. All too often, black churches and churchmen and churchwomen have been drawn off course by these arguments of deception.

At the same time, the black church and its people have not pursued the unique theologies birthed (albeit out of their unlettered minds) by the rustic preachers from the backwoods' praying ground of slavery's plantations. What of the socio-theological connotations of "freedom," "heaven," "Beulah Land," the birth of Jesus, the crucifixion and resurrection of Jesus, Sunday, judgment, the church, Jesus the Sufferer, Jesus the man, Jesus the Son of God? All of these terms were born out of the limited understanding of unlettered leaders of the black church. Few of the children of former slaves have bothered to probe into the minds of those black and unknown theological bards of Christian faith and freedom to understand the unique interpretations they sifted out of the polluted soil of a tightly protected Christian gospel. While black preachers in slavery, Henry Highland Garnet, Richard Allen, and Frederick Douglass, to name only a few, still flinching from the oppressive chains of servitude, wrote prolifically of the Christian gospel's message of the freedom and dignity of every person, there is little interest or writing activity today in theological investigation of the Bible and its message of freedom. In fact, the perversion of the Christian faith by the white church has led many black people to hold in utter contempt the Christian faith.

With a few rare exceptions, practically every black theologian today holds the apostle Paul up to venomous derision; not because of what the apostle has done or said, but because of what white preachers and the white church have done with his theology and said about him (e.g., the alleged statement, "slaves, be obedient to your masters," a statement he did not make, denoting a position he did not hold). And so; without exercising the discipline of tediously examining the apostle Paul and his theology for themselves, most black theologians have dismissed him out of hand. Therefore, refusing to examine the Christian faith for themselves and to inquire into the faith of their forebears, many black people are abandoning the Christian race and are opting for movements, such as the Black Muslims and the Moonies, spiritual cults, and religious cliques, and many have drifted back into the white church where there is "courteous" conceit, "hospitable" hostility, vacillation and isolation, and an obsession with the rapture.

This is the plight of the contemporary black church. It has strayed from the path of Christian duty so clearly marked by its forebears, Paul the apostle and Jesus the Christ. It is wandering in the wilderness of this world, floundering in a turbulent sea of social change, not knowing which way to go. All this is because the black church has abandoned its training and self-control for the long, long road to ultimate Christian freedom, the race so nobly begun by its forebears, and has opted for the sprint mentality,

The apostle Paul's statement in 1 Corinthians 9:25a stands as a haunting criticism of the manner of running of the Christian race by the black church today. But there is also hope and promise, for if the black church is willing to submit itself to discipline, to engage itself in training and self-discipline, it can prepare itself for the long, long road that leads to ultimate Christian freedom and the preservation and perpetuation of the Christian faith.

The Nature of the Prize

Paul's strategy for following the long, long road to ultimate Christian freedom continues in the latter part of verse 25: "They do it to receive a perishable wreath, but we an imperishable." It was not enough for the Corinthians to know that they were in a peculiar kind of race, the Christian race, and that they were to pursue the prize and exercise self-discipline in the process; they had to know the kind of prize, the goal, for which they were in pursuit. Unlike the prize of the runners on a racecourse, the Corinthians' prize was not to be a wreath of pine or celery; theirs was to be an imperishable wreath, an eternal crown.

It was probably Paul who first introduced the idea of an incorruptible or imperishable wreath or crown *(aphtharton stephanon)* as the prize for those engaged in the Christian race. Other writers after him picked up the concept and implemented it in their writings (e.g., 2 Timothy 4:8; 1 Peter 5:4; James 1:12; Revelation 2:10). But what was this imperishable crown for which Paul was running and toward which he was encouraging the Corinthians to run? Was it some eternal ethereal garland with which he was to be adorned at the journey's end? Hardly so! It was eternal life itself. It was that everlasting life of perfection, peace, and ultimate freedom, the beauty of which he had received only fleeting glimpses, the aroma of which he had enjoyed only faint whiffs (e.g., 2 Corinthians 12:1-4). He didn't altogether know what it was like, but he did know that the resurrection of Christ had made it possible and he knew that it must be beyond anything he had known while living according to the flesh *(kata sarka)*. It was this, then—the crowning of life itself with eternal life in peace and freedom with God—for which Paul was in hot pursuit and to which he urged the Corinthians to run so that they might attain it.

Hope for eternal life was one of the themes that held together Paul's letters to the Corinthians, one of the elements of the matrix of his message. Paul opens his first letter to the Corinthians by informing them of the incredible, indescribable future that God has prepared for his own:

> "What no eye has seen, nor ear heard,
> nor the heart of man conceived,
> what God has prepared for those who love him. . . ."
> —1 Corinthians 2:9

Had the rulers of that age known that it was this for which Jesus came, they would not have crucified the Lord of glory. Yet it was precisely the crucifixion of Jesus, by the hands of the wicked, and his resurrection that made this indescribable future certain for the ones who believe. Had the crucified Christ not been raised from the dead, then those who had fallen asleep in him would have perished; and further, "If for this life only we have hoped in Christ, we are of all men most to be pitied" (15:19).

To be relegated forever to the battlefield of mortal misery was for Paul an imponderable thought. But by faith, for Paul, this was not the case. As God raised the Lord Jesus, so God also would raise Paul up to be with him in his presence (cf. 2 Corinthians 4:14). It was for eternal glory beyond all comparison which this world with momentary afflictions was preparing Paul (4:17). In fact, Paul longed to move out of his earthly tent into his heavenly dwelling place (cf. 5:2; Romans 8:18), knowing that a house had been prepared for him, not made with hands and eternal in the heavens. There, in that heavenly abode, he would dwell in ultimate freedom and be forever with the Lord (cf. 2 Corinthians 5:6-9; 1 Thessalonians 4:17). There the righteous and the unrighteous alike would stand before the judgment seat of Christ and receive the reward of good or evil, according to what they had done in this life (2 Corinthians 5:10; cf. Matthew 25:31-46). There the wrongs done by the ruthless would be condemned and the righteous would be rewarded. When the final abode of ultimate freedom is achieved, Paul perceived that his perishable nature would put on the imperishable and his mortal nature would put on immortality (1 Corinthians 15:51-55). This is the imperishable wreath for which Paul was running, and it is the goal, the prize, he was encouraging the Corinthians to pursue.

The Important Element of Living in Hope

Living in hope of finally realizing the imperishable wreath has been perceived to be a prominent theme in Pauline theology by many popular theologians, Rudolf Bultmann and Albert Schweitzer to name only two. It is significant that Bultmann and Schweitzer, among others, pointed out its very important function in Paul's life. Because he was in pursuit of the prize of an imperishable wreath, i.e., eternal life, does not mean that he excused himself from his responsibility in the world.

In Rudolf Bultmann's treatment of Pauline eschatology, the acceptance of the eschatological promise of the cross-resurrection event of Jesus Christ by the believer in grace through faith places the believer in a state of freedom; he or she is justified before God, free from the law, free from sin, and free from the fear of death now.[21] Living out of this eschatological occurrence, Paul/ humankind walks not according to the flesh *(kata sarka)*, but according to the Spirit *(pneumati peripateite*, "walk in the spirit," Galatians 5:16). The eschatological future is that toward which Paul/humankind walks in the Spirit. The Spirit is the power that takes control of the self and opens it up to the future toward which Paul/humankind is walking.[22] The glory that is anticipated in the eschaton is that power that pours out of the future and determines the present for Paul/humankind.[23]

Because of the eschatological promise of the cross-resurrection event and the acceptance of that fact by faith through grace, Paul/humankind had already established citizenship in heaven (Philippians 3:20). As such, Paul/humankind is free (cf. 1 Corinthians 9:1; 3:21-23; 4:3-4; Galatians 5:1). Although the cross-resurrection event has freed Paul/humankind and the eschatological future draws him/humankind to it, walking in the Spirit, Paul/humankind is not totally free but is a "slave to all" (1 Corinthians 9:19): although all things are lawful, not all things build up (10:23). Although Paul is free to eat meat offered to idols, if doing so offends the conscience of a weaker brother or sister, Paul will not eat such meat lest he cause his brother or sister to stumble (1 Corinthians 8:12-13). The thesis that Bultmann proposes is this: though eschatologically free and living in possession of and in expectation and pursuit of eschatological freedom, i.e., the imperishable wreath, Paul/humankind still has a responsibility to this world.

Albert Schweitzer sees the function of eschatology in Paul's theology a bit differently. For Schweitzer, eschatology is seen best in Paul's theology in his "being-in-Christ" mysticism.[24] Mystically being in Christ, Paul/humankind is experiencing, according to Schweitzer, the eschatological future while not being free of temporal, worldly existence. Paul/humankind then is the human being who looks ". . . upon the division between earthly and super-earthly, temporal and eternal, as transcended, and, feeling himself, while still externally amid the earthly and temporal, to belong to the super-earthly and eternal."[25]

Admittedly, Pauline eschatology is an enigma, especially as it relates to its influence in Paul's/humankind's life in the world. Generally, contemporary theologians come short of seeing Pauline eschatology as influencing the entire life existence of Paul/humankind in the world. The tendency is to perceive Pauline eschatology, Paul's/humankind's possession/pursuit of the imperishable wreath, as having already been achieved, thus, freeing a person entirely from the world or elevating one above the world and its effects. Especially is this true of Schweitzer. For example, Schweitzer says, "The fundamental thought of Pauline mysticism runs thus: I am in Christ; in Him I know myself as a being who is raised above this sensuous, sinful, and transient world and already belongs to the transcendent; in Him I am assured of resurrection; in Him I am a Child of God."[26] But this perception of the achievement of the "already" leaves us dangling when it comes to what to do about the "not-yet" existence with which Paul/humankind has to deal, the existence which constitutes the long, long road that leads to ultimate freedom in Christ.

Both Bultmann and Schweitzer, and most other contemporary theologians, see the impact of Pauline eschatology, i.e., the pursuit of the imperishable wreath and its effect on the life of the church and on the individual Christian's life and ethic, in nothing more than individualistic and subjective terms. Their understanding of the Pauline eschatological phenomenon had little to do with Paul's/humankind's/the church's relationship to the society and world about them. For example, both Bultmann and Schweitzer insist that Pauline eschatology has nothing to do with freeing Christian slaves from their masters, whether the masters were Christian or pagan. Bultmann argues,

Consideration for one's brother does not mean dependence upon his judgment (I Cor. 10:29b; Rom. 14:5). On the contrary, Christian freedom is *freedom from all human conventions and norms of value.* The social distinctions of freedom and slavery as well as those of sex and race have lost their significance "in Christ" (Gal. 3:28; I Cor. 12:13) and "do not become slaves of men" (I Cor. 7:23) applies to all desires for emancipation, for they stem from human evaluations. The Christian, then, is free from all men, and yet there is a proper subjection of himself as "slave to all" (I Cor. 9:19) and the imperative, "be servants of one another" (Gal. 5:13) still stands. Here again, however, this is no surrender of freedom, but precisely the exercise of it.[27]

But to say this, according to Bultmann, means that slavery becomes unimportant and the disparity of an inferior slave and a superior slave master becomes insignificant. Incredibly, Bultmann argues that slavery is only a human evaluation, that the Pauline dictum, ". . . do not become slaves of men," does not suggest emancipation for the Christian slave but that the Christian slave should endure slavery because it is of human evaluation. Similarly, this erroneous reasoning is followed by Schweitzer.

If Paul is exposed to the reproach that he did not in the Spirit of Christ oppose slavery, and consequently for centuries lent the weight of his authority to those who regard it as compatible with Christianity, the blame rests on the theory of the *status quo*. His mysticism did not permit him to hold a different view. For what need has one who is already a free man in Christ Jesus, and momentarily expects to enter as such into the Messianic glory, to be concerned about release from slavery for the few moments that he has still to spend in the natural world? Accordingly Paul enjoins upon Onesimus, the escaped slave whom he had come to know during his imprisonment, that he should return to his master Philemon, and although as a believer he is now a freeman like his master, nevertheless to continue to serve him.[28]

As we have contended in an earlier chapter, to argue in this manner would mean that Paul made legitimate the institution of slavery and the idol worship that accompanied it. To insist on this position would mean that for Paul eschatological freedom meant not freedom of the body from the menacing shackles of human servitude but salvation of the self, freedom of the soul, a soul that was fit for nothing but heaven. Ludicrous! Paul would have none of this.

Yet this is the kind of interpretation of Pauline eschatology that the Bultmanns and Schweitzers and the white church have held and espoused to this day. It was because of such an interpretation that the white church of American slavery stood by in righteousness while white slave masters viciously abused and held in utter contempt their chattels, black African slaves, even those who had come to be Christians. The same is true today of those white churches in South Africa who stand under the shelter of their piety while their government holds captive millions of native South Africans with the shackles of apartheid. It is because of this interpretation that the contemporary white church and, in too many instances, the black church have stood by or participated in the emergence of the Ku Klux Klan, the Nazi party, and others whose intent is to eliminate black people, Jewish people, and other nations of the world.

As I have shown in a previous chapter, although eschatological freedom has already been assured in the cross-resurrection event, for Paul and for the church human slavery had to be dealt with, the same as bondage to law, sin, and immorality. Helping to secure freedom for slaves who became Christians and were added to the church was one of the obstacles along the terrestrial path over which Paul and the church had to travel as they traversed the long, long road to the imperishable wreath (cf. 1 Corinthians 9:24c). By no means did Paul perceive the freedom in Christ, that he already enjoyed and that ultimate freedom for which he was ever in pursuit—the imperishable wreath—in terms of selfish subjectivity. In order to maintain freedom in Christ and to acquire that ultimate freedom, Paul was constrained to manifest that freedom and its power in the social and even political context of the world about him and the church. The glory, perfection, peace, hope, fulfillment, presence with the Lord, freedom, and all that was held in the eschatological future was the motivation that impelled Paul to revolutionize, not only himself but the world itself, and to try to rid it of its evils. Paul did not excuse himself with the notion that ". . . the form of this world is passing away" (7:31b) so that he need not engage in a struggle with the world in an attempt to rid it of its evil. For Paul it was as Jürgen Moltmann intimates: "Peace with God means conflict with the world, for the goad of the promised future stabs inexorably into the flesh of every unfulfilled moment."[29] This, it seems to me, is what it meant for Paul to "run" in pursuit of the imperishable wreath.

Other Significant Elements

An abundance of evidence points out the sometimes vicious encounters Paul had with the social and political elements of the world as he moved along the long, long route of righteousness on the way to the imperishable wreath. These encounters were met by Paul with power, power he derived from the pull of the eschatological future made available to him by the cross-resurrection event in Jesus Christ. In Philippians 3:10-11, Paul expresses the desire to have the same power that was manifested in the cross-resurrection event of Jesus Christ: ". . . that I may know him and the power of his resurrection, and may share his sufferings, becoming like him in his death, that if possible I may attain the resurrection from the dead.'' The power that was manifested at Calvary and at the open tomb on Easter morning was that power for which Paul hungered and thirsted; and it was that power by which he wished to live each day in the world. It is the power *(dunamis)* by which he dealt with the church and the world (cf. 1 Corinthians 4:19-20; 6:14; 15:43; 2 Corinthians 4:7; 13:4; Romans 1:16).[30]

It is not strange then that as part of his discussion of the pervasive and all-impelling power of the resurrection of Christ, Paul asks the question, ''What do I gain if, humanly speaking, I fought with the beasts at Ephesus?'' (1 Corinthians 15:32). What else could this mean than that because Paul had been assured by grace through faith of the resurrection from the dead, the imperishable wreath, he was free to engage in physical fisticuffs with Roman soldiers? Hardly would that engagement be reasonable if in this life only Paul had hoped; those who do live hoping only in this life are conditioned by the maxim ''Let us eat and drink, for tomorrow we die.'' But having the assurance of eternal life and the resurrection of the dead, Paul shrank not from engaging in physical warfare, especially when it was for the sake of the glory of Christ and the freedom of the church in the world. It was part of his attempt to make the world better as he passed through it on his way to the finish line where awaited his imperishable wreath.

The power of the future that was drawing Paul through the world caused him to be in conflict not only with those in the church but with Gentiles as well (2 Corinthians 11:26). Paul refers to a political situation when he refers to his escape from Damascus (when the governor under King Aretas guarded the city in an attempt to apprehend him [11:32-33]). Hardly would political authorities seek out the apostle unless his activities in the name of Christ had caused political problems. But Paul was willing to be subject to such political pressures because of the power of the resurrection that impelled him.

And what of the question of slavery? The subject itself was

political and social in nature. It was an issue that put Paul in conflict with the political world of Rome. As I have previously shown, by Roman law certain classes of people in the Roman Empire were relegated to peonage and servitude. In the Roman Empire it was a matter of social status and luxury for Romans to have large numbers of slaves at their disposal. So, then, it was not a small matter—but, socially and politically even volatile and dangerous—for slaves seeking freedom to come into the church and for Paul to tell them, "But if you can gain your freedom, avail yourself of the opportunity. . . . You were brought with a price; do not become slaves of men" (1 Corinthians 7:21b-23). It was significant as well as humiliating to Philemon for Paul to send Onesimus back to him, not as a slave, but as a brother in the Lord.

All of this—political encounters, social challenges, manumission of slaves, and disruption of a lucrative slave business—was part of the long, long road that leads to ultimate freedom in Christ, the imperishable wreath. But none of these things moved Paul to fear death or to feel trepidation at the thought of suffering. The eschatological cross-resurrection event had given him the faith to conquer all things, even the fear of death, and the pull of the imperishable wreath had given him the wherewithal to endure the sufferings he encountered along the long, long road of this world.

The eschatological future of which Paul had already been assured and the imperishable wreath toward which he was running mandated another assignment alongside the raw encounter with the world and worldly institutions. Calling men and women into the church and giving shape and meaning to the church through theology and ethics were also part of that long, long road that led to ultimate freedom in Christ. After all, for Paul it was the church, the *ekklesia*, the people of God, that would spread out into the world, permeating it, saturating it with righteousness, and revolutionizing it to the glory of Christ. And so, faced with the fact that eschatological existence with God consisted not only of an imperishable wreath but also of righteous judgment in which each person must give an account of the deeds done in the body, Paul says, "Therefore, knowing the fear of the Lord, we persuade men . . ." (2 Corinthians 5:11). Paul, then, spent his life on the long, long road to ultimate freedom, preaching so that people might be saved and called into the church (cf. 1 Corinthians 1:17; Romans 1:16). The folly of the cross was the content of his preaching (1 Corinthians 1:21-25). His preaching called into the *ekklesia* those who were not wise according to worldly standards, those who were not powerful or of noble birth, those who were weak and of low esteem (1:26-29). Even the morally despicable were won to Christ through his preaching (6:9-11). Preaching that people might come to know Jesus Christ and be added to the church was a necessity for Paul (9:16).

Yet this was only the beginning of the task. There was the faithful transmission of the tenets of the faith, e.g., the cross (1:17-25), the resurrection (15:1-58), baptism (Romans 6:1-14), justification by faith (4:1–5:21), and the Lord's Supper (1 Corinthians 11:17-34).

Faithful transmission of the tenets of the faith was still not all that constituted the long, long road that led Paul to ultimate freedom in Christ; maintenance of the health, stamina, strength, and freedom of the church as it moved through the world was also part of the journey. The church had to be healthy in order to withstand the "slings and arrows of outrageous fortune" that were hurled against it. It had to be strong if it was to endure threats of heresies and moral degeneration from within and persecutions and perversions that attacked from without. It had to be free from the entangling snares of the conventions of this world. By virtue of the race he was running and the crown he was pursuing, Paul had to set things in order in the church. This was important for Paul because he saw the church, the *ekklesia*, as a microcosm of the kingdom of God, the spatial entity of freedom in Christ in the world. It is little wonder that he would strain with every ounce of his energy and resources to maintain its health, strength, and freedom in the world. It was for this reason, according to Luke's story, that Paul paid, out of his own financial resources, the rent for the Hall of Tyrannus for a period of two years in order to preach the gospel of Jesus Christ at Corinth (see Acts 19:9-10).

Paul fought diligently to make the church (at Corinth, as is the case in the discussion of this chapter) healthy to withstand the many misfortunes that would come upon it. Therefore, he forcefully dealt with the divisions within the church (e.g., 1 Corinthians 1:11-13; 11:18-19); he caustically criticized the Corinthians for taking their ecclesiastical matters before pagan courts with church member contending against member (6:1-8); and he called them to unity as the body of Christ (cf. 12:1-31).

Paul worked harder than all of the other apostles to weed out the heretical elements that threatened the church at Corinth with perversions and weakness. He attacked the Gnostic elements within the congregation that flaunted knowledge *(gnosis)* as the principle thing (cf. 2:12-16; 3:18-20; 2 Corinthians 11:5-6), perceived the body as being of no importance (cf. 1 Corinthians 5:1-13; 6:15-20), and renounced the resurrection of the dead (cf. 15:12-19).

Paul indefatigably strove to keep the church at Corinth free from the entangling influences of the conventions of the world. In a society that was saturated with the philosophy of divorce, Paul labored tirelessly to maintain the dignity of marriage within the context of the church (cf. 7:1-16, 25-40). He sought endlessly to keep the church free from idolatry and from eating meat offered to idols (e.g., 10:14-22). With every ounce of measurable strength, Paul sought to cull out from within the church the adultery, homosexuality, thievery, avarice, drunkenness, and debauchery that was so prevalent in the society about it.

Had the church at Corinth been splintered by division, dismembered by heresies, or weakened by immorality, there never would have been a church at Corinth to read about centuries later. Paul set out to make the church at Corinth strong and united so that it, too, could run its race unhindered. Although Paul had established his citizenship in the heavens, he had his work cut out for himself on earth. He shrank not from it, for this work was part of the long, long road that led him to the imperishable wreath of eternal life of peace and freedom in God.

So then this, and much more is what Paul meant when he said that every Christian runner exercises self-control in all things as he or she pursues, not the perishable wreath pursued by the runners on a racecourse (or the citizens of this world) but the imperishable wreath of eternal life, a life of freedom and peace with God. It is unimaginable that Paul could have done all that he did, as catalogued in 2 Corinthians 11, had he not exercised self-control and discipline and had he not had in clear view and was totally possessed by the pull of the imperishable wreath of eternal life. Without this he would have utterly failed, but with it the centuries testify of his towering success for the sake of the gospel of Jesus the Christ.

Paul Uses Himself to Illustrate Discipline

In verses 26 and 27, Paul discontinues the analogy of racers on a racecourse, relating the lessons of that experience to the Corinthians' situation. He now uses himself as the example *par excellence,* the Christian archetype, running the race of life on his way to the imperishable wreath.

"Well, I do not run aimlessly, I do not box as one beating the air. . . ." Here, again, Paul demonstrates a terrific knowledge of the secular writings of his day and earlier writings. The imagery used here can be found in Virgil's *Aeneid* when Dares lashes the air with blows[31] and in *Georgics* when Sila, while rehearsing for battle, "buffets the winds with blows."[32] But this action is not Paul's, for he knows his objective, the goal, and he knows the road over which he must run to pursue it. He does not wildly lash the air with errant blows or swing blindly at his target. His every punch is calculated, and his blows reach their mark. Every juncture along the long, long road that leads to ultimate freedom in Christ is marked with challenges that must be met, situations that must be mastered, and dangers that cannot be avoided but must be met head-on. Paul cannot afford the luxuries of losing time by racing aimlessly, now in this direction and then in that direction, or of the costly expenditure of psychological energy with his mind running here and there. And so, with his goal clearly in view, Paul runs to pursue it and strives to make his every effort count.

But more than this, as is pointed out in verse 27a, Paul pommels his body and keeps it under subjection. This is his way of exercising self-control in order to obtain the prize for which he is running. A cursory glance at Paul's life makes the point. Although he was single and had the right to have a wife (cf. 1 Corinthians 9:1, 5), Paul chose not to have one (cf. 7:7). To be married meant for him to be anxious about the affairs of the world; but this he could not do, for he wished to be anxious only about the affairs of the Lord (7:32-34). He could contain his desire for a wife and womanly companionship through self-control.

This is not to say that Paul was not shaken by temptations of the flesh and perhaps succumbed to some of those temptations. Of Paul's own admission, there were times that he did the very thing he hated (cf. Romans 7:15). Every day of his life he was vexed with a veritable thorn in the flesh (cf. 2 Corinthians 12:7-9). One can only wonder what the affliction was, whether it was some embarrassing moral impediment or simply some physical ailment; but we do know that Paul agonized over it and prayed for deliverance and was assured that God's grace was sufficient.

It was through discipline that Paul kept himself free from greed and desire for the financial security due him (cf. 1 Corinthians 9:8-18). Rather than be free from the drudgery of work and earning his living by the sweat of his brow, Paul would labor with his hands (cf. Acts 18:3; 1 Corinthians 4:12; 9:12, 15) so that he would have no obligations to persons that would prevent him from preaching the gospel of God. It was through discipline that he could do this so that no one could deny him of his ground for boasting and making full use of his right in the gospel.

It took self-control and a virtual buffeting of his body to take the disappointment and punishment meted out to him as he "brought life," i.e., preached and ministered, to others while death was at work in him (cf. 2 Corinthians 4:7-12; 6:3-10). It took a continuous pommeling of his body and mind for him to endure a series of dangers (2 Corinthians 11:23-33) and deny the self-exaltation that could have come as a result of having endured them. Rather, he boasted of his weaknesses and the strength he gained from the Lord because of his weaknesses (cf. 2 Corinthians 11:30–12:10).

What else could it have been but discipline that kept Paul from succumbing to the many temptations that courted him at every turn in the road, the tests he encountered from his own people, the debilitating persecutions he endured at the hands of the Jews and Gentiles, and the debasement he received from his arrogant opponents?

Following the protracted list of bone-shattering experiences he had in his travels while preaching the gospel (cf. 11:23-27), Paul concludes his tale of horror by disclosing the burden of his never-ending worry about the churches: "And, apart from other things, there is the daily pressure upon me of my anxiety for all the churches" (11:28). To add to his physical and mental torture, there was the gloom of growing blindness. Such is the conjecture behind his statement to the Galatians, "See with what large letters I am writing to you with my own hand" (Galatians 6:11).

What kept Paul from going completely insane from the mental, spiritual, and physical consternation that enveloped him on every mile along the road to ultimate freedom? What was it that kept him pushing on, pressing forward toward the high calling of God to make it his own? Nothing but discipline! So Paul sets down on record that in order to run the race successfully, he pommeled his body and kept it under subjection.

He concludes the chapter (1 Corinthians 9:27b) by citing why discipline is necessary: ". . . lest after preaching to others I myself should be disqualified." It was an imponderable thought for Paul, one that caused a weariness of the soul, to consider the distant but very real possibility that after proclaiming the salvation event of the cross and resurrection of Jesus Christ, he himself might be disqualified and denied the wreath of eternal life. It was this grave and unsavory possibility that Paul kept ever before him and that kept him battering his body, keeping it under subjection. By no means did he wish to be disqualified at the end of the race. He did the one so that he might avoid the other.

What I have tried to show in this discussion is Paul's view of the race that is before the Christian and the church as they pursue the long, long road to ultimate freedom and the discipline that must be employed in order to reach the goal successfully. I have attempted to show how the promise of the prize of eternal life, the imperishable wreath, gave Paul the power to navigate through this world and encounter face-to-face the dangers it held for him. I have considered how Paul sought to make better, to reform, to revolutionize the world with his theology and the church while he was moving through the world. I have shown that Paul worked tirelessly with the church, the people of God, the *ekklesia,* in order to shape its theology, to assure its unity, to maintain its independence from the world, and to develop its strength as it moved through the world as an agent of redemption. I also have explained that Paul strove hard to exercise self-discipline, that he insisted the church must also exercise self-discipline if it is to run a creditable race. I have observed that one of the foremost concerns for Paul was keeping himself under subjection so that while declaring salvation's story to others, he himself would not be disqualified at the end of the journey.

Paul's Piercing Word for Today

For almost twenty centuries now, Paul's operational principle, his *modus operandi,* has stood. The wash of the waves of time has not swept away his testimony. The gathering storms of theological and social controversy have not weakened his witness. The disciples of disparagement and disillusionment have not obscured the way Paul left for generations to travel. In fact, at the very times in history when it seemed that the church was about to drop the baton and forfeit the race, there emerged the likes of Augustine, Thomas Aquinas, Martin Luther, John Calvin, Karl Barth, Rudolf Bultmann, Albert Schweitzer, Ernst Käsemann, Martin Luther King, Jr., Jürgen Moltmann, Günther Bornkamm, and others who took the baton and continued the race according to the logic and principles laid down by Paul.

What this means for us today is that the theology of Paul, his manner of running the race in pursuit of the imperishable crown, comes before us once again as a most viable option. Paul's recommended manner of running the race along the long, long road that leads to ultimate freedom in Christ stands before the contemporary church, in all of its variety, as both caustic criticism and catalytic encouragement.

America's Indictment and Hope

Paul's manner of running the race with the imperishable wreath before him stands before America as a caustic criticism, for the nation has made itself its own end. Because it has no imperishable wreath to pursue, the nation has come to the place at which there is little hope for a better future for its people. The nation has no national spirit, no corporate objective beyond itself and the individual selves that make up the nation. For the nation and the people who make up the nation, the present is shattered and the future is uncertain. Chaos holds the people captive. The national fabric is ruptured along racial, economic, and social lines. Nuclear war looms around every corner and at the dawn of each new day. Swelling arsenals of weaponry and bloated budgets for law enforcement have not brought under control the flood of crime that madly rushes through the streets of our society. The insatiable greed on the part of a few of the power elite has brought about a disparity in the distribution of fiscal and physical resources among the people of the land, so much so that there are now islands of wealth surrounded by oceans of poverty. All this has occurred because there has been a radical departure from the philosophical and theological objectives formulated at the early infancy of this nation and a departure from the principles in the Bible and Paul's theology. There has been a long-standing movement away from the race as Paul perceived it, the pursuit of the imperishable crown, and the self-discipline needed to run the race.

Paul's message, which provides the locus of the discussion in this chapter, gives the nation of America more than a caustic criticism; it offers a wellspring of hope and renewal. If this nation, which prides itself on the motto "In God We Trust," can grasp anew the salvation of the cross-resurrection event of Jesus Christ, then it can claim the power to reform itself and become truly a "nation with the soul of the church." If America can wipe from its eyes the myopic matter of materialism, it may catch a clear view of the future of God and the imperishable crown that awaits it at the end of the road. If this is done, this nation might willingly give itself to the relentless pull of that future so that it will correct its flagrant racial, social, economic, and political inequities. If this is done, there is the likelihood that America will win the wreath of eternal life that awaits it at the end of the road. But if it is not done, even though preaching democracy and Christianity to the world, America could be disqualified at the end of the race. America alone can accept or reject the challenging option that Paul lays before it.

The Church's Criticism and Challenge

The contemporary church, both white and black, is confronted with the criticism and challenge of the message the apostle Paul sets before it. The white church has understood Pauline eschatology in terms of heaven being pie-in-the-sky-after-awhile. The church has chosen not to understand eschatology as the pull of God's future empowering it to do battle with the evils and inequities of this world. It has refused to see itself as the light of the world, the salt of the earth. Because of this, it has not seen fit to be partner in the battle for full human and civil rights of its darker Christian brothers and sisters. It has not seen the necessity to exercise self-control in sharing its material resources with Christians of a darker hue. The white church has seen fit only to accumulate wealth and riches for its own sake and to share such with black Christians and the black church only if obligatory strings are attached. The white church, in too many instances, has manipulated theological issues in order to use them as facades to veil insidious motives. This being true, it is highly possible that while preaching to others the message of salvation, the white church could pull up to the finish line and be disqualified.

This does not have to be. The white church can wipe the matters of prejudice, selfishness, theological narrowness, and materialism from its eyes and view anew the message of Paul the apostle as a challenge, allowing the message to jolt it from its theological and social lethargy. It can hear Paul's message as a challenge to view God's eschatological future not only as a reality already achieved but also the power by which it can move determinedly and triumphantly over its course toward it. The white church is challenged to employ the self-discipline needed to correct the twisted, perverted, racist, and flagrant theology it has spawned over the years, theology that has been utilized to deceive, mislead, and even incarcerate hundreds of thousands of men and women. It can correct the misuse of the theology of eschatology that makes heaven a religious opiate which keeps people longing for a nebulous life after death while being insulated from or having to endure the hell of the evils of this world. It can desist from senseless arguments about the Bible, such as biblical inerrancy, which often provides a shield behind which conservatives can hide to make political power plays.

If this bit of corrective theological housekeeping can be done, then Paul's message presents the white church with the challenge to move from proclamation to implementation. The white church can move to bridge the division that is rending its ranks and reducing it to impotence, such as the rupture that has emerged among Southern Baptists over conservatism and liberalism. If the white church can get its theology in order and unify its ranks, it can then move to correct the problems of marriage and divorce, sexuality and homosexuality, child abuse, racism, greed and graft, selfishness and solipsism that exist within it. Only until this is done—and that through rigorous self-discipline—can the white church move out into American society to heal it of its ills. The white church could very well be the agent of redemption for America, if it is willing to exercise the self-discipline, about which Paul spoke, as it moves along its long, long road toward the imperishable crown of eternal life.

Paul's challenge is one that the white church alone can accept or reject. If it accepts the challenge, good! But if it rejects it, it could be in the same situation as those who said to Jesus, "Lord, Lord, did we not prophesy in your name, and cast out demons in your name . . . ?" and the Lord will answer, "I never knew you; depart from me, you evildoers" (see Matthew 7:22-23). Its lot will be that of running an ostensibly creditable race but being disqualified at the end of the journey.

Paul's message in this chapter presents the black church with a similar criticism and a healthy challenge. His message criticizes the black church for not freeing itself from its crippling sprint mentality so that the church can proceed with the noble mission its forebears began when in slavery. In failing to do this, the church has failed to pursue or be pulled by the power of the imperishable crown as it moves through a very evil and hostile world. With the goal blurred in its vision, the black church has proceeded as one running aimlessly and as one lashing the air with futility. It has failed to exercise self-discipline in theological reflection so that it has been lured haplessly from the race into the dreaded regions of idolatry, superstition, and intrigue. Without self-discipline for the long, long road to ultimate Christian freedom, it has allowed its ranks to be ruptured by rapacious ribaldry, churlish chicanery, and opulent obsession for material possessions. Divisions within the ecclesiastical ranks, marital and family fissions, rampant immorality, and perverted personalities have all enervated the black church to the point that it is little more than a sounding gong and clanging cymbal. The black church stands before the very real and frightening possibility of pulling up at the finish line only to be declared disqualified by the judge of all the earth.

This does not have to be the lot of the black church in America. Paul's message challenges the black church to wipe from its eyes the blinding vitriolic fumes of racist oppression, self-pity, and self-indulgence and to view anew the imperishable crown of ultimate freedom in Christ and to run victoriously through the world of evil to claim it. Paul challenges the black church to rid itself of its gullible acceptance of effete and errant theologies spawned by deceptive theologians and heralds of nebulous truth and to recapture the liberating gospel of the Bible, the New Testament, the theology of Paul and those unlettered religious leaders of its noble past. Paul urges the black church to mend its cleavages, and to heal its disparities, to unify its ranks, and to stand forth as a true and undivided church, an *ekklesia,* the people of God.

Once all of this is in place, the black church can set about eliminating the debilitating ravages of immorality and idolatry in all of its forms. Once it has recaptured the essence of the liberating gospel of the Bible, the New Testament and the theology of Paul the apostle and its forebears, once it has reorganized its ranks in unity and gotten back on the road to ultimate freedom in Christ in pursuit of the imperishable crown, the black church can get on with the task of marshalling its fiscal resources to match its spiritual resources in order to fight better the battle of liberation in the world. But all this must be set in the context of self-discipline for the long, long road that leads to ultimate freedom in Christ. This is the challenge Paul sets before the black church. If the black church can meet the challenge, it could emerge as the true light of the world and the salt of the earth, the church in which the salvation of the Christian faith occurs in the world. But it is the black church and the black church alone that can respond to Paul's challenge.

The Choice That Is Left to Us

Understandably, Paul caustically criticizes and presents a difficult challenge before America and the contemporary church, both black and white. The church since Paul's time has had tremendous difficulty making sense out of his time-eternity continuum; that heaven gives direction, meaning, and power to the church's struggle for righteousness on earth and that without heaven all of the church's battles are insignificant and futile. All along the road of the history of the church, the church in all of its versions opted for either revolutionary quest of this world or righteous repose, waiting for another nebulous world. But neither option has been successful. It is time, then, to look anew at the apostle Paul and consider his use of self-discipline in all facets of the Christian life as the church proceeds toward the imperishable crown of ultimate freedom in Christ.

Understandably, it is a difficult alternative—it was difficult for Paul himself—but it is one that beckons us to follow on. As I have reexamined the route over which Paul traveled, it is obvious that to follow him is extremely difficult. It is as Günther Bornkamm says: ". . . not a few who yield themselves to his gospel are left feeling like a traveler overcome by vertigo in an Alpine region surrounded by steep, cloud-covered peaks, who often does not know how to follow on and how he is going to last the journey."[33] If America and the contemporary church, both black and white, are to realize the ultimate freedom that awaits in eternal life, they must in self-discipline follow after Paul through the labyrinth of this world. The victory and the imperishable wreath will be awarded only to the ones who endure.

5

2

The Body of Christ: Unity in the Free Community

The freedom of a people is greatly contingent on the unity they can maintain. It is inconceivable that the early church could have maintained its freedom and movement in a hostile Roman Empire had it not had unity. This chapter concerns itself with the position that, for Paul the apostle, the freedom claimed and maintained by the early church and its individual members by arduous efforts of self-discipline could not have been accomplished without unity within the Christian community.

From its inception, the early church existed in a world of religious and political fragmentation, a world dominated by the Roman Empire, which encouraged and sustained social fragmentation and a multitude of disparate religions and philosophies. The early church existed in a world that perpetrated violence and persecution against it. From at least two camps, the early church received blows aimed at dividing it. The political power of the time, the Roman Empire, sought to destroy it with persecution from without. Fanatical religio-philosophical groups sought to undermine the new faith from within the church and without.

With its references to Jews and religio-philosophical groups, such as Gnostics, Stoics, and Epicureans, the New Testament gives some indication of the extent to which the early church was confronted with attempts to divide and undermine it in its early days. Paul's notation of the persecutions experienced on behalf of the gospel and Luke's narration in Acts of the punishment the early church suffered at the hands of Jewish religionists and political authorities are scriptural indications of this.

One can also perceive the devastating attempts to divide and destroy the early church by means of religious hegemony and political hatred by exploring Eusebius' *Ecclesiastical History*. Here are detailed the efforts aimed at undermining the early church by many groups and heresies that made their mark on distant history. The sinister and sordid persecutions of the Neronian, Domitian, Diocletian, and other periods of Roman history are painfully detailed by Eusebius to demonstrate the bone-racking punishment suffered by many in the early church, punishment designed to divide and conquer it, punishment designed to decimate and destroy it. The means by which the early church withstood these assaults was that of unity; and in maintaining its unity, the early church maintained its freedom and the freedom of its individual members.

In his masterfully written book *The Mission and Expansion of Christianity in the First Three Centuries*, Adolf Harnack traces the expansion of the early church through all of its precarious paths and lays the success of its movement to the unity that evolved out of preaching. The objective of all preaching, according to Harnack, was not only to evangelize individuals but also to unite those who became believers in Jesus Christ. ''Christian preaching aimed at winning souls and bringing individuals to God, 'that the number of the elect might be made up,' but from the very outset it worked through a community and proposed to itself the aim of uniting all who believed in Christ.''[1] Although each local Christian community was a unit, it also was a paradigm, a reproduction of all other communities of the Christian faith[2] so that the church at Corinth and the church at Thessalonica were both known as the church of God. Individual members of Christian communities were subordinate to the body.[3] Harnack observes that the uniqueness of the Christian community, self-contained, with individuals who had come from the surrounding society now being welded into an entity without political or national basis, "was a novel and unheard-of thing upon the soil of Greek and Roman life."[4] But it was "the mere existence and persistent activity of the individual Christian communities" according to Harnack, that did "more than anything else to bring about the extension of the Christian religion."[5]

Johannes Weiss drew the conclusion that unity was an important characteristic of the early church. Engagement in daily prayers, participation in communal meals, and submission of its members to daily teachings of the apostles, Weiss suggests, reflect the unity that characterized the early church.[6] Weiss and Harnack represent a large list of scholars who picked up the important fact that unity was a major characteristic in the early church, one that allowed it to maintain its freedom and the freedom of its members in a fragmented and hostile world.

Unity: A Major Strategy for Freedom

The origin and emphasis of unity as a major component of freedom for the church in the New Testament is in the theology of the apostle Paul. A serious reading of the genuine writings of Paul discloses considerable concentration on the concept of unity.[7] This is true especially in the first letter to the Corinthians. The twelfth chapter of that letter, is the locus of Paul's model for unity in the believing community. Everything Paul says leading up to chapter 12 in First Corinthians anticipates this model of unity for the church and everything in the following chapters builds upon what has been said in chapter 12. It is because of this intense emphasis on unity in First Corinthians and in Paul's other letters that I conclude that unity is one of the major strategies for freedom for the church in Pauline theology. Paul's model of unity as an expression of freedom in the Christian community is especially important for us because unity is not apparent in the Christian church in America in our time.

Paul's Call to Affirm Unity

The fact that Paul's treatment of unity for the church consumed the entire twelfth chapter of First Corinthians indicates not only that the subject was an important one to include in the church's portfolio but that something gravely serious had occurred in Corinth that necessitated the subject's discussion. The occasional nature of Paul's letters tells us that, in every case, his writing was in response to some condition, situation, or question that had arisen within a particular church community. Looking at the letter from a holistic perspective, one can draw the conclusion that disunity within the Corinthian community was precisely the reason Paul wrote the letter.

Immediately following his glowing greetings and accolades, Paul raised the issue of division within the fellowship at Corinth: "I appeal to you . . . that all of you agree and that there be no dissensions *(schismata)* among you . . ." (1 Corinthians 1:10). The report had been conveyed to Paul by people who associated with a certain woman named Chloe that quarreling was going on among the church members (1:11). Some were claiming identification with theological or ideological camps, represented by Paul, Apollos, Cephas, and even Christ (1:12). Paul's rejoinder is the rhetorical question, "Is Christ divided?" (1:13a); the answer of which is obviously no! Paul is concerned about the rumored division within the Corinthian fellowship because the end result could very well empty the cross of Christ of its power (cf. 1:17).

Other divisions also afflicted the Corinthian church. Some of the fellowship considered themselves to have superior spiritual wisdom over others within the church and some claimed to have arrived already at whatever state of prominent knowledge they felt was theirs (cf. 2:14-16; 3:1ff.; 4:6ff., respectively). A deep and yawning chasm was cut into the community when one member took another member to trial before a pagan judge of the Roman civil court (6:1-b). Paul's discussion of marriage and divorce (7:1-16, 25-40) and slavery (7:17-24) is strong indication that these issues threatened a serious rupture in the relations of the membership of the Corinthian church. Some in the Corinthian community claimed the power to speak in tongues *(glossalalia)* and elevated themselves over those who could not (14:1-33). This, too, brought about the threat of division.

One of the most blatant and painful demonstrations of division at Corinth was that which occurred during the observance of the Lord's Supper. In astonishment Paul says, "I hear that there are divisions *(schismata)* among you . . ." (11:18). The Corinthian church community (cf. 1:22) came together to eat the Lord's Supper, and the rich or more well-to-do proceeded to eat all the food and drink all the wine before the poor could get their share. Along with desecrating the Lord's Supper and eating until they were sick and drinking until they were drunk, the rich also brought about a rupture in their relations with the poor, thus bringing about division in the church.

Following his discussion of the divisive activity surrounding the Lord's table, Paul provides profound theological advice designed to unify and liberate the church at Corinth. Set in the context of his discussion of the variety of gifts enjoyed by the Corinthians is Paul's argument for unity: "For just as the body is one and has many members, and all the members of the body, though many, are one body, so it is with Christ" (12:12). He follows with what seems to be an unalterable conclusion: "Now you are the body of Christ and individually members of it" (12:27).

Before I attempt to unpack the meaning of what Paul has said here, it should be stated that this is the first time in the New Testament that the church has been symbolically styled as a "body." Paul was the first to introduce such a notion, one that claimed the unalterable unity of the church and the members within it. Paul obviously borrowed the idea from the classic philosophers of Greek thought, especially the Stoics. Greek philosophers thought of the state, for example, in a corporate sense as a "body," which was comprised of various members.[8] As he had done on numerous occasions (for example, the athletic symbolism of 1 Corinthians 9:24-27), so now Paul borrowed again from pagan cultures. In using the symbol of the "body" to describe the unity of the church, Paul gave the church this theological understanding of unity in the church, a unity that results in liberation for both the church and its individual members.

What does Paul mean in 12:12 when he says, "For just as the body is one and has many members . . . so it is with Christ," a maxim which he caps with "Now you are the body of Christ and individually members of it" (12:27)? He means that the church at Corinth (not only the church at Corinth, but also the church at Galatia, Thessalonica, Philippi, and everywhere) is similar to the human body, a body composed of many and various members that are equal though different in nomenclature, nature, and function.

First, Paul is calling the Corinthian church and the members thereof to be what they have been called to be. Paul is not simply reminding them of who they are, but he is urging them to be, in fact, what and who they have been called to be by God through Jesus Christ. Placing in his exhortation the force of the affirmative, he says, "Now you are . . . ." "You are" indicates a unit. This is Paul's way of affirming the entity of the Corinthian church and its members. It is his way of reminding the proud and prosperous within the Corinthian church that they are a part of the ecclesiastical unit which he calls the "body of Christ"; and it is his call for them to be that, in fact. It is also his way of reminding the rejected among the Corinthian fellowship that they, too, are part of the "body of Christ"; and they, too, are called to be that.

The thrust of what Paul is saying here is similar to what Jesus said to his disciples in his Sermon on the Mount. Jesus said, "You are the salt of the earth" and "You are the light of the world" (Matthew 5:13, 14). As the disciples were preparing to go out to evangelize a hostile and oppressive world, Jesus wanted them not to be in doubt about who they were and what they were to do. Therefore, he affirmed their identity, "You are. . . . You are!" As Jesus affirmed his disciples' identity, so Paul affirms the Corinthians' identity: *"You are* the body of Christ."

Paul's affirmation and call for church members to be the body of Christ is a forceful point made throughout his other letters. The unity that is effected by the act of baptism into Christ is expressed in his letter to the Romans.

> Do you not know that all of us who have been baptized into Christ Jesus were baptized into his death? We were buried therefore with him by baptism into death, so that as Christ was raised from the dead by the glory of the Father, we too might walk in newness of life.
> For if we have been united with him in a death like his, we shall certainly be united with him in a resurrection like his (Romans 6:3-5).

A strong statement of the unity that is brought about by baptism into Christ is made in Galatians 3:26-28:

> . . . for in Christ Jesus you are all sons of God, through faith. For as many of you as were baptized into Christ have put on Christ. There is neither Jew nor Greek, there is neither slave nor free, there is neither male nor female; for you are all one in Christ Jesus.

The Corinthians are to be the body of Christ because they have all eaten and drunk the same sacred meal which is, in effect, participation in the blood and body of Christ. This position is clearly taken by Paul in 1 Corinthians 10:16-17:

> The cup of blessing which we bless, is it not a participation in the blood of Christ? The bread which we break, is it not a participation in the body of Christ? Because there is one bread, we who are many are one body, for we all partake of the one bread.

The Corinthians are to be the body of Christ because they have been unified by the Spirit of Christ:

> For by one Spirit we were all baptized into one body—Jews or Greeks, slaves or free—and all were made to drink of one Spirit (1 Corinthians 12:13).

Having been baptized in the Spirit and given the Spirit (cf. Romans 8:9), the Corinthians are exhorted like the Galatians to "live by the Spirit" and to "walk by the Spirit" (Galatians 5:25). It is through the power of the Spirit of Christ that the church at Corinth and the members thereof have been united and liberated.

Being unified by the Spirit, baptism, and participation in the Eucharist, the Corinthians are to be the body of Christ because through these means they have become a family in which each member stands on equal ground with the other. There is no stronger term describing the relationship between members within the church fellowship than that of "brother" (cf. 1 Corinthians 5:11; 6:5). For Paul, to be a member of the fellowship of believers in Christ means to be a member of the "brotherhood" (6:5). As a member of the brotherhood, one member is not to wrong or defraud another member (cf. 6:8; 1 Thessalonians 4:6). A member is not to exploit or make use of another, e.g., as a slave (cf. Philemon, v. 16). A member is not to indulge in immorality, greed, idolatry, revelry, drunkenness, robbery, or the like (cf. 5:11). In the brotherhood, the strong are not to exploit the weak, causing the weaker to sin (cf. 8:7-13), but the stronger member is to bear the infirmity of the weaker one (cf. Romans 15:1; also 14:13-21). As a member of the fellowship of believers, a member is not to take another to court but is to settle differences with the other within the fellowship (cf. 1 Corinthians 6:1-6).

Participation in the unifying power of the Spirit, in baptism, in the Eucharist, and membership in the brotherhood are what Paul means when he says to the Corinthians, "You are the body of Christ." The Corinthians, as is the case with all churches, are called to be united. This is a truth they should know, but because of the instances of division reported to Paul by Chloe's people, he is constrained to remind them again of their calling.

Members Are Components, Not Detachments

Having said, "just as the body is one and has many members, and all the members of the body, though many, are one body, so it is with Christ" (12:12), and climaxing his exhortation with "you are the body of Christ and individually members of it" (12:27), Paul must say something of what this does not mean. When Paul says that the members of the Corinthian church, all of them, compose the body of Christ, he does not mean that detachment is allowed. On the contrary, each member of the church is a component part of the body. Therefore, no individual has the right to say, because he or she may not be like another or does not think the same or agree with another (although this should not be) that he or she is not a part of the body or the church. Paul states this in anatomical language:

> If the foot should say, "Because I am not a hand, I do not belong to the body," that would not make it any less a part of the body. And if the ear should say, "Because I am not an eye, I do not belong to the body," that would not make it any less a part of the body (12:15-16).

The point that Paul sets forth here simply is that no component of the body can have the luxury of detaching itself from the body simply because it is not the same as another component of the body. Even if this were attempted, the detached component would be no less a part of the body. Stating it ecclesiastically, Paul would say that no member is at liberty to say, because he or she is not like another member or does not appreciate another member, that he or she therefore is not a part of the church, the body of Christ. Detaching himself or herself from the body of believers because of this would make him or her no less a part of the body. The unspoken argument that Paul makes here is that if a member of the church were to detach himself or herself from the rest of the body because of dissimilarity with another component, that detachment would constitute a division within the body, the church, which the church at Corinth, or any other church, can ill afford. The detached member is no less a member of the body, the church.

Members Are to Integrate, Not Dominate

Paul takes his argument a step further to say that the concept of the body of Christ does not mean that some components of the body can enjoy dominance in the body and therefore constitute the body itself. He states it thus,

> If the whole body were an eye, where would be the hearing? If the whole body were an ear, where would be the sense of smell? But as it is, God arranged the organs in the body, each one of them, as he chose. If all were a single organ, where would the body be? As it is, there are many parts, yet one body (12:17-20).

The thrust of the argument here is that there can be no dominance of one component of the body over the rest of the body. It would be illogical, Paul argues, for the eye to be in and of itself the whole body. The same would be true of the ear or any other component of the body. The body is composed of many members; yet in its composition of many members, it is one body. Similarly, the church, the body of Christ, is not composed of one member or individual. What if the body of Christ were composed of only the rich or only the poor? What if it were composed only of the enlightened or the unenlightened? Or what if it were composed only of the strong or the weak? Were it of such, the church would be a society of the opulent or of paupers, a coterie of supercilious eggheads or of effete ignoramuses, or a mass of plundering giants or a horde of heartless parasites. On the contrary the body of Christ, according to Paul, is comprised of neither one nor the other, but of both strong and weak. The body of Christ is composed of many and varied parts, all of which are united into one body.

Paul concludes this segment of his argument by saying that there is no logical rationale or sustainable justification for one component of the body of Christ claiming existence without need for, relationship to, or support of the other components of the body. Hence, Paul says,

> The eye cannot say to the hand, "I have no need of you," nor again the head to the feet, "I have no need of you." On the contrary, the parts of the body which seem to be weaker are indispensable, and those parts of the body which we think less honorable we invest with the greater modesty, which our more presentable parts do not require. But God has so composed the body, giving the greater honor to the inferior part, that there may be no discord in the body, but that the members may have the same care for one another. If one member suffers, all suffer together; if one member is honored, all rejoice together (12:21-26).

Two important points are made here. The first is that one component of the body cannot claim self-sufficiency and exist exclusive of other components of the body. A second point, and one that is greatly profound, is that the weaker and inferior components of the body are indispensable to the body and in fact are given greater honor than the stronger and more presentable parts of the body.

The Weaker/Stronger Dynamic in the Body

The thrust of Paul's second point here is brought into clearer focus when set in the context of the concrete situation that existed in Corinth, e.g., the wise and the ignorant (or the strong and the weak), husband and wife (marriage and divorce), slave and free, rich and poor, the ones who were spiritually gifted to speak in tongues *(glossalalia)* and those who were not. It may be well to look at each of these categories to make the point more forcibly.

The Indulgence of the Spiritually Wise

Paul's initial concern in his first letter to the Corinthians is with those who claimed superior wisdom *(pneumatikoi)* in the Corinthian church community. "Where is the wise man? Where is the scribe? Where is the debater of this age? Has not God made foolish the wisdom of the world?" (1:20). There were those within the Corinthian church community who claimed the "wisdom of this world." Paul's concern is, however, "that your faith might not rest in the wisdom of men but in the power of God" (2:5). For Paul, possession of the wisdom of this world is for naught; it is better that one has the wisdom that comes from God, for with such wisdom ". . . the rulers of this age . . . would not have crucified the Lord of glory" (2:8). But there were those who obstinately claimed this worldly wisdom (hence Paul's discussion in chapters 2, 3, and 4), and claimed it as if it were not a gift to them from God (cf. 4:7). Albeit equipped with this worldly wisdom *(pneumatikoi)*, they were "puffed up in favor of one against another" (4:6c). So much was this the case that one brother took another brother to civil court, an act that was reprehensible to the church and the name of Christ and threatened to divide the church and empty the cross of its power (1:17c). So Paul responds to the situation, "Can it be that there is no man among you wise enough to decide between members of the brotherhood, but brother goes to law against brother, and that before unbelievers?" (6:5-6).

The spiritually wise of the Corinthian church community violated the principles of the body of Christ in that they said to the unwise of the fellowship, "I have no need of you." Because the unwise and weak were dispensable and useless to the wise, the wise took the liberty to carry the unwise before the civil court for settlement of differences that occurred within the church. In the first place, this was an indictment against the church members for not being able to settle differences among themselves. In the second place, such action by the so-called wise men caused a rupture within the body of Christ and disharmony within the fellowship.

The whole matter could have been avoided had the spiritually wise (*pneumatikoi*) men of the Corinthian church community considered the unwise and the weak to be as useful and valuable to them as they themselves were to the unwise. The body of Christ would have been spared the disruption and disharmony had the spiritually wise demonstrated to the unwise a spirit of forbearance and forgiveness rather than a spirit of impatience by marching them off to civil court. Further, the wise would have received the boon of redeeming the errant brother from his misdeeds, an act of liberation and salvation. This would have effected what Paul says in Romans 15:1, "We who are strong ought to bear with the failings of the weak, and not to please ourselves." This is what Paul meant when he said that the parts of the body that people think less honorable are to be given greater honor. This is done so that there might be no discord in the body of Christ.

In two other instances, Paul discusses the possible misuse of the unwise by the wise or the weak by the strong. In the first instance, Paul observes that while the strong among the Corinthian fellowship are wise enough to know that meat offered to idols makes one no worse off if it is eaten, there are those within the fellowship who are weak and not wise enough to eat such meat without thinking they are defiled. In the first passage (1 Corinthians 8:7-13), Paul concludes that food, whether offered to idols or not, will not commend one to God. However, he points out that the wise or strong among the fellowship should not become a stumbling block to the weak by eating meat offered to idols (8:9). Indications are that the wise and strong, in fact, had taken advantage of their knowledge and had eaten meat offered to idols and, by their action, the ". . . weak man [was] destroyed, the brother for whom Christ died" (8:11). This constitutes a sin against the brother whose conscience is weak; and it also is a sin against Christ (8:12). Paul concludes his argument here by injecting himself into the discussion and offering for a solution what he himself would do: "Therefore, if food is a cause of my brother's falling, I will never eat meat, lest I cause my brother to fall" (8:13).

The same point is made in 10:23-33 in a similar discussion. In this case, Paul concedes that it is permissible to eat all meats, even those sold in the marketplace that are offered to idols. However, if a question about eating the meat is raised by someone who points out that the meat has been offered to idols, for the sake of the inquirer's conscience, the meat should not be eaten (10:28).

In both cases of the permissibility of eating meat offered to idols, Paul's advice to the strong and wise is to be considerate of the conscience of the weak and unwise and not eat meat because it would be offensive to the weak and unwise and cause them to stumble. The wise and strong have a responsibility to the weak and unwise—to seek not their own good of self, ". . . but the good of [their] neighbor" (10:24; cf. 10:33). This is Paul's way of undergirding what he has said in 1 Corinthians 12:22-26, when he insists that those parts of the body of Christ that are less honorable be invested with greater honor and that this be done so that there will be no discord in the body.

Marriage Affects/Reflects the Body of Christ

The point of Paul's statement in 12:21-26 can be seen a bit more clearly when we focus on the situation of a husband and wife or marriage and divorce, which he treats in 1 Corinthians 7 and 11. Paul's desire is that everyone in the Corinthian community be as himself, i.e., remaining unmarried and exercising self-control (7:7). But, if this is not possible, it is better to marry than to engage in promiscuity (7:9). Paul urges those who have married to remain together in marriage. The wife should not separate herself from her husband and the husband should not divorce himself from his wife (7:10-11). Paul does not deal with husband and wife in terms of stronger and weaker (as is the case in 1 Peter 3:7). He does conclude that the woman was made for man (cf. 1 Corinthians 11:8-9) and that the woman is the glory of man (cf. 11:7b). Yet the man is not independent of the woman and the woman is not independent of the man (cf. 11:11). In this sense, neither the woman nor the man can say, "I have no need of you" (12:21).

Paul's concern here is that married couples be aware that they, too, comprise the body of Christ (cf. 12:27) and that their attitude toward each other—resulting in their remaining with each other or separating from or divorcing each other—either builds up the body or does violence to it. The emphasis, however, is on married couples remaining together. (However, if they agree to separate, to do so only for a season and then be reconciled with one another lest they both be tempted through lack of self-control.) To separate from one another would not only bring division to the family but also bring division within the body of Christ, the church. To remain together would mean the preservation of unity and harmony in the family as well as in the body of Christ, the church. To stay together for the sake of unity within the body of Christ is of paramount importance for Paul.

Paul felt this to be true even for those within the believing community who were married to unbelievers. They cannot say, "I have no need of you" (12:21), for the believing husband or wife has a responsibility to the unbelieving wife or husband (cf. 7:12-14). If a man has a wife who is an unbeliever, he should not divorce her; likewise, the unbelieving husband should not be divorced by the believing wife. But here again, such action is recommended by Paul so that greater honor can be given to the weaker and inferior partner of the marriage, who, because of marriage to the believing partner, has a connection with the body of Christ. The responsibility of the believing husband or wife is to remain with the unbelieving husband or wife in an attempt to save the unbeliever. Paul states his case in a rather enigmatic phrase, "Wife, how do you know whether you will save your husband? Husband, how do you know whether you will save your wife?" (7:16). Such missionary or evangelistic behavior on the part of the wiser and stronger husband or wife reflects the "I have need of you" mentality that exists within the body of Christ. It also reflects the "greater honor" that is given to the weaker and inferior parts of the body of Christ. The bearing with the unbelieving husband or wife by the believing wife or husband would, in effect, be a possible act of liberation and salvation for the unbeliever. It would also preserve harmony and unity within the body of Christ, the church.

The Relationship of Former Slave and Free Person

The meaning of the body of Christ, as stated in 1 Corinthians 12:21-26, is made even clearer when consideration is given to the relationship of the slave and the free within the believing community. Paul's treatment of slave and free is tersely done in 7:20-24. As has been discussed in chapter 2 of this book, Paul urges those slaves coming into the believing community to claim their freedom (7:21). As a convert to Christ and a member of the body of Christ, the slave becomes "a freedman of the Lord." At the same time, the one who is free in the church is "a slave of Christ" (7:22). In such a relationship, neither the former slave nor the free person can say, "I have no need of you" (12:21).

In Paul's discussion of the former slave's relationship with the free person, the responsibility of the wiser and stronger of the two (the free person) to the weaker and unwise of the two (the former slave) is implicit. This is seen more clearly in Paul's letter to Philemon. In that discussion Paul is returning the former slave, Onesimus to his former owner, Philemon. As a slave, Onesimus was "useless" to Philemon. But now as a believer, he is "indeed useful" (see Philemon, v. 11). Philemon cannot say of him, "I have no need of you." In fact, now that Onesimus has been converted to Christ by the preaching of the gospel and has become a member of the body of Christ, Paul returns the former slave to his former master, telling Philemon of his responsibility to treat Onesimus no longer as a slave but as a "beloved brother" (v. 16). This means that now Philemon is to give this fledgling believer, this weaker, less honorable, and inferior part of the body of Christ, the greater honor so that there may be no discord in the body. The entire episode is an act of liberation both for Philemon and Onesimus, for in the church there is no place for slavery. Philemon is liberated from his penchant for lording over a brother as a slave master, and Onesimus is liberated from servitude and accepted as a free man and a brother in the believing community.

Rivalry of the Poor and the Rich

Still another situation in the Corinthian church community makes clear the meaning of 1 Corinthians 12:21-26, viz., the friction between the rich and the poor. The question is addressed by Paul when he deals with the Lord's Supper in 1 Corinthians 11. Here is the second place in his letter where he specifically states ". . . I hear that there are divisions among you" (11:18). It seemed to be the case that when the church gathered to participate in the Lord's Supper, the rich proceeded to eat the bread and drink the wine before the poor arrived. Paul states it thus,

> For in eating, each one goes ahead with his own meal, and one is hungry and another is drunk. What! Do you not have houses to eat and drink in? Or do you despise the church of God and humilate those who have nothing? (11:21-22).

By going ahead with the meal, the rich were saying to the poor, "I have no need of you; you are not important." Paul does not commend them for this (cf. 11:22c). He proceeds with his classic formula of the Lord's Supper, a tradition which he has received from the Lord. This is his way of reminding the Corinthians that when they participate in the Lord's Supper they are, in fact, participating in the body and blood of the Lord (cf. 10:16). In addition to this, they are "proclaiming the Lord's death until he comes" (11:26). Paul follows with a dreaded "therefore." "Whoever, therefore, eats the bread or drinks the cup of the Lord in an unworthy manner will be guilty of profaning the body and blood of the Lord" (11:27).

There seems to be a cryptic meaning here. Eating and drinking in "an unworthy manner" is that which is done without the presence and participation of an integral part of the body of Christ, the poor. Profaning the body and blood of the Lord is not simply denigrating the body of Jesus, which was hanged on a cross, but denigrating also the body that represents him now, the body of Christ, the church. The act of disregarding the poor and neglecting them in observance of the Lord's Supper is profaning the body of Christ. It is as if to say that they are not "brothers," that they have not been baptized into the body of Christ, or that they have not received the Spirit just as the rich had. The rich profane the body of Christ by saying of the poor, "I have no need of you."

Here Paul injects a warning for the rich: "For any one who eats and drinks without discerning the body eats and drinks judgment upon himself" (11:29). The judgment is not described. But it must be some dreaded thing, for in proceeding with the meal without the poor, the rich have not discerned the body of Christ; they have disregarded one of the important components of the body of Christ; they have failed to give the greater honor to the less honorable and inferior part, thus imposing division upon the body. Paul concludes by saying, "So then, my brethren, when you come together to eat, wait for one another . . . " (11:33).

Hence, in Paul's treatment of the Lord's Supper, the argument in chapter 12 of the inseparability of the members of the body of Christ is undergirded. There must be unity and harmony within the church, the body of Christ. This unity must be guaranteed by the attitude of the rich toward the poor, which grants greater honor to the weaker and inferior parts of the body.

The Contention Between Tongues and Prophecy

A final situation in the Corinthian church makes clearer the meaning of 1 Corinthians 12:21-26, viz., the contention that existed between the ones who spoke in tongues and the ones who prophesied. Chapter 14 is the locus of Paul's discussion of this situation at Corinth.

Apparently, there were those in the church in Corinth who claimed that speaking in tongues (*lalon glosse*) made them better off than those who prophesied. The problem with this claim was that it was causing a schism within the church, the body of Christ.

The speakers in tongues were saying of those who could not, "I have no need of you." Their spiritual gift to mouth unintelligible utterings made them something special in the congregation, according to their thinking. But Paul's rejoinder to those speaking in tongues is that "one who speaks in a tongue speaks not to men but to God; for no one understands him, but he utters mysteries in the Spirit" (14:2). Paul argues that one who prophesies is "greater than he who speaks in tongues" (14:5b) because the one who prophesies "edifies the church" (14:4b). The one who speaks in tongues "edifies himself" (14:4a), thus causing a rift in the fellowship.

Paul really has no problem with those who wish to speak in tongues, as long as the church is edified (14:5c), i.e., built up (14:12). But edification of the church and building up of the church by those who speak in tongues is possible only if there are interpreters to decipher what is being said (14:5c, 13, 27). Although the weight of Paul's argument falls on the side of prophecy, he allows those who wish to speak in tongues to do so; but, he says, whatever is done, "Let all things be done for edification" (14:26c). If Paul had his way, however, there would be no speaking in tongues, for speaking in tongues tends to generate confusion, and God is not a God of confusion (cf. 14:33). Paul would prefer for "all to prophesy" so that a distinct sound and a unified voice can go out from the church announcing the message of the liberating gospel.

Clearly Paul's argument here is in line with what he has said in chapter 12 about the body of Christ. Those who speak in tongues cannot say to those who prophesy, "I have no need of you." Neither can those who prophesy say the same about those who speak in tongues. Each must compliment the other ". . . that there may be no discord in the body, but that the members may have the same care for one another" (12:25).

Concluding Paul's Argument

What is emerging out of Paul's discussion of the body of Christ in 1 Corinthians 12 is Paul's passion for a unified church. The apostle's incessant concern is that the church at Corinth, and all churches, be unencumbered from the ravages of division, division that results from pious individualism, quests for power, greed for riches; that churches not be hamstrung by social stratification nor bloated with selfish spiritualism. There would be no way for the church to withstand the onslaught of persecution that was imminent if it were itself divided. Further the church could not be an agency of liberation for wandering and powerless souls, souls hopelessly divided and fragmented by a ruthless society, if the church itself was divided.

Therefore, Paul calls upon the church at Corinth to be what, in fact, it has been called to be: ". . . the body of Christ" (12:27). In the church the strong must give reinforcement to the weak; the husband must not divorce himself from his wife nor the wife from her husband; the free man is not to lord over the one who once was a slave; the rich are obligated to support the poor; and those who speak in tongues have no prominence over those who prophesy. Not one of these can exist apart from the other; one cannot say to the other, "I have no need of you," and neither can one member of the body, the church, expect all others to be the same as he or she, "for by one Spirit we were all baptized into one body—Jews or Greeks, slaves or free—and all were made to drink of one Spirit" (12:13).

It cannot be deduced from this line of reasoning that Paul disregarded church order. It must be said that Paul conceptualized the church as containing an ordering of positions of various functions. Paul is the first in the New Testament to raise to visibility and prominence the offices of bishop and deacon (cf. Philippians 1:1). In 1 Corinthians 12 he concedes that God's own arrangement of ministries in the church allows for apostles, prophets, teachers, workers of miracles, healers, helpers, administrators, and speakers of various kinds of tongues (cf. 1 Corinthians 12:28). But according to his discussion of these positions in the church, "All these are inspired by one and the same Spirit, who apportions to each one individually as he wills" (12:11). And so, although there are various gifts, the gifts are given by the same Spirit and the various services that are performed by people in the church are given by the same Spirit (cf. 12:45). The underlying argument here is that the church is one unified body of believers in Christ. It is the body of Christ.

Contributors to Divisiveness Today

Paul's model for church unity as an expression of liberation and salvation is especially important for the church today. It is particularly needed in a country such as America where the church has a gaping chasm of cultures and an assortment of social schisms. The weak need the reinforcement of the strong; the slave needs the affirmation that he or she is free; the husband needs the wife and the wife needs the husband; the poor need the support of the rich; and the lesser endowed with gifts and talents need the ones who are more endowed. The church as the body of Christ, as it is described by Paul, offers this liberating interaction between cultures, classes, and castes. The irony of our day is, however, that though Christianity in America is prominent and ostensibly flourishing, the church has a glaring lack of unity, unity as prescribed by Paul the apostle.

Although there seems to be some common agreement among the churches in America on the theological understanding and articulation of God, Jesus, the Holy Spirit, salvation, eternal life, and the like, there is an all-too-obvious, mitigating, and devastating disunity among the churches in America. Similar ecclesiastical structure in churches and denominations in America fails to hide the gaping chasms of disunity within and between them. The problem of disunity emerges in the sociological, political, economic, and racial application of Christian theology and ecclesiastical structure. And so, while the Christian churches in America appear to be similar or the same in theology and structure, they are divided along sociological stratifications, national politics, economic distribution, and racial lines.

The fact of sociological influences as an ultimately divisive force within the Christian church in America is addressed in a powerful statement by H. Richard Niebuhr in *The Social Sources of Denominationalism*. Niebuhr makes the point that Christian churches in America are divided by what he calls the evil of denominationalism. He says,

> The evil of denominationalism lies in . . . the failure of the churches to transcend the social conditions which fashion them into caste-organizations, to sublimate their loyalties to standards and institutions only remotely relevant if not contrary to the Christian ideal, to resist the temptation of making their own self-preservation and extension the primary object of their endeavor.[9]

According to Niebuhr, the Christian church in America is divided by the social realities of differing ethnic groups, e.g., black and white. To extrapolate further, denominationalism exists because of the failure of churches in America to rise above the tendency of aligning with social standards and institutions—such as economic stratification and political parties—alignments which in many instances are diametrically opposed to Christian ideals. Another evil of denominationalism that evolves into division is a church or group of churches choosing self-preservation or self-extension as the major objective. While Niebuhr's judgment about the evils of denominationalism was made in the late 1920s, it sheds insight on the current situation in America.

Racial Division

There could be no greater demonstration of the division of the Christian church in America than its division along racial lines. For some time now, historians of the development of the Christian church in America have conceded that slavery and racism have been the major cause of division within the church. William Warren Sweet's telling statement underscores this conclusion:

> The most important of the many schisms which have occurred among the American churches were those growing out of negro slavery, while some of the most difficult problems facing the churches today are due to the negro and the bitter contests which have risen in the churches because of him.[10]

The truth of Sweet's sweeping conclusion is corroborated by the fact that in 1845, or thereabout, virtually every major denomination in America split over the issue of slavery: whether black people in America should remain slave or be set free. This was the white church's way, especially the white church of the South, of saying to black people, "I have no need of you." The result of this devastating division was a Methodist Church of the North and a Methodist Church of the South, a Northern Baptist Convention and a Southern Baptist Convention, and so forth.[11]

These denominational demarcations still remain, with few exceptions. Further, while a United Methodist Church has emerged, there still are predominantly black and predominantly white congregations. Racial differences exist to the extent that black Methodists have formed an organization that is called Black Methodists for Church Renewal. The American Baptist Churches in the U.S.A., formerly the Northern Baptist Convention, is comprised of both white and black congregants. The black constituents of the American Baptist Churches in the U.S.A., however, have seen the need to form caucuses within the convention. In both cases of the Methodists and Baptists, black constituents have experienced racial inequality, the feeling of not standing on equal ground with their white counterparts because of their race. This kind of division, in which whites unquestionably demonstrate that they have no need of blacks, exists in virtually every Protestant denomination in America.

There is, to be sure, a white church and a black church in America. The theology and the ecclesiastical structure for both have been the same for the most part but the *praxis* of them has been altogether different and for different reasons. The theology and the ecclesiastical structure of the white church have had, by and large, a conservative bent. They have been designed and articulated to preserve the status quo, i.e., maintaining black Christians in particular and black people in general in a position of inferiority and servitude. This has been a blatant way of the white church saying to black Christians and black people, "I have no need of you."

As a response to this rejection and discrimination on the part of the white church, black Christians formed their own churches. Such a move could be construed as the black Christians' way of forming their own identifiable component of the body of Christ, a church that became an agent of shelter, affirmation, and liberation for the ebony souls rejected by the white church. The organization of the black church was done with raging discontent swelling in black bosoms and yearning for freedom surging in the souls of black folk.

The chronicling of this historic development was done by the unmatched Carter G. Woodson in *The History of the Negro Church*.[12] Black Baptist churches sprang up in Georgia and South Carolina and all over the South in 1774 and later. They eventually formed associations, state conventions, and, finally in 1880, the National Baptist Convention. In 1797, Richard Allen led a group of black Methodists from St. George's Methodist Episcopal Church in Philadelphia, Pennsylvania, and formed the African Methodist Episcopal Church.

One cannot read the works of Benjamin E. Mays, E. Franklin Frazier, James H. Cone, and Gayraud S. Wilmore[13] without coming to the conclusion that the black church in America has been and is very much a part of church life in this land. Yet its very presence is a reflection of the division within the Christian church: it is a separate entity in itself and it is diametrically opposed to the white church in its sociological, political, and racial application of theology.

Denominational Division

Division within the Christian church in America, however, has not been relegated to the categories of black against white. Division in church life in America has occurred within white denominations as well. As has been stated previously, white denominations have been divided all along over the race issue. Other divisions have occurred within the white church that appear on the surface to be the result of differing theological views, but even these have racial undertones.

White denominations tend to be divided along the lines of liberalism, conservatism, and fundamentalism. Liberal whites tend to be more socialistic in their outlook, i.e., they recognize the relative equality of all people and more or less contend for equal sharing of the wealth of the community and country. Conservative whites, while recognizing the equality of persons to a relative degree, would rather that people be relegated to a place with their own kind, e.g., whites with whites and blacks with blacks. Fundamental whites lean more toward rigid racism and otherworldliness and biblicism.

In each of these cases, the problem of race is an underlying factor. For example, the Presbyterian Church (U.S.A) is divided over the problem of race; while one sector is more favorable toward black people, the other is not. The Lutheran Church-Missouri Synod, known for its less-than-favorable attitude toward black people, has had running conflicts with other Lutherans in America. Within the Southern Baptist Convention, an open conflict has emerged between the conservatives and so-called liberals over the issue of race. These are some examples of the division that exists within the white denominations. The fact that the underlying cause of such division is race reflects the nagging persistence of an "I have no need of you" mentality toward black people within a large segment of white denominations.

Black denominations are divided as well. The division in black denominations, however, follow along the lines of power struggles and personality differences. Probably the greatest example of this is the split that occurred within the National Baptist Convention in 1915. The split was not over theological differences but over ownership of the convention's publishing house. This split changed the name of the older group to the National Baptist Convention, U.S.A., Inc., and formulated a new group that drew the name National Baptist Convention of America. A later split within the National Baptist Convention, U.S.A., Inc., occurred in 1961 over personalities and power struggles. Out of that skirmish emerged the Progressive National Baptist Convention. These epochal divisions within the black Baptist church could very well have been because of the "I have no need of you" mentality instead of political power struggles and personality clashes.

"Divide and Conquer"—The White Church's Strategy

Another divisive force moves within the black church community. It has been present from the days of slavery in America.

It is the continuing influence of the white church and its various denominations on the black church and the black community, inflicting upon them both the terrible malaise of division.

Since the days of American slavery, the white church has provided the theological matrix for the tactic of "divide and conquer" imposed upon black slaves and the black church. During slavery, the white church played a major role in separating the "field nigger" from the "house nigger," the "garden nigger" from the "barn nigger." Slaves within these categories were separated from each other and were not allowed to talk with one another without incurring severe punishment. When the black church began to organize, this division was perpetuated by means of denominations. As black Christians began to organize their church structure, they found themselves organizing as denominations, which were the same as the ones to which their white masters belonged. And in doing so, they found themselves divided by a wedge of denominationalism, denominationalism which was accompanied by the disparate theologies and ecclesiastical practices of the comparable white denominations that limited and even eliminated communications between black Christians. This process disallowed the black church and its various denominations the opportunity to weld themselves into a strong entity and viable component of the body of Christ.

Another leftover from American slavery was that the white church sought to maintain control over the emerging black church. Never was the nascent black church allowed to congregate or the black preacher allowed to preach unless there was supervision by a white preacher from the white church. This provided control over what transpired and what was said in the black church gathering. Even when black churches began to organize into associations and episcopal districts, they were not allowed to do so without the supervision of the white church. Especially was this true with the black Baptist churches. This practice allowed for white church control over the ever-growing black church and its attempt to organize itself into an important component of the body of Christ. Putting this process in the context of the Pauline criticism of the Corinthian church, it could be said that this was the white church's attempt to bring about a situation in which the whole body would be the eye (cf. 1 Corinthians 12:17), that is, to make the black church, even though separate from the white church, an ebony replica of the white church.

Control of the black church has always been a major objective of the white church. The die was cast in slavery. Slave masters provided emerging black congregations a place to worship without cost. The black congregation was allowed to use the land and the building constructed thereon free of charge as long as the building was used as a church. If at any time the building stopped being used as a church, the building and land reverted back to the white slave master (or landowner, as he later came to be known). This was a means of maintaining control.

The white church continues attempting to maintain control over the black church in a similar manner by providing financial assistance for the construction of church buildings and technical assistance for educational and mission programs. Black church-related colleges, organizations, and institutions have been founded with money from white church philanthropists ostensibly for the education and cultural development of black Christians. But white church philanthropists have always maintained control over these black churches and institutions by loading the boards of trustees and holding boards with representatives from the white church. In some cases, the land on which the black college stands is owned by the white church and the stipulation for its use is similar to the stipulations placed upon the black slave congregation's use of land for a church: The black college is allowed to utilize the land as long as it is operated as a college; once the college discontinues that use, the land reverts back to its owner, the white church. All this is done to assure that the black church and its institutions stay in line with the ecclesiastical nomenclature and theological norms of the providential and controlling white church group. But it also disallows the development of the black church from becoming a strong, independent, and unique component of the body of Christ.

Efforts on the part of some white churches and their various denominations and sects to divide and control the black church are continuing to this day with devastating results. Some white churches are luring black churches into their communions while at the same time isolating those black churches from the rest of the black community, both Christian and non-Christian. Under the guise of representing the "right doctrine" and the "right church," these white groups convince unsuspecting black Christians and black Christian congregations that because they are identified with the "right church" (which has the "right doctrine") they are the only ones going to heaven and, therefore, are better than other black persons, be they Christians or non-Christians. The effect of this is division within the black church community because persons in the "right church" (which has the "right doctrine") have nothing to do with those of other church communities, albeit they all are black.

A grotesque example of this is the now-defunct People's Temple and the infamous Jim Jones who lured hundreds of black and poor people away from their black churches and alienated them from their families and communities. A less dramatic example of this is the activity of the electronic churches and evangelists of television, the PTL Club, the 700 Club, Rex Humbard, Oral Roberts, Robert Schuller, and others, and the endless number of evangelistical, fundamentalist movements that are drawing heavily from the black church community. A more sophisticated example is the increased missionary and evangelical efforts within black communities across the nation on the part of conventional white church denominations. This hegemenous activity weakens the Christian witness within the black community. It also divides the black community so that it makes ineffective the political, social, and economic strength of the black community and the black church. The underlying reason for the white church's action is the white church's declaration, by its creeds and deeds; unless the black church and black people are like themselves, blacks are not a part of the body of Christ—an assumed interpretation of Paul's complaint with the Corinthians in 1 Corinthians 12:14-18.

The Challenge Intrinsic in Unity

The truth of the matter is that the Christian church in America is divided. The cleavages that afflict the Christian church in America are along the lines of race, economics, sociology, and politics. This ought not be! Paul's model for a united church comes before the church in America as a relevant and challenging one. It even smacks of condemnation. Ideally, the relationship between the white church and its various denominations, between white churches and black churches, and between the black church and its various denominations should be that of relative separateness but unity of purpose as the body of Christ. It should be that the white church and its various denominations work together as the body of Christ, albeit they exist separately. It should be that the white church and its various denominations work together with the black church and its various denominations without paternalism or absorptionism as the body of Christ, albeit they exist separately. It should be that the black church and its various denominations compliment each other and work together as the body of Christ although they exist separately. This should be done for the sake of the integrity of the church as the body of Christ so that the church in America can indeed be a church of unity and power.

There have been rare epochs in America's history when large segments of the church and its denominations have joined together as the body of Christ for the common good of a weaker member of the body. The most salient of these in recent history is the civil rights era. In order to claim equal rights and knock down barriers of racial discrimination against black people in America, Martin Luther King, Jr., formed a coalition of churches and churchmen of all races and creeds in the 1950s and 1960s. There probably has not been another time in recent American history when Jews, Protestants, and Catholics merged together to aid a weaker part of the body of Christ, the black church, in the cause of justice and righteousness. This was probably the most hopeful of times, for the church was demonstrating itself to be the body of Christ.

A Subtle Delusion of Unity

Most recently, there have been isolated instances of unity within limited enclaves of the church for the sake of political and social change in a particular segment of the American population. Most noted is the group of fundamental religionists known as the Moral Majority. The Reverend Jerry Falwell of Lynchburgh, Virginia, forged a nationwide group that radically influenced the presidential electoral process and served as a primary force for the election of President Ronald Reagan. This group also addressed the issues of abortion, divorce, violence on television, and other immoralities that plague American society.

One preponderant area that was not addressed by this august group was the lingering monstrous tentacles of racial discrimination that still exist within a significant part of the body of Christ of which it is a part. There seems to be a silent contempt for the black church and black people within the Moral Majority, as if the black church and black people are not a significant part of the body of Christ. The Moral Majority seems to say by its creeds and deeds, "I have no need of" the black church and black people. Even for those black churches and black people who have joined the ranks of the Moral Majority, and other such groups and sects, there seems to be a benign neglect and callous contempt.

Some ecclesiastical groups in America, on the face of things, seem to incorporate the black church and its various denominations and form some semblance of the body of Christ. The National Council of Churches, the World Council of Churches, and the Religious Education Association are among these. But even here, incorporation of the black church and its various denominations really amounts to nothing more than lip service and window dressing. No real effort is made to provide genuine assistance to the black church and its various denominations to strengthen them and assist them to become a unique part of the body of Christ. Further, these groups have made no serious attempt to make use of the black church's unique understanding and demonstration of the Christian faith, to benefit from the ways the black church and white church complement each other. In fact, the white churches who hold membership in these organizations have unabashedly announced their intentions to impose ecclesiastical hegemony upon the black church and the black community.

At a meeting of the Religious Education Association during its celebration of the two-hundredth anniversary of the Sunday school, held on the campus of Scarritt College in Nashville, Tennessee, in the summer of 1980, virtually every major Protestant denomination represented stated that its missionary and evangelical efforts for the 1980s would be the ghettos of the inner cities of America. This meant that the white church was launching contrivances to evangelize from the inner-city black communities of America those black persons who either held membership in black churches or are prospective members of the same. The end result of this ecclesiastical raid of the inner cities of America would be, if effective, the decimation of the black church and its various denominations and the economic and numerical strengthening of the white church.

The success of this movement would mean the realization of that dreaded thought expressed by Paul to the Corinthians, that the whole body would become an ear or an eye. If successful, in the words of Paul, ". . . Where would be the hearing? . . . where would be the sense of smell?" (12:17). Expressed in the language of the present situation, "Where would be the brilliance of black church theology, the likes of which introduced to the ecclesiastical community the theology of freedom? Where would be the excitement of black church worship? Where would be the power and romance of preaching, which are widely known in the black church and unmatched outside of it?"

What I have tried to show in this brief discussion is that for Paul the apostle, the model for the church is the unity of the body of Christ. However, I have seen that the image reflected in the church in America has been that of division. Only in rare instances in recent American history has there been any semblance of the church demonstrating itself to be the body of Christ, e.g., the civil rights era. And American history's most recent unified church effort, the Moral Majority, has been selective in the issues it has addressed, leaving out the pressing issues of discrimination against the black church and black people.

And so what we have today in America is not the church being the body of Christ as Paul the apostle described the body of Christ to the Corinthians, but a church of disparate parts and disjointed members that have often warred against one another at worst, attempted to absorb each other, or ignored each other at best. The question becomes, how can this state of division be overcome?

Overcoming Division—Subtleties and All

To begin, there must be a recognition of the real situation. That is, the reality is that there is in America a white church and a black church. This is unmistakably clear.

In all likelihood, competition within the white church between liberals, conservatives, and fundamentalists will continue. However, this probably will not affect the strength of the white church inasmuch as when one white church or denomination might lack numbers, it is likely to have the power of wealth; while when another white church or denomination might lack wealth, it would have the power of numbers. Whatever the case, the white church with its variety of denominations will remain strong as an entity of the body of Christ.

Another thing that is likely to continue is the ecclesiastical hegemony of the white church and its various denominations over the black church and black community. If this continues successfully, it will greatly diminish and may even destroy the black church as it is known today. This would be a great and horrible loss of one of the significant components of the body of Christ in America. If such were to happen, the body of Christ in America would be tremendously weakened and disfigured because one of the significant component parts of the body of Christ, albeit a less honorable part, would be missing.

For many and obvious reasons, the black church and its various denominations cannot allow this to happen. It has too much to offer the rest of the members of the body of Christ in America.

To use Paul's analogy, the eye cannot perform the function of the hand nor can the head perform the function of the feet. In like manner, the white church and its variety of denominations cannot perform the function of the black church and its variety of denominations; neither can the black church perform the function of the white church. The black church has provided the rest of the members of the body of Christ its theology of freedom, a theology hewn out of its experience in slavery and racial discrimination in America. It offers an excitement in worship, strong preaching and unexcelled music, political prowess, power, and potential. The rest of the members of the body of Christ in America have been complemented by the contributions of the black church. The church in America would be poorer without the black church. The white church can continue to be complemented by the black church only if the black church maintains control over its peculiar talents and contributions and guards against the hegemenous efforts on the part of the white church to abolish the black church and to absorb its constituents into the white church, to become faceless and anonymous.

The church in America cannot be truly the body of Christ and manifest itself in strength unless and until the black church develops and controls its talents and resources. This is not to espouse a doctrine of separatism because the black church cannot exist without the white church and the white church cannot exist without the black church. However, both can and must exist as separate entities or members of the body of Christ; the two are one body, having drunk of the same Spirit of Christ.

The black church must realize that in black-white church relations in America Paul's formula in 1 Corinthians 12:22-26 is not applicable at this point in time, though it should be. Although the black church is weaker, inferior, and the less honorable part of the body of Christ, it cannot expect the stronger parts, the white church, to consider it indispensable, to treat it with greater modesty, or to give it greater honor. This is not the way things work in the ecclesiastical world in America. Just as it is in the world of politics, economics, and war, so it is in the world of the church—only the strong survive.

The black church must develop itself to a point of strength so that it can make its rightful claim as a respected member of the body of Christ. In fact, it must do this if it wishes to survive, by the help of God. If this can happen, it will be an act of liberation for both the black church and the white church. It will liberate the black church so that it can become a strong independent entity, cultivating its own resources and ministering effectively to its constituents and functioning as a complementary component of the body of Christ. It will liberate the white church in that it will free it from its spirit of dominating paternalism and mitigating absorptionism, which are the result of rapacious racism. The end result will be a strong and united body of Christ.

Working Toward Unity in the Black Church

How can this be done? The issues at Corinth that provided Paul the matrix out of which he could write his letter and call that church to unity can provide unity for the black church today.

Dissolving False Levels of Knowledge

In the first place, just as Paul called the Corinthians to resolve differences between those who claimed superlative wisdom over those who did not have it, so must the black church resolve the division that exists within it due to falsely constructed levels of knowledge. This must occur within and between the various black denominations whether they be Baptist, Methodist, African Methodist Episcopal, Christian Methodist Episcopal, Churches of Christ, Catholic, Church of God in Christ, Apostolic, Church of God, Presbyterian, Primitive Baptist, or whatever the case might be. The denominations must realize that they are all one in fact, regardless of falsely constructed levels of knowledge.

There are those within the black church community, for example, the Black Churches of Christ in the southeastern section of the United States, who claim superior knowledge of the Holy Writ over that of other denominations. They spend their time promenading their time-worn doctrine of superior knowledge and self-righteousness and, at the same time, separate themselves from the rest of the black church community. The Black Churches of Christ, and other sects who hold this persuasion, must recognize that while they enjoy one particular level of knowledge, other denominations within the black church community enjoy other levels of knowledge, whether greater or lesser; but whatever level of knowledge each one enjoys, they all are part of a significant component, the black church, of the body of Christ.

There must be a recognition that black church denominations function similarly to fingers on the two hands of the body with each finger or denomination serving in its peculiar capacity. Although they are many, they all make up the hands which the rest of the body cannot effectively do without. Each segment of the black church must come to grips with the truth of what Paul says to the Corinthians in 1 Corinthians 4:7, "What have you that you did not receive? If then you received it, why do you boast as if it were not a gift?"

Eliminating Ecclesiastical Court Fights

A second area in which division within the black church can and must be ameliorated or eliminated is its tendency to resort to court fights to resolve its ecclesiastical power struggles. This was one of the problems Paul confronted in the church at Corinth, as is indicated in the sixth chapter of his first letter. In utter disgust, Paul says to the Corinthians,

> I say this to your shame. Can it be that there is no man among you wise enough to decide between members of the brotherhood, but brother goes to law against brother, and that before unbelievers?
> To have lawsuits at all with one another is defeat for you. Why not rather suffer wrong? Why not rather be defrauded? (6:5-7).

Paul's dictum clearly indicates that in the church there ought to be persons wise enough to settle any difference among members. If this is not the case, it is better to suffer wrong or be defrauded than to go to court against another church member.

Too often, however, black churches have multiplied by dividing, and that after an agonizing, painful, and embarrassing appearance before the courts of the land. For Paul, court fighting was an abomination in the church at Corinth. While it may not be the case that the courts of America are conducted by unbelievers, for the church with its ecclesiastical problems to appear before the court does constitute a situation in which the state is given the luxury of ruling over the affairs of the church. Plus it brings the odium of shame upon the body of Christ as well as the black church. The black church must desist from this or suffer the ignominy of dissipating its energies in litigation and emptying the cross of Christ of its power. Wise persons within the black church must make themselves available to settle the controversies that arise between members within the black church, or those who have been defrauded or made to suffer wrong must, for the sake of the church, suffer it rather than take a church member to court.

Venerating Marriage and the Family

A third area in which the black church must ameliorate or eliminate division and strengthen its ranks is marriage and the family. The black church must venerate marriage and the family and stem the rising tide of divorce and broken homes in the black church and black community. The problem of marital separation and divorce was one that seriously threatened the unity of the church at Corinth. And so Paul devoted the entire seventh chapter of First Corinthians to marriage, with the exception of verses 17 through 24 in which he discusses circumcision and slavery. With the exception of injecting his personal opinion that everyone should remain single like himself, Paul strongly recommends to the Corinthians that those who are unmarried should marry, that it is better to marry than to be aflame with passion (7:8-9). To the married, Paul says that the woman should not separate herself from her husband and the husband should not divorce his wife (7:10-11). Just as unity is demanded in the church, so it is demanded in the family. If families within the church are rent by separation or divorce, inevitably the church will feel the effects; a divided family will eventuate into a divided church. For Paul this cannot be, for Christ is not divided.

There is within the black church and its variety of denominations an inordinate number of divorces and marital separations. Fifty percent of all marriages in America end in divorce, and black families have more than their share of this percentage. The black church cannot allow this to continue, for a divided family in the church ultimately results in a divided church.

Pastors and responsible persons in the black church must keep ever before its members the fact that American slavery never encouraged and in many cases did not allow black men to marry the black women they loved and who bore children for them. Marriage was an unattainable state for black slaves on the plantation. Black men and women were used as breeders to populate the plantation with more slaves. This historical reality must be kept before black people. Further, the black church must remind its people that the honorable estate of marriage was something that was fought for with pain, agony, and tears; and now that it is a privilege and right, it should be maintained with dignity and pride. But more than this, the black church must constantly guard against the massive efforts, seen on television, in movies and the general American life-style, to divide the black family.

The black church must be engaged in a constant vigil and even declare war against those doctrinal differences that emerge out of the white church which precipitate dissolved and decimated homes. Following the warped views and parochial preachments of the white church, some sects and groups espouse the tenet that if one of its members is married to a person belonging to another denomination or faith, although the second person is a Christian, that marriage is not Christian nor acceptable. The person to whom the first member is married is a sinner and is doomed to go to hell unless he or she is converted to the particular sect or group in question. When marriages such as these are permitted to continue, they do so under great strain. The husband and wife go their different ways to worship, and sometimes these marriages end in divorce because of the irresolvable theological and ecclesiastical differences.

The black church must vigilantly and militantly guard against such ideologies and practices, or else shame and impotence will be its lot. Not only will its families and church be divided but also the cross of Christ will be emptied of its power. The black church must subscribe to the position of the apostle Paul. Although he had his personal opinion about marriage, for him it was in the best interest of the church for the man and woman within the church to marry. So it must be for the black church if it is to be a strong and independent component of the body of Christ.

Removing Prohibition Against Certain Foods

Still another area in which division in the black church must be ameliorated or eliminated is the prohibition of certain kinds of foods by various segments of the black church. This fourth area, in which concerted effort is needed, once again reflects the influence of the church of the larger culture. For example, black members of the Jehovah's Witnesses and Seventh-Day Adventists expend enormous amounts of energy campaigning within the black community against eating certain kinds of meats and foods. This is done only because it is the stated policy of the administration of those sects, which generally is comprised of whites.

Not in all instances, however, has the church of the larger culture been the cause of division within the black church and the black community. The Black Muslims is one example of division due to prohibition of certain kinds of foods originating from the black church and black community. Generally speaking, persons who became devotees of the Black Muslim sect were those who either came out of conventional black Baptist or Methodist churches or were descendents of those who did. This means that Black Muslims are well acquainted with the slave necessity of eating pork fatback, pig feet, pig ears, and chittlins. Black Muslims know that black slaves ate such a diet, not because it was nutritious but because it was the only food they could get. But when black people began to gravitate to the Black Muslims because of the mystique of Messenger Elijah Muhammad, all of a sudden eating pork was wrong, although black people spent more than three hundred years eating it. Black Muslims began to spread their teaching prohibiting the eating of pork. The end result has been division within the black church and the black community.

The black church can ameliorate and even eliminate this menacing, divisive wedge by resorting to Paul's method of dealing with the problem in the church at Corinth. In 1 Corinthians 10:27-30, Paul says, "If one of the unbelievers invites you to dinner and you are disposed to go, eat whatever is set before you without raising any question on the ground of conscience. . . . For why should my liberty be determined by another man's scruples? If I partake with thankfulness, why am I denounced because of that for which I give thanks?" In another place he says, "I know and am persuaded in the Lord Jesus that nothing is unclean in itself; but it is unclean for any one who thinks it unclean" (Romans 14:14).

But Paul is not incorrigible on the acceptability of eating meat of any kind, offered to idols or not. For him, although eating meat is acceptable as long as it is done with thankfulness, for the sake of another's conscience it may be expedient in some cases *not* to eat certain kinds of meats. In what appears to be an aside on the subject, he says in 1 Corinthians 10:28-29, "But if some one says to you, 'This has been offered in sacrifice,' then out of consideration for the man who informed you, and for conscience' sake—I mean his conscience, not yours—do not eat it." The conscience of the other, not the rightness or wrongness of eating prohibited meat, is the thing of most importance for Paul.

The idea here is, it seems, that of preserving the conscience of the other, maintaining the other's harmony of mind and thus maintaining harmony in the community and the church. Paul believed this so strongly that he thought to violate another's conscience was tantamount to sinning against Christ: "Thus, sinning against your brethren and wounding their conscience when it is weak, you sin against Christ. Therefore, if food is a cause of my brother's falling, I will never eat meat, lest I cause my brother to fall" (8:12-13). Here then is another plausible remedy, a functional strategy for ameliorating and even eliminating the nagging, divisive nemesis of the black community and the black church over the question of eating certain kinds of food and meat.

Keeping Redemption the Theological Crux

A fifth and extremely important area in which the black church must unify itself is its theology. Here, again, the apostle Paul gives inestimable assistance. The crux of Paul's theology was the crucifixion and resurrection, the unjust murdering of Jesus on the cross and his victorious resurrection on Easter. The whole of Paul's theological system revolved around these two historic phenomena. Christology, eschatology, soteriology, ecclesiology, and history all hung on the hinges of the political crucifixion and victorious resurrection of Jesus Christ. Paul never talked about baptism, the Lord's Supper, or eternal life except as they related to the cross and resurrection. The organizational structure of the church, if there was such in Pauline churches, and the ethical behavior of the members of the church were contingent on the understanding of the crucifixion and resurrection of Jesus Christ. For Paul, there was no other theological matrix out of which the church could work.

A close reading of Paul's letters and a reasonable acquaintance with the historical and theological developments surrounding the early church informs one of the serious encroachment upon the church by aberrant philosophies and pseudotheologies of false apostles and those with selfish motivations. Gnostics, Stoics, Epicureans, Neo-Platonists, Ebionites, Manicheans, and Nicholaitans were only some of these. Many of the problems of division in the Corinthian church were caused by eccentric philosophies, ideologies, and theologies. A reading of Eusebius' *Ecclesiastical History* gives a clearer picture of the devastating impact they had upon the early church. When we read Paul's letters, especially First Corinthians, which is our point of reference, we get only the undercurrents of the thinking that caused division. The genuine Pauline letters, the Pastorals, deutero-Pauline literature, the epistle of James and the epistle of Hebrews, and the apocalypse of John all reflect grave concern over the influence of the heretical thinking that had invaded the church.

Paul vigorously combated the heresies that raised their heads in the church, especially in the church at Corinth, with his theology of the crucifixion and resurrection of Jesus Christ. The first indication of heretical influence at Corinth surfaces in the first chapter of First Corinthians. In his discussion, which starts at 1 Corinthians 1:17, Paul forcefully attacks the Corinthians for the prominence that they had allowed wisdom to play in their lives as Christians. Possibly this occurred due to the influence of Gnosticism and/or Stoicism. But Paul countered it unequivocally with what was his theological foundation stone, "When I came to you, brethren, I did not come proclaiming to you the testimony of God in lofty words or wisdom. For I decided to know nothing among you except Jesus Christ and him crucified" (2:1-2; see also 1:23). To make use of wisdom when preaching the gospel of Jesus would have been, for Paul, tantamount to emptying the cross of its power (see 1:17).

Another example of the centrality of the crucifixion of Jesus Christ for Paul was in his eschatology. In chapter 15 of First Corinthians, Paul's rehearsal of the cross-resurrection tradition leads into his discussion of how the cross-resurrection event prepared him and all believers for service in the church, giving them the will and courage to fight for righteousness in the world with the assurance of victory in the fight (cf. 15:24-32b) over death and of eternal life.

Finally, the centrality of the cross-resurrection phenomenon manifested itself throughout both of Paul's letters to the Corinthians in the *theologia cruxis,* a term made popular by theologians such as Ernst Käsemann. Käsemann posited that in Corinth an attitude was at work that through knowledge of Christ, individual members of the Corinthian church already had experienced ultimate salvation. Individual members already had been saved and, therefore, had no need for physical, moral, or ethical restraints; hence the reason for so many moral and ethical problems in Corinth. They were living out of what Käsemann called a *theologia gloria* (theology of glory), a theology that maintained that the glory of salvation had already been attained. However, Paul argued that the *theologia cruxis* (theology of the crucifixion) kept the church, of which the believer was a part, continually struggling against moral, ethical, and spiritual imperfection within as well as social and political persecution without (cf. 13:11-12 and Philippians 3:12-14).

One can understand, then, why Paul unswervingly clung to the centrality of the *theologia cruxis,* the theology of the political crucifixion and victorious resurrection of Jesus Christ. He doggedly set that theology before the Corinthians as their defense against raging heresies, heresies that were weakening their ranks and wreaking havoc and division upon them. The unifying gospel of the cross and resurrection was for Paul the spiritual mortar that bound together the disparate elements of the Corinthian church within the context of a very fragmented world.

As the cross-resurrection theology provided the central unifying matrix for Paul and the Corinthian church, so it can for the black church today. There is no question that the black church is besieged by a barrage of aberrant and eccentric theologies that weaken its ranks and wreak havoc and division within it, as happened in Corinth. An emphasis of wisdom and knowledge— a kind of neo-Gnosticism—is sweeping through the black church. Segments of the larger religious community are bombarding the black church and the black community with a theology of the ultimate significance of the salvation of the individual, a salvation that disregards the individual's relation to the local or larger church community. Effortless salvation that fits the individual for heaven-after-death while ignoring the evils perpetrated against the black church and black people in the world about them is another theological twist binding the minds of black people in uncontrovertible confusion. The political crucifixion and victorious resurrection of Jesus Christ and participation in the act of baptism and in the Eucharist, which symbolize participation in the unjust suffering, dying, and victorious rising of Jesus Christ, ought to communicate something altogether different to the black church and its members than the gospel of the salvation of the individual. By participating in the act of baptism and the Eucharist, the individual participates in the suffering, dying, and resurrection of Christ; and, as regards the church, the individual becomes a participant in and even a subordinate to the church which is, for Paul, the body of Christ.

The black church must continue to combat the surging theological forces that militate against it by stringently adhering to the crucifixion and resurrection of Jesus Christ, the center of Paul's theology. The crucifixion and resurrection of Jesus Christ is not a new theology for the black church and the black community. It has been the dynamic force and unifying power of the black church since American slavery. Personal and communal salvation, regulation of ethical behavior of members of the believing community, assurance of an inevitable victory over the evils of servitude, dehumanization, political and social injustice, and assurance of eternal life after death were all basic to the slave understanding of the crucifixion and resurrection of Jesus Christ. The evolution of time and the assiduous efforts of those who have "no need of" the black church and black people have whittled away at the tenacious grip this church and these people have had on the theology of the crucifixion and resurrection of Jesus Christ. If the black church is to ameliorate or eliminate its division and forge itself once again into a strong element of the body of Christ, it must cling fast to the belief in and proclamation of the gospel of the crucifixion and resurrection of Jesus Christ. It must believe in the contemporary hermeneutic reality that even though the Jewish sacerdotal hierarchy in collusion with the Roman government killed Jesus on a cruel tree, nothing they could do could keep him in the grave, for early on Sunday morning he got up with all power in his hands. The black church must say, as did the apostle Paul, "Since we have the same spirit of faith as he had who wrote, 'I believed, and so I spoke,' we too believe, and so we speak, knowing that he who raised the Lord Jesus will raise us also with Jesus and bring us with you into his presence" (2 Corinthians 4:13-14). In this the black church will find unification and salvation.

Respecting the Preacher/Pastor

The final area in which the black church must ameliorate or eliminate division is its respect for and allegiance to its leader, its undershepherd, the preacher/pastor. It is the preacher/pastor in the black church who is under a divine mandate to divine rightly the Word of truth and to call the church to unity. It is he or she who interprets and declares the Word of God. It is he or she around whom the church revolves and upon whom its unity depends. This is true for the black preacher and the black church as it was true for Paul and the early Christian church.

The indispensability, prominence, and authority of the preacher/pastor in the black church has become a serious problem for the forces of division both within and without the black church. So it was with the apostle Paul. The black preacher/pastor and the black church must take grave measures to retain the indispensable, prominent, and authoritative position of the black preacher/pastor or the dissolution of the black church and black community is assured. Here, again, the means by which this can be done can be learned from Paul.

From reading all of Paul's genuine letters, there is no question that every church to which he wrote had serious problems with him as a preacher and pastor. Although Paul was responsible for establishing the churches to which he wrote, with the exception of the church at Rome, there were those who immediately sought to undermine his influence in those churches once he had departed. People questioned his legitimacy as an apostle (cf. 1 Corinthians 9:1-2), made mockery of his personal appearance and inability to articulate as a *genuine* preacher (e.g., 2 Corinthians 10:10), derided his authority (e.g., 1 Corinthians 4:14-18), and catered to the flamboyant and arrogant preachments and leadership of Paul's opponents, the superlative apostles (see 2 Corinthians 11:5, 13). If there was not another reason for division within the churches to which Paul wrote, the anti-Pauline attitude introduced by opponents from outside the church surely was one.

In at least four ways, Paul shows how he combated this anti-Pauline, anti-preacher/pastor attitude that had painfully and divisively emerged within the church. First, Paul always boldly introduced himself as an apostle called of God, not of humankind (cf. 1 Corinthians 1:1; Galatians 1:1; Romans 1:1). In contrast to those apostles who had been confirmed at Jerusalem (Galatians 1:17) or those who had made themselves apostles (e.g., 2 Corinthians 11:4-5, 12-15), Paul received his call to be an apostle from God. There was no need for him to be accepted or confirmed by people in order to be a legitimate apostle; this was done by God alone. Thus, he was not beholden to any person, the church, or any worldly authority. In any and every instance, Paul defended his call to apostleship by God, a call that freed him from the restraints of the will of humankind (1 Corinthians 9:1ff).

Second, Paul unswervingly clung to the theology that had been delivered to him. In fact, he pronounced judgment upon anyone who preached or taught a different gospel than his own. In Galatians 1:8, Paul angrily says, "But even if we, or an angel from heaven, should preach to you a gospel contrary to that which we preached to you, let him be accursed." He meant this so emphatically that he repeated it a second time (Galatians 1:9). It was this kind of dogged authority that Paul wielded against those surging, divisive, heretical, theological doctrines that were wreaking havoc in all of the churches. So irrepressible was his hatred for heretical, theological doctrines that he openly declared war against them and pronounced heaven's curse upon them. This was his way of maintaining unity in the church—by driving out divisive and devastating teachings that had worked their way into the church.

Third, Paul the preacher/pastor demonstrated his unifying influence in his handling of the ethical problems that emerged in the church, possibly as a result of the superlative and false apostles and the false doctrine they introduced into the church. Paul did not deal with the problems at Corinth in a weak and willy-nilly manner but in a forceful and oftentimes brutal way. For example, in 1 Corinthians 4, Paul responds to those who had broken ranks to follow the countless guides in Christ who had shown up in Corinth by saying,

> For though you have countless guides in Christ, you do not have many fathers. For I became your father in Christ Jesus through the gospel. I urge you, then, be imitators of me. Therefore I sent to you Timothy, my beloved and faithful child in the Lord, to remind you of my ways in Christ, as I teach them everywhere in every church. Some are arrogant, as though I were not coming to you. But I will come to you soon, if the Lord wills, and I will find out not the talk of these arrogant people but their power.

> For the kingdom of God does not consist in talk but in power. What do
> you wish? Shall I come to you with a rod, or with love in a spirit of
> gentleness? (1 Corinthians 4:15-21).

Here Paul is seen at his best as one who wields the high-
handed authority of a pastor. He behaves as though he felt that
some of the members of the church at Corinth had to be whipped
into line for the sake of unity. Their unethical and arrogant
behavior would have rent the church in pieces had they not been
roughly pulled back into place. The fact of the matter is that for
the sake of unity in the church, Paul utilized his pastoral authority
to pronounce anathema against anyone in the church who had no
love for the Lord (cf. 16:22) and to drum them out of the church
(cf. 5:11-13). The church would be better off and its unity assured
without them.

Fourth, Paul utilized his power and authority to unify the
church and drive out the forces of division through his incessant
preaching of the gospel of freedom, a gospel that was grounded
in the cross-resurrection event of Jesus Christ. Paul was forever
reminding the churches to which he wrote that because of the
execution of Jesus on Calvary and his victorious resurrection on
Easter, they all were free. They were free, not only from Jewish
law but also from the social and political institutions of this
world, the entanglement of ethical and moral norms of heretical
teachings, and from the fear of death. The gospel of freedom
was Paul's trademark. To the slave, he announced freedom in
Christ (cf 7:20-24). To the one laboring under the bondage of
the law, Paul announced freedom from the law (cf. Galatians
5:1, 13). In fact, Paul announced freedom for anyone who was
in Christ Jesus and who was walking according to the Spirit of
Christ, for he said in 2 Corinthians 3:17, "Now the Lord is the
Spirit, and where the Spirit of the Lord is, there is freedom."
Such a message certainly had a profound liberating and unifying
effect wherever it was heard, especially at Corinth.

Once again Paul invaluably aids the black church in its effort
to strengthen itself and dispel the reigning night of division that
holds captive its ranks. If the black church can take Paul's lead
here, it then must unapologetically project its preacher/pastor as

one whom God has divinely called and whom it respects and unfalteringly follows. The black preacher/pastor must claim this himself or herself.

This may be said in all too facile a manner, for the churches of the larger religious community and the people of the larger American population have done literally everything conceivable to mitigate the black preacher's respectability and responsibility, his or her authoritative influence and forcefulness in the black church and black community. It began in slavery when the sermons of black slave preachers were monitored and laws were passed in state legislatures to prohibit them from proclaiming the gospel of freedom. It continued when an unknown and unnamed assailant killed Martin Luther King, Jr., for preaching a gospel of freedom and for leading black people in America from bondage to freedom. The black preacher is still under assault in varied and even indescribable ways. The preacher is being spied upon and intimidated by government authorities. His or her character is being reprehensibly slandered and caricatured by movies, television, and secular music. As a result of this, the preacher's authority is forever being questioned by his or her followers, followers whose flirtations with outsiders have made them mutiny-minded. His or her efforts to develop a pastor-led congregation of unity is being dislodged by cumbersome but rigid ecclesiastical structure imposed from without and designed to neutralize and even nullify his or her power.

The black preacher/pastor stands to lose his or her congregation of today and the church of the future because the white church community has declared war on the inner city. It is bombarding the ghettos with buses, executing every-Sunday sorties, carrying black children away to white churches in the suburbs to be drilled with the doctrine of division. The preacher is even faced with the grave possibility of becoming a non-being himself or herself, for denominations of the larger culture are feverishly recruiting black preachers so that he or she becomes an anonymous and faceless figure.

The black church must vigilantly combat this savage assault

against the black preacher. It must do so by unapologetically projecting its preacher/pastor as one whom God has divinely called and whom it respects and unfalteringly follows. If the black preacher is not given this common courtesy by the people he or she pastors, he or she must take the initiative. The preacher/pastor must declare his or her unequivocal call by God. The preacher/pastor must be undaunted in the proclamation of the gospel of liberation that is grounded in the theology of the cross and resurrection of Jesus Christ. The preacher/pastor must assert authority as a pastor to unify the people by giving will to the weak and by controlling the mania of the maverick, by calling into session the councils of ethical behavior and ruling out of order the disciples of immorality. By seizing the reins of control of the black church as a general must do with an army at war, the black preacher/pastor can shape the black church into an entity of unity and strength. Under the leadership of a determined and indefatigable black preacher/pastor the black church can become, not a controlled clone of the larger church community, but a complementary and strong member of the body of Christ.

Finding the Way to Unity

In conclusion, I have cited Paul's model of the church as the body of Christ as one that is relevant for the liberation of the church in America today. I have tried to show that Paul's theology of the church as the body of Christ emerged out of the difficulties he encountered in the churches that he visited and to which he wrote, especially the Corinthian church. I have tried to show, moreover, that Paul clung to that theological model as his prescription for division that was afflicting the church at Corinth from within and without. Inasmuch as the affliction of division is a nasty nagging nemesis in the Christian church in America, I have argued that Paul's description of the church as the body of Christ is both relevant and necessary for it.

It is without question that the deep and abiding hunger of serious theologians and churchmen and churchwomen today is for a church that is unified, a church that is bereft of racial rifts, cultural cleavages, social schisms, ecclesiastical chasms, and religious ruptures. Eduard Schweizer dreams that

> . . . the members of the church belong together, as members of the body exist only as parts of the one body and are nothing if severed from that body. Thus participation in Christ's body, i.e., in Christ's sacrifice and victory, which blesses and challenges us, means at the same time participation in the life of all fellow members.[14]

Rejecting exclusivism, mysticism, isolationism, and individualism, Hans Küng muses that "The believers 'abide' within the fellowship of the disciples, within the Church. . . ."[15] Jürgen Moltmann envisions a church which is truly a community of brethren, a community in which "social, cultural, racial and sexual privileges lose their validity. . . ."[16] He hopes for a church in which "fellowship among the congregation's rank and file" will be the foundation stone for unity.[17]

The prayers, songs, and theology of the black church reflect an incredible hope and dream for one church. But the fact of the matter is that in America today there are many churches in general and a white church and a black church in particular. Paul's model for the church as the body of Christ stands in stark contrast to and condemnation of the manner in which the Christian church manifests itself in America. The white church historically has attempted to control the black church or ignore it. It now has come to the point of attempting to absorb it and even eliminate it, a gross violation of Paul's understanding of the church as the body of Christ. I have taken the position that for the body of Christ truly to be so in America, the black church will have to strengthen itself by controlling its membership, its resources, its theology and by having a strong, independent, and authoritative black preacher/pastor. By doing this, it will fulfill its role as a unique, strong, and independent member of the body of Christ. It will serve as an indispensable and independent member of the body of Christ, liberating the white church from its penchant for paternalistic control and insatiable greed for power over the black church. It will serve as an agent of liberation for black people and the black community by providing them a haven of refuge from a cold and hostile world about them.

6

Economic Independence as a Strategy for Freedom

It is interesting to note that in the theological developments of the post–Martin Luther King, Jr., civil rights era virtually no consideration was given to the need for economic development and independence on the part of black people, the poor, and oppressed. A plethora of liberation literature burst upon the theological scene following the assassination of Martin Luther King, Jr. Much of it was reactionary in nature. That is, it literally lashed out against the system of white racism and oppression.[1] Such was James H. Cone's *Black Theology and Black Power*. In a similar vein, Albert Cleage set out to build a *Black Christian Nationalism* that would be based on *The Black Messiah*.

In a publication, *Quest for a Black Theology,* edited by James J. Gardiner, S.A., and J. Deotis Roberts, Sr., there seems to have been the attempt to make some theological sense of the Bible for black people in the wake of the theological mess made of it by their white theologian counterparts. Many similar publications made their way into the theological marketplace with the hope of being subscribed to by black people as their theological *modus operandi* for liberation. But of all of the publications launched by black theologians, hardly any dealt with the theological significance (as well as sociological and political significance) of economic development and independence as a *modus operandi* for liberation of black people.

What to Have and What Not to Have

The problem with black theology of the post–Martin Luther King, Jr., civil rights era was that it was reactionary in nature. In a recent retrospective evaluation of that era, Gayraud S. Wilmore concluded that "Cone and other black theologians are clearer about what ought *not* to exist than they are about what *should* exist."[2] This is an important observation because it has been the failure of shapers of black thought, including black theologians, to deal with the question of what should exist within the social nexus of black existence that has spawned a situation in which black and poor people could be dangerously at the economic mercy of the larger culture. It is not that black theologians have caused the economic condition that black and poor people face today; rather, it is that they have failed to provide these people with a theologically designed master plan for economic development and independence. Hence, the black church and black and poor people in America are dangerously at the economic mercy of the larger culture.

A case in point is the aftermath of the social explosion that occurred in the Liberty City section of Miami, Florida, in 1980. It is painfully remembered that following the acquittal of four white policemen charged with the brutal beating death of Arthur McDuffie, blacks in Liberty City burned and destroyed the businesses and industries located in that section of Miami. In a conversation with a black service-station owner who survived the conflagration, the owner was queried as to what blacks would do for jobs now that many of the businesses and industries had been destroyed. The response was that black people in Liberty City had no businesses or industries to provide jobs for themselves. They had no banks that could provide the money needed to rebuild the burned-out hulks that remained. The only alternative was to go downtown to government agents and businessmen and solicit financial assistance to rebuild the community, their very own, which they had burned down.

Although black people in Liberty City were enraged (and rightly so) over the racially unjust acquittal of four white policemen who beat to death a black man, so enraged that they burned and destroyed as their way of reacting to what ought not exist, they did not have the economic wherewithal to deal with the question of what should exist. To address that question, they had to turn to the very people against whom they were reacting. In effect, because Liberty City could not respond to its own economic needs following the conflagration, the liberation of its people was less sure in the aftermath; they had to depend on the larger culture for economic assistance to rebuild their community. As a result, Liberty City today is in worse economic condition than it was prior to the 1980 social explosion.

It is without question that Martin Luther King, Jr., led black and poor people a long way up the road to liberation during his lifetime. In his writings, he made suggestions, assignments as it were, of what black and poor people must do to secure and sustain their liberation. One salient suggestion was to develop economic independence. Black theologians have not dealt with Martin Luther King, Jr.'s suggestion of how to deal with the question of what ought to exist.

The Call of Economic Independence

The thesis of this concluding chapter is that for the contemporary Christian church to sustain its freedom and the freedom of its people, it must be economically strong and independent. The thesis is particularly applicable to the contemporary black church in America. No other denominational expression of the Christian faith in America demonstrates economic dependence on outside assistance, be it sacred or secular, as does the black church.

There are approximately twenty-five million black Christians in the major denominations and churches in America, and thousands and possibly millions more in various sects and cults. These numbers represent millions and billions of dollars that are handled by these churches and denominations. But the millions and billions of dollars handled by black churches and denominations have not factored out into jobs for black people or security for institutions that exist in black communities and cater to black and poor people.

Many of the black male youth who make up the more than 50 percent unemployed in that age and sex category in America are in the black church or have had connections with it. However, the black church seems unable to respond to their employment needs. There is the ever-bellowing cry from the black church for the government to provide employment for these black youth.

Many private black educational institutions are in the throes of economic distress, but the black church seems unable to come to their aid. These institutions must depend on foundations, businesses, and industries of the larger culture and the government for their existence. Medical institutions and hospitals that cater primarily to black and poor people have not been able to depend on the black church for support; they have had to call upon the government and outside philanthropists. Even for black church-related educational institutions, such as Bible colleges and theological seminaries, basic financial support comes from the larger white church community, foundation grants, and government assistance.

It is not to say that the Christian community cannot be self-supporting. There are too many examples in which it is self-supporting. In the state of Tennessee alone, the Tennessee Baptist Convention of the Southern Baptist Convention operates several colleges and hospitals. These institutions provide education, health care, and employment for the persons identified with the churches of that convention. In Salt Lake City, Utah, and surrounding cities and states, the Church of the Latter Day Saints (Mormons) has an economic system of its own that provides education for its children and health care and jobs for its people. Other examples are too numerous to mention. The fact is that the black church, with all of its wealth, is failing to support those institutions that provide education and health care for its people and is failing to utilize its economic resources to provide jobs for its constituents.

The threat that is before the black church in America, and thus black people, is that it is on the verge of surrendering itself to total dependence on outside assistance, be it sacred or secular. If this happens, a significant component of the Christian church will be terribly weakened, the Christian faith will become a mockery, and the gospel of Christian freedom will be a farce and colossal failure. The contention of this chapter is that the Christian church in America, especially the black church, must remain economically solvent, strong, independent, and free. If this happens, the black church will render a tremendous service to its people, the poor and oppressed, and Christianity as a whole. If this does not occur in the evolution of things, the future of the black church could be no future at all and the Christian church could be dealt a serious and unrecoverable blow.

Paul's Directive for Being Economically Strong

From the most cursory study of the documents of the New Testament, it is easily concluded that the early church was economically independent. There is not the slightest indication that the early church or any of its members were recipients of Roman economic assistance (which probably did not exist) or economic assistance from any of the municipalities in which they existed or from the Jewish temple or synagogue from which many of the early Christians had emerged. Had the early church been dependent upon outside economic assistance, there would be no Christian church to speak of today. As it was, the early church was economically independent; and because it was thus, it was free. Its economic independence allowed it to wage its pretentious battle to establish Christianity in a cruel world without fear of intimidation or reprisal from unfavorable contributors. The early church not only had to claim its freedom, to prepare itself faithfully for the long road to freedom and to do this in the context of unity; it also had to be economically strong and independent. And being thus, it truly was free.

When we peruse the New Testament for models and instructions as to how the church can become economically strong and independent, we are driven to the writings of the apostle Paul. It is here that we find strong emphasis on the need for the early church to engage itself in economic development and arm itself in economic independence. Even when we forage the pages of the New Testament outside the genuine Pauline writings for statements of economic development and independence on the part of the early church, I highly suspect that the statements we find have all been influenced by Paul's thinking. One of the reasons for this, of course, is that all the other writings of the New Testament were written after Paul's time and the writers of those documents were familiar with his writings and were influenced by them one way or another.[3]

Although the Synoptic Gospels and the Gospel of John are not as detailed in their discussion of economic development and independence, it is obvious that they portray Jesus and his twelve disciples as totally independent of pagan assistance. This writing perspective could be attributed to Paul's influence inasmuch as the Gospels were written about 70 A.D. or after. The Acts of the Apostles reveals a church that is totally independent (cf. Acts 2:43-45; 4:33-35). Herein Paul's teaching is exemplified.

In the Acts of the Apostles, Paul is portrayed as a tentmaker (18:3). It is believed by some that it was from the revenue generated by his tentmaking trade that Paul was able to rent the Hall of Tyrannus at Ephesus so that he could teach the Word of God unhindered (19:9).[4] The maxims found in Second Thessalonians, "If any one will not work, let him not eat . . ." and that believers should ". . . do their work in quietness and . . . earn their own living" unequivocally bear the stamp of Pauline influence (2 Thessalonians 3:10-12). The same can be said of the deutero-Pauline epistle of Ephesians when it says, "Let the thief no longer steal, but rather let him labor, doing honest work with his hands, so that he may be able to give to those in need" (Ephesians 4:28). Similar statements born out of Paul's influence can be found in the Pastoral and catholic epistles.

Paul himself provides for us a model *par excellence* of an economically strong and independent Christian. He is economically independent not only of outside pagan assistance but of assistance from the church as well. He refused assistance from the members of the Corinthian church so that he could be free to preach the gospel without the slightest fetter (cf. 1 Corinthians 9). It was only from the church at Philippi that he received and accepted gifts of assistance (cf. Philippians 4:15-18). So it is to Paul that we must look in the New Testament to find that model of economic strength and independence that allows us not simply to make a claim of Christian freedom but to sustain it as well.

My interest here, however, is not to portray Paul as the model for economic strength and independence. (Stretched beyond its limits, such an enterprise would leave breathing space for one to forge a philosophy of economic individualism. Rational conjecture is that this is not what the New Testament is about.) My concern is to grasp Paul's directive to a people, the church, to see what his instructions are to them on how they should secure and sustain their freedom by being economically strong and independent.

In order to do this I am drawn to chapter four in Paul's first letter to the Thessalonians; verses 9 to 12, especially, are of utmost concern.

There are several reasons for my use of First Thessalonians, Paul's classic directive to the early church on how to be economically strong and independent. One reason is that it is the first of Paul's letters and it lifts up economic development and independence as one of the concerns of the early church in its early days. Another reason is that the church at Thessalonica suffered tremendous religious and political persecution from the Jews and Romans. Another particularly strong reason for my use of the Thessalonian letter is that some of the members of the church there had become overly enthusiastic about eschatology, i.e., the coming of the end of time and the return of Jesus Christ. This resulted in some of the members of the church becoming idle and mischievous, and, according to the reading of the text, some of them became dependent on members within the church and possibly on persons outside the church.

The History of Thessalonica

A brief look at the city of Thessalonica will allow us to set the scenario for the political persecution suffered by the church there. Thessalonica was a large port city of Macedonia, situated at the mouth of an inlet from the Aegean Sea. Its fourth century B.C. name was Therme, which was derived from the hot springs of water that were nearby. Cassander refounded the city in 315 B.C. and named it after his wife, Thessalonica, who was the sister of Alexander the Great. The location of the city made it a thriving seaport and a bustling center of commerce. Aside from seaport trade, products of food from the fertile watered plains that were in the vicinity were also sold in the marketplace. In addition, the great *Via Egnatia,* the Roman highway, passed through the heart of the city. This highway brought much traffic through the city, e.g., commerce and military troop movement.

When Thessalonica came under Roman dominance, it was made the capital of one of the four provinces into which Rome divided Macedonia. Eventually, it became the capital of the entire nation of Macedonia. Because Thessalonica threw its favor on the side of Octavian and Antony in their struggle against Brutus and Cassius, the city was rewarded by Roman authorities with the honor of being a free city, *civitas libera.* This allowed the city to have its own political govenment, albeit it was loyal to Rome. Magistrates ruled the political affairs of the city; these were known as politarchs (cf. Acts 17:6, 8).

Herein is the point at which some of the political oppression began. Luke's version of the visit of Paul and Silas to Thessalonica gives us a superficial view of what that oppression was like. During the three weeks that Paul and Silas spent in Thessalonica—though some commentaries surmise that Paul's stay in Thessalonica could very well have been more like several months rather than three weeks as Luke reports—he preached the gospel of Jesus Christ, saying, "This Jesus, whom I proclaim to you, is the Christ" (17:3). Luke reports that his preaching stirred up the Jews of the city who sought to find Paul and Silas. When they could not find the two men, they apprehended Jason, in whose house Paul and Silas were staying, and carried him before the city authorities (i.e., politarchs; 17:6). The charge brought against Jason was, "These men who have turned the world upside down have come here also, and Jason has received them; and they are all acting against the decrees of Caesar, saying that there is another king, Jesus" (17:6b-7). So it can be concluded that the persecution that was experienced by the members of the church at Thessalonica was due to some degree to their being charged by Roman authorities with *maiestas*, disloyalty to the Roman-backed government in Thessalonica, and irreverence to the Roman gods, the chief of which was the deified Caesar.

The Specific Problem at Thessalonica

The city of Thessalonica was a bustling seaport, bristling with commerce, opulently prosperous, a privileged puppet of the Roman government, and possibly occupied with Roman military troops or at least troops that were loyal to Rome. It was into such a city that Paul and Silas went to introduce the gospel of Jesus Christ, the gospel of freedom. Specifically, Paul's preaching was to a group of people—as Ernest W. Saunders suggests, "an inner city congregation"⁵—that was composed of some Gentiles, Macedonian Greeks, and maybe some Jewish Christians.

Suffering was part of the price that had to be paid for accepting the gospel as preached by Paul, as was shown in Acts 17:6. Paul remarked that the Thessalonians' acceptance of the gospel was accompanied with "much affliction" (1 Thessalonians 1:6). To the credit of the Thessalonian Christians, they withstood the persecution inflicted upon them on account of the gospel. Sitting in Corinth, Paul became increasingly worried about the stamina of the faith of the Thessalonian church, so much so that he sent Timothy to them ". . . that I might know your faith, for fear that somehow the tempter had tempted you and that our labor would be in vain" (3:5b). Timothy carried back the news that their faith was holding fast (3:6-8). Thus, all indications are that the Thessalonian church fared well in its stance against political presecution on account of the gospel.

Although Paul had a concern that the Thessalonians might wilt under the heat of political and religious persecution, he had another concern also. Reports had come to him that the church had an overabundance of enthusiasm over eschatology, i.e., the Parousia, the imminent second coming of Christ. Paul's concern was that this obsessive excitement and anticipation of the end time was causing instability within the fellowship at Thessalonica. Such excitement and anticipation in abandon could wreck the church if it were not checked.

Preoccupation with Parousia

Paul's concern with the overabundance of enthusiasm for the Parousia was probably one of the foremost reasons, if not the primary reason, for writing his first letter to the Thessalonians. His concern with this emerges in 1 Thessalonians 4:13ff., when he addresses the question concerning those who had fallen asleep. Some members were grieving over fellow church members who had died. Their worry was whether those who had died would be raised from death to experience the Parousia, which they thought, as they had been taught by Paul, was very close at hand. Paul reassured them that those who had died would be raised first at the Parousia, followed by those who were alive. Then they all would be caught up with the Lord in the air to be forever with the Lord.

It is conceivable to conclude from this obsession with the imminent Parousia, that those who were alive in the Thessalonian church were not only worrying about the status of those who had died but were also drifting into a dreadful situation of simply waiting for the coming of the Lord. As such, they inadvertently slipped into immorality (cf. 4:1-8), living boisterously, meddling in other peoples' affairs, and refusing to work (cf. 4:9-12). With such reprehensible behavior going on in the church, it is understandable that Paul perceived that the ecclesiastical glue was losing its effect and the church was threatened with internal dissolution. Such a horrible thought drove Paul to respond in his correspondence with a pastoral edict which included, among other things, telling the members of the church to work with their hands and be economically strong and independent. Hence, it is for this second reason (i.e., the Thessalonians' slip into carnality) that I have chosen this passage in Paul's first letter to the Thessalonians as the basis of my argument for a strong and economically independent contemporary church for black and poor people.

As we focus primarily on the text of 1 Thessalonians 4:9-12, it appears that the troubles in the church at Thessalonica had been communicated to Paul by a letter.[6] Reference is made by Paul to the fact that there was no need for anyone to write to the Thessalonians on the subject which he is now discussing. Although it could have been the case that someone wrote to Paul about such problems, it is hardly so. There is not the slightest indication that a letter was written to him from the Thessalonians.[7] The tremors that were taking place within the little congregation were probably reported to Paul by Timothy on his return to the apostle.

Addressing himself to the problem as it stands before him, Paul says to the Thessalonians that there is no need for anyone to write to them on the subject of "love of the brethren" *(philadelphias)*. The reason is that they have been "God-taught" *(Theodidaktoi;* cf. also John 6:45) to love one another (1 Thessalonians 4:9). Although Paul assures them of his awareness that they love the brotherhood, not only in Thessalonica but in all of Macedonia, he urges them to do so more and more (4:10). Paul's addendum of "to do so more and more" is the harbinger of some additional comments. Such follow in verses 11 and 12. It begins to emerge that the message Paul received from Thessalonica bore with it an inquiry about the appropriate demonstration of love for the brethren. While this still is sheer speculation, the fact remains that in the following verses, Paul provides further explication of what he meant by the paraenesis of loving the brethren and to do so more and more.

Three Exhortations

And now Paul plunges to the heart of the matter. His first of a catena of paraeneses is somewhat obtuse. In 4:11, the Greek construction is *philo timeisthai esuxazein.* J. B. Phillips's translation strangely renders this to read, "make it your ambition to have, in a sense, no ambition!" This makes no sense at all. This rendering of the meaning of *esuxazein* seems to stretch it to the point of absurdity. To be sure, the meaning of the word could be "being quiet," "resting," or even "abstaining from work." If this were the case, I would be inclined to agree with the Phillips translation and conclude that Paul was urging the Thessalonians to be ambitious to have no ambition, i.e., to be lazy or idle. According to what follows though, Paul has no intention of making such an assertion. What is more likely here is the translation of the RSV, "aspire to live quietly."

If we accept this latter translation, we can assume, from what is said here and in the previous verses (4:1-8), that with time on their hands as they waited for the Parousia, the Thessalonians fell into boisterous arguments over women with whom they possibly were having erotic affairs (4:4-5), or arguments erupted when one brother sought to be the paramour of the wife of another brother (4:6). If such were the case, it is imaginable that it caused quite a ruckus in the church, a disruption of the peace within that was heard outside the church. This disquiet that eventuated into disharmony was a result of idleness that resulted from anxious anticipation of the immediate return of the Lord.

Paul follows hard on the heels of his first upbraiding with another exhortation: "to mind your own affairs" *(prassein ta idia)*, literally, "to take care of the things that are your own" or "to take care of your own business." The implication is that when the members of the Thessalonian church dismissed themselves from meaningful activity (e.g., work) they became busybodies, meddling in everybody else's affairs. Here again the exhortation seems to be related to 4:4, that the men of the Thessalonian church should take wives for themselves in holiness and honor and not meddle with wives of other brethren. It could be speculated that Paul's exhortation to the Thessalonians to mind their own affairs had to do with things other than erotic affairs; but the thought would be just that—speculation. His discussion, which precedes the concerns of verses 9 to 12, is about male-female, erotic activity.

Whatever it was that caused Paul to call them into account about idleness and meddling into other people's business, the

root of the problem was the Thessalonians' eager over-antici-
pation of the return of the Lord that was to happen almost any
day. And so, they found themselves waiting for the return of the
Lord. But their waiting was not constructive. Their waiting brought
them to idleness, and their idleness brought upon them the temptation to meddle in other people's affairs.

The third of Paul's paraeneses drills to the core of our concern,
viz., work and the development of financial means that would
make the church at Thessalonica independent and secure. In verse
11c, Paul chastens the Thessalonians "to work with your hands,
as we charged you." Here Paul uncovers not only the nerve
center of the disruptive problem, but a development that threatened the economic strength and independence of the Thessalonian
church. It seems that in their anxious anticipation of the immediate return of the Lord, the Thessalonians desisted from productive work. Ernest Best suggests that these persons, while
ceasing their labor, busied themselves in "excessive missionary
activity" and spent much time "in prayer and the pursuit of
personal holiness so that the community [might] be fit to greet
the coming Saviour."[8] While this is altogether possible, it is not
probable. As I intimated earlier, the drift of Paul's discussion
causes me to conclude that the Thessalonians spent their time
quarreling and bickering over one another's wives.

Both Frame and Best postulate that the Thessalonians who
failed or even refused to work possibly turned to other members
of the church for support.[9] It was such a development that pro-
voked the writer of Second Thessalonians to admonish, "If any
one will not work, let him not eat. For we hear that some of you
are living in idleness, mere busybodies, not doing any work.
Now such persons we command and exhort in the Lord Jesus
Christ to do their work in quietness and to earn their own living"
(2 Thessalonians 3:10b-12).

So what we have here in the church at Thessalonica was a
situation in which people, while waiting for the immediate return
of the Lord, resorted to idleness and meddlesomeness but also
had become dependent on other members of the church and maybe

even outsiders for support. Paul's harsh reminder to them is that they should work with their hands as he had charged them on a previous occasion.

The concept of "work" linked to "hands" is peculiarly Pauline and peculiar to the early church. Unlike the Greco-Roman society about them—which sought to graduate quickly from manual labor to sumptuous living and an opulent life through adroit maneuvering and business manipulations—Paul and the early church made a life, earned their living, and gained political leverage through manual labor, working with their hands. Further, it is to be remembered that the early church, and particularly the church at Thessalonica, was in its infancy, trying to make a place for itself in a very hostile world. Those who composed the church were not rich, powerful, or possessors of earthly means (cf. 1 Corinthians 1:26); rather, they were society's scrubs, social rejects, former slaves, and women. With the exception of gaining support from outsiders (a thought to be abhorred), there was no way for the church at Thessalonica to nurture itself, grow, and sustain itself with necessary provisions unless its members worked with their hands.

It is for this reason, viz., that of charging the Thessalonians to work with their hands, that Paul called them to imitate him inasmuch as he had toiled and labored with his hands while with them (cf. 2 Thessalonians 3:7-8). Paul presented himself in the same manner to the Corinthians, e.g., 1 Corinthians 4:12, ". . . and we labor, working with our own hands." This is implied in 1 Corinthians 9:7-15. It was by working with his hands that Paul sustained himself and, most importantly, maintained his freedom and independence.

Theological power is uncapped in Paul's charge to the Thessalonians to work with their hands. Paul transforms the understanding of work from the Old Testament conception of work being the result of sin into something new. In the third chapter of Genesis, because of Adam's sin, God curses the ground and tells Adam, ". . . in toil you shall eat of it all the days of your life" (Genesis 3:17). But here, Paul seems to be venerating work with the hands, redeeming it from ignominy, and raising it to nobility.

Indeed not only is Paul lifting work with the hands from its sinful connotation, but he is also pointing the Thessalonians to its divine nature. For imbedded in the Old Testament is the theology of God working with his hands. For example, in Psalm 19, the psalmist opens with the words,

> The heavens are telling the glory of God;
> and the firmament proclaims his handiwork.
> —Psalm 19:1

In Psalm 95:3-5, the psalmist speaks once again of God's work with his hands:

> For the Lord is a great God,
> and a great King above all gods.
> In his hand are the depths of the earth;
> the heights of the mountains are his also.
> The sea is his, for he made it;
> for his hands formed the dry land.

Similarly, in Psalm 102:25:

> Of old thou didst lay the foundation of the earth,
> and the heavens are the work of thy hands.

In the creation story in the book of Genesis, it is implicit that the creation of the heavens and the earth was the work of God's hands:

> Thus the heavens and the earth were finished, and all the host of them. And on the seventh day God finished his work which he had done, and he rested on the seventh day from all his work which he had done. So God blessed the seventh day and hallowed it, because on it God rested from all his work he had done in creation (Genesis 2:1-3).

Certainly many theological interests are packed into these three verses, e.g., the hallowing of the seventh day, but explicit in the language is that God created the heavens and earth with his hands. Thus, even though Adam is consigned to earn his living by working with his hands in and with the cursed earth, the fact that God engaged his hands in the creation of the heavens and earth elevated work to a divine level.

Even in the ministry of Jesus, the Evangelists noted his work with his hands. It is highly likely that because he was the son of a carpenter, Jesus himself was a carpenter (cf. Mark 6:3; Matthew 13:55). Further, Mark reports the comments made by those who observed Jesus in the synagogue in Nazareth, "Where did this man get all this? What is the wisdom given to him? What mighty works are wrought by his hands!" (Mark 6:2). In Jesus' resurrection appearance, the Evangelist John paid special attention to the fact that when Jesus appeared to the disciples in the upper room, ". . . he showed them his hands" (John 20:20). It is conceivable that one of the many things the Evangelists intended to convey in referring to the hands of Jesus was the veneration Jesus gave to physical labor with his hands.

Another dimension to this matter of working with the hands is implicit in what Paul says in 1 Thessalonians 4:11, that such labor is a demonstration of the community's faith in God and its faithfulness to God. Further, it is a demonstration of God's working through the church and its members. Such a position is posited by Georg Bertram in his treatment of *ergon* (work) in Kittel's *Theolgical Dictionary of the New Testament*.[10] In focusing on 1 Thessalonians 4:11 and passages pertaining to it, Bertram states, ". . . work is sacred to the degree that at least indirectly it serves the Christian community as the *Soma Xristou* [body of Christ] in respect of its good repute in the world."[11] Bertram perceives Paul's understanding of work to be that it makes no difference whether it is temporal or spiritual. He says,

There can be indeed no final distinction between work in temporal avocation and direct work in the service of the community. All *ergon* in the Christian community (and not merely in the organized Church) is finally God's work through men. With this insight of faith the problem of work is solved in the NT. For Paul and for all believers all work is the fruit of faith.[12]

And so if we were to adopt Bertram's understanding of Paul's perception of work, we cannot see "work" to be spiritual in nature only, i.e., engagement in prayer and fasting; work is understood to be those things as well as manual labor with one's hands. The latter is just as much a demonstration of a person's faith in God, a person's faithfulness to God, and God's working through that person as are prayer and fasting. It is all of this that Paul is alluding to when he strongly urges the Thessalonians ". . . to aspire to live quietly, to mind your own affairs, and to work with your hands, as we charged you . . ." (1 Thessalonians 4:11).

To Command Respect from a Hostile World

But why is this emphasis made on manual labor with the hands? Is it to polish the church community's piety? Is it to give reinforcement to the church's status before God? Hardly so! Paul's grave concern with the Thessalonians' working with their hands is ". . . so that you may command the respect of outsiders" (1 Thessalonians 4:12a).

The RSV's translation of what Paul says here does not conform directly to what is read in the Greek text. However, it catches the spirit and intent of it. The Greek text reads *hina peripatete eusxemonos pros tous eksw.* The word *eusxemonos* can variably be translated to mean "something that is done decently, becomingly, or in an orderly fashion" (see 1 Corinthians 14:40). It has the import of behaving with dignity, decorum, and in a manly or womanly manner. Paul intends, then, that the Thessalonians should walk or work, as is intimated in the previous verse, so that in their walking or working they will demonstrate as a group (viz., the church) dignity, decorum, orderliness, and unquestionable behavior. This, in turn, elicits and even commands the respect of those outside of the church. This explains the RSV translation.

This is a powerful statement on Paul's part, for in truth, the early church was seen in a negative and obnoxious light. In the Roman society, the early church was an anathema, comprised of the scoundrels of the earth. There was a total lack of respect for Jesus and the early church on the part of the society in which they existed and operated. For example, in Luke's portrayal of the trial of Jesus, he is charged with the criminal act of ". . . perverting our nation, and forbidding us to give tribute to Caesar

. . ." (Luke 23:2). In the Acts of the Apostles, Saul and Barnabas, after spending a year teaching a large company of people at Antioch, were labeled with the stigma-ridden epithet of "Christians," a name of derision and ridicule (Acts 11:26).

Secular literature written during the time of Paul and the early church discloses that Christians were shown little respect; in fact, they were viewed as criminals, disturbers of the peace, profaners for their refusal to worship the Roman gods and the deified Caesar, and the disease of the earth. In Suetonius' *Lives of the Caesars,* it is reported that Emperor Claudius expelled Christians from Rome because they caused disturbances " . . . at the instigation of Chrestus."[13] In his historical portrayal of the time of Emperor Nero, reference is made to Christians as ". . . a class of men given to a new and mischievous superstition."[14] Tacitus, another Roman historian of early church times, is no more respectful of the church. The following is his description of Christians in light of their role as scapegoats for Emperor Nero after he had burned Rome with fire:

> But neither human help, nor imperial munificence, nor all the modes of placating Heaven, could stifle scandal or dispel the belief that the fire had taken place by order. Therefore, to scotch the rumour, Nero substituted as culprits, and punished with the utmost refinements of cruelty, a class of men, loathed for their vices, whom the crowd styled Christians. Christus, the founder of the name, had undergone the death penalty in the reign of Tiberius, by sentence of the procurator Pontius Pilatus, and the pernicious superstition was checked for a moment, only to break out once more, not merely in Judea, the home of the disease, but in the capital itself, where all things horrible or shameful in the world collect and find vogue.[15]

And so outsiders held early Christians in derision. They saw them as violators of the laws of Rome and Roman religious practices. The religion of Jesus was seen as a "mischievous superstition" and a "disease" by Nero; its adherents were called "disturbers of the peace" by Claudius.

It was against this negative and destructive perception that Paul and the early church were struggling. If such malignant and negative labeling was allowed to prevail, violent extinction of the church would be sure. Thus, it was necessary for Paul to instruct the church members at Thessalonica to work with their hands and demonstrate unquestionable behavior so that they could command the respect of outsiders. There was no way that they could expect respect for their piety and virtue; their very existence was an insult, an aberration, and a contradiction to Roman life and politics. They had to command the respect of outsiders.

The literature that chronicles the horrors, suffering, ignominy, and death of Christians at the hands of the Roman Empire is voluminous indeed (a good example is Eusebius' *Ecclesiastical History*). However, in spite of the heinous treatment imposed upon the early church by the authorities of the Roman Empire, buried within the literature of that time is a faint, albeit grudging Roman respect for the Christians. An example of this is found in secular writings, one of Pliny the Younger's letters to the Emperor Trajan. Pliny's letter to Trajan inquired what to do with Christians who refused to bow reverently before the statue of the deified Emperor. Pliny says of the Christians:

> . . . they had met regularly before dawn on a fixed day to chant verses alternately among themselves in honour of Christ as if to a god, and also to bind themselves by oath, not for any criminal purpose, but to abstain from theft, robbery and adultery, to commit no breach of trust and not to deny a deposit when called upon to restore it.[16]

Another example of the respect the early church grudgingly extracted from Roman society is seen in the secular writings of Julian the Apostate. Julian observed the unquestionable work and behavior of the Christians in their care for one another as well as those outside of the church community. He attempted to duplicate the church's system, only to fail. His grudgingly given respect for the Christians and their behavior seeps through a letter he wrote to Arsacius (Sozom. v. 16) when he said: "These godless Galileans feed not only their own poor but ours; our poor lack our care."[17]

This is the kind of respect Paul demanded that the Thessalonians command of outsiders. The very fact that the early church survived the inhumanities imposed upon it by the Roman Empire and drove Emperor Constantine to acknowledge Christianity as *the* religion of the empire in about 325 A.D. is indicative of the respect Christians won.

Working with their hands so that they could command the respect of outsiders is not the final step in Paul's strategy for freedom for the Thessalonians; the final, forceful, and most significant step is stated in 1 Thessalonians 4:12b when Paul says, ". . . and be dependent on nobody." This dimension of Paul's strategy for freedom is not separate from the community's living quietly, minding its own affairs, and working with its hands so that it could command the respect of outsiders; it is part and parcel of that entire process.

However, there is a controversy in the translation of the phrase that appears in 1 Thessalonians 4:12b, *medenos xreian exete*, "you have need of nothing." We need to deal with this controversy momentarily in order to see more clearly what Paul is demanding of the Thessalonians so that we might apply the concept to the situation of the church today, especially the black church. The KJV renders a literal translation of the phrase to read, "and that ye may have lack of nothing." J. B. Phillips and the *New English Bible* follow somewhat this literal translation; "and you will never be in want" (Phillips), and "and at the same time may never be in want" (NEB). But these renderings, albeit faithful to the literal translation of the phrase, fail to grasp the meaning in light of what is said prior to and following the phrase itself. The RSV grasps the spirit of the phrase as it stands in the context of what is said before and after it, "and be dependent on nobody." This rendering is followed by the relatively new New International Version of the Bible, "so that you will not be dependent on anybody." The *Jerusalem Bible* particularizes its understanding of the phrase to mean that the Thessalonians should be free from dependence on assistance from outsiders; hence, "so that you are seen to be respectable by those outside the Church, though you do not have to depend on them." The Moffatt translation is somewhat in line with the spirit of the RSV's translation when it says "so that your life may be respected by the outside world and be self-supporting."

The literal translators of the phrase imply their understanding of an independent church at Thessalonica but the obtuseness of their translation indicates their obvious dismissal of the problems that were plaguing the church, viz., idleness, resulting misbehavior, and subsequent dependence of those waiting for the Parousia on people either within or without the church. The *Jerusalem Bible* goes a bit far in concluding that the Thessalonians should guard against becoming dependent on outsiders. This fails to grasp the possibility that the problem could have been that certain ones within the church at Thessalonica were becoming dependent, not necessarily on outsiders, but on those within the church. The Moffatt translation seems to conclude subtly that it is outsiders upon whom the church should avoid becoming dependent. Although all translations cited indicate their agreement on the need for the church to be independent, only the RSV and the New International Version reflect an understanding of this needed independence in the light of both outside and inside support.

Paul's discussion in chapter 4, especially in verses 11 and 12, and his emphasis in 5:14 to "admonish the idle," indicate that there was something amiss within the church at Thessalonica that was causing dependence of some on others within the church and this could easily develop into dependence on those outside the church. Hence, the RSV translates correctly, "and be dependent on nobody," as does the New International Version, "so that you will not be dependent on anybody."

So Paul admonishes the Thessalonians to live quietly, mind their own affairs, and work with their hands so that they can demand the respect of outsiders and be dependent on no one, whether inside the church or outside. This implies that the Christians at Thessalonica were charged to utilize whatever skills they had to engage in productive labor. By doing this, they would be free from encumbrances and fetters from anyone outside the church; also, by utilizing their skills in productive labor, they would lessen the economic burden of others within the church. It is not certain what modes of manual labor they were to employ, but whatever they had, the Thessalonians were to employ them in order to maintain their freedom.

Paul's Contribution to Economic Freedom

This underlying principle of independence and freedom, of providing the needs of individuals and the Christian community through hard work is a prominent contribution of the apostle Paul. It became a guiding principle for the emerging church in the Roman society. It can be concluded that this principle of independence and freedom through hard work underlies statements referring to work by those New Testament writers after Paul. It is reasonable to conclude that they were following Paul's lead. It is evident that the emerging early church made work mandatory for those who became a part of it.

In fact, there was an increasing emphasis on the church's providing work for those who were a part of it. For example, in the pseudo-Clementines, there is the admonition, "For those able to work, provide work" (Clem. viii). In *The Didache*, a traveler who entered the church community claiming to be a Christian and who wished to remain more than two days was made to work:

> "If he who comes is a traveller, help him as much as you can, but he shall not remain with you more than two days, or, if need be, three. And if he wishes to settle among you and has a craft, let him work for his bread. But if he has no craft provide for him according to your understanding, so that no man shall live among you in idleness because he is a Christian" (*Didache* xii).

The underlying principle is that the church should remain independent and free by not allowing its members or the church itself to become dependent on those either inside the church or outside of it.

This does not mean to say that in the early church of Paul's day and afterward there was no concern for those within the church who genuinely could not work, maybe because of some physical ailment. There was provision for such. Adolf Harnack's treatment of "The Gospel of Love and Charity" is a sound statement of the church's dedication to its responsibility to take care of the widows, orphans, travelers, the infirm, and elderly.[18] Further, one church community would go to the aid and assistance of another when the other was in some dire distress. The truth of this is seen in Paul's passionate appeal to the church community at Corinth to lift an offering for the saints at Jerusalem who had been smitten by a famine (cf. 2 Corinthians 8 and 9). For Paul and the emerging early church, hard work was a necessity, a divine duty for each healthy member of the church. It was necessary so that the members of the church in particular and the church in general would not become dependent on one another within the church or, heaven forbid, those without the church. Work was necessary in order to have the economic resources to operate, to provide relief for those within the church who were in need, and to remain autonomous. It was necessary even for those caught up in the rapture of the Parousia and those, who, as alluded to in the pseudo-Clementine *de Virgin,* i, II, tended to become lazy while chattering about religion instead of taking care of their own business.

Ecclesiastical history discloses that it was through hard work by the members of the early church, manual labor such as tent-making, leatherwork, artistry, and craftsmanship of all sorts, that Christians generated the economic revenue needed to maintain their freedom from disintegration within and intrusion from without. In fact, as Shirley Jackson Case argues, through this process, the early church and many of its members became extremely wealthy.[19] It was with this accumulation of wealth realized from labor performed with their hands that the early church was able to sustain itself and be dependent on no one and at the same time gain respect from outsiders. As Case concludes:

> Largely as a result of its attainment of economic prestige the new religion was able to forsake the rough and dusty bypaths which formerly it had been forced to pursue and could now boldly emerge a dignified traveler upon the main highway to social respectability.[20]

In concluding this segment of our discussion, Paul the apostle must be recognized as the one responsible for providing the early church with the theology and philosophy of economic development and independence that factored out into a church of power and freedom, a church that commanded the respect of outsiders and was dependent on nobody.

His Word to Us

What does Paul's theology of economic development and independence as a strategy for freedom have to say to the Christian church in America today, especially the black church? To the white church and its denominational expressions, it already has provided a *modus operandi* for economic development, independence, and employment for its constituents. The Protestant work ethic of John Calvin, the man and his theology certainly being influenced by Paul, has been central to the white church. The white church, and all of its denominational expressions, has become wealthy and independent by following the theology of Paul as it has been filtered through the eyes of Protestant theologians such as Calvin. As a result, white churches operate schools, hospitals, bookstores, farms, camps, manufacturing companies, television and radio stations, and many other businesses that generate revenue and employment for their constituents. It is not to the white church and its many expressions in America that Paul's theology of economic development and independence poses a particular challenge.

It is to the black church in America that Paul's theology speaks and before which it stands as a strident challenge. The black church has not come to the point at which it can command the respect of those inside the church (i.e., the white church) or those outside the church (viz., the white political and economic community). The black church has not arrived at total liberation so that it can pride itself in the fact that it is not dependent on anybody. And so Paul's exhortation to the Thessalonians stands before the black church in America as a forceful challenge. His challenge is that the black church must put itself and its money to work for the liberation of its people so that it can command the respect of those inside the church and those outside and be dependent on nobody.

Notes

Chapter 1

[1] Ernst Käsemann, *Jesus Means Freedom*, trans. Frank Clarke (Philadelphia: Fortress Press, 1970), p. 9.

[2] *Ibid.*, p. 65.

[3] See Heinrich Schlier, "Eleutheros," *Theological Dictionary of the New Testament*, ed. Gerhard Kittel and Gerhard Friedrich, trans. Geoffrey W. Bromily, 7 vols. (Grand Rapids: Wm. B. Eerdmans Publishing Co., 1964), 2, pp. 496-502. While Schlier deals only with freedom in the context of sin, law, and death, the point here is that he verifies the preponderant usage of the term in Pauline writings. It is interesting that Martin Luther's open letter to Pope Leo X, *The Freedom of a Christian*, begins with several references to Pauline passages to make his case that the Christian is free. See Martin Luther, *Christian Liberty*, ed. Harold J. Grimm, trans. W. A. Lambert (Philadelphia: Fortress Press, 1943), p. 7.

[4] An understanding of Paul's theology comes only after one wrestles with his mind. The neoorthodox theologian, Karl Barth, responding to his critics, came to this profound conclusion. See Karl Barth, *The Epistle to the Romans*, trans. Edwyn C. Hoskyns, 6th. ed. (London: Oxford University Press, 1968), p. 12. By way of inference, Latta R. Thomas draws a similar conclusion, i.e., black people must wrestle with Paul to understand his position on slavery and freedom. See Latta R. Thomas, *Biblical Faith and the Black American* (Valley Forge: Judson Press, 1976), pp. 112-113, *passim*.

[5] The first letter of Paul, First Thessalonians, was written ca. 50 A.D., some twenty years before the Gospel of Mark, the first of the Gospels, was written, ca. 70 A.D. With the exception of the genuine writings of Paul, the remaining writings of the New Testament were written after 70 A.D. See the dating of the New Testament by Paul Feine and Johannes Behm in Werner Georg Kümmel, *Introduction to the New Testament*, trans. A. J. Mattill, Jr., 14th. rev. ed. (Nashville: Abingdon Press, 1966); and Willi Marxsen, *Introduction*

to the New Testament, trans. Geoffrey Buswell (Philadelphia: Fortress Press, 1968).

[6] Martin Luther King, Jr., *Where Do We Go from Here: Chaos or Community?* (New York: Bantam Books, 1967). See especially pp. 125-134.

[7] Wayne A. Meeks, ed., *The Writings of St. Paul*, A Norton Critical Edition (New York: W. W. Norton & Co., Inc., 1972), p. 437.

[8] See Howard Thurman, *Jesus and the Disinherited* (Nashville: Abingdon Press, Apex Books, 1949), pp. 30-31.

[9] Howard Thurman is a prime example here, *ibid.*, pp. 31-35. Although he tries to offer reasons for Paul's seeming proslavery position, he never really sees in Paul strong themes that lend themselves to a plan for liberation.

[10] While James H. Cone caustically maligns Paul for what he thinks is Paul's contribution to slavery in America, his approach to Paul is not one of complete dismissal. He stealthily utilizes Paul where he wishes but avoids him otherwise. See James H. Cone, *Black Theology and Black Power* (New York: The Seabury Press, 1969) and *A Black Theology of Liberation*, The C. Eric Lincoln Series in Black Religion (Philadelphia: J. B. Lippincott Co., 1970); and Albert B. Cleage, Jr., *The Black Messiah* (New York: Sheed and Ward, 1968) and *Black Christian Nationalism: New Directions for the Black Church* (New York: William Morrow & Co. Inc., 1972). My discussion on the position of these two black theologians on the apostle Paul is "In Defense of the Apostle Paul: A Discussion with Albert Cleage and James Cone" (unpublished dissertation, Vanderbilt Divinity School, 1975), pp. 42-87.

[11] It is commonly known by serious scholarship that white preachers, slave owners, and guardians of the institution of slavery distorted the Bible (including Pauline and deutero-Pauline writings) to make a defense for slavery; see Kyle Haselden, *Mandate for White Christians* (Richmond: John Knox Press, 1966), pp. 34-35. For a historical example of how Paul was used for the enforcement of slavery for blacks, see John Lofton, *Insurrection in South Carolina: The Turbulent World of Denmark Vesey* (Kent, Ohio: Kent State University Press, 1964), p. 161. The setting here is Denmark Vesey's trial for leading an insurrection in the Charleston, South Carolina, area. Included in the judge's sentencing statement is reference to statements attributed to Paul regarding slaves' obedience to their masters. This is reminiscent of the Roman Caesar who functioned both as chief magistrate and Pontifex Maximus. It also is a flagrant misreading and misuse of the New Testament.

[12] Barbara Hall, "Paul and Women," *Theology Today*, XXXI (April, 1974), pp. 50-55.

[13] Theological concern with the religion of nationalism as an opponent of Christianity in America goes back as far—and maybe farther—as 1943 with H. Richard Niebuhr's concern with rising henotheism, social religions, that was threatening to subvert the church. See H. Richard Niebuhr, *Radical Monotheism in Western Culture* (New York: Harper & Row, Publishers, Inc., 1943). A similar concern is expressed later by Sidney E. Mead, *The Nation with the Soul of a Church* (New York: Harper & Row, Publishers, Inc., 1975), pp. 11-28, 48-77.

[14] For a thorough discussion of the historical development of this phenomenon up to the time of Richard M. Nixon and its future implications, see Arthur M. Schlesinger, Jr., *The Imperial Presidency* (Boston: Houghton Mifflin Co., 1973).

[15] *Newsweek*, June 3, 1974, p. 24. See also *The Nation*, June 8, 1974, p. 707.

[16] For a discussion of Paul's cross-resurrection theology and the Corinthians' violation of it, see Käsemann, *Jesus Means Freedom*, pp. 68-78.

[17] Jürgen Moltmann, *Theology of Hope*, trans. James W. Leitch (New York: Harper & Row, Publishers, Inc., 1967), pp. 20-21.

[18] *Ibid.*, p. 21.

[19] Günther Bornkamm, *Paul*, trans. D. M. G. Stalker (New York: Harper & Row, Publishers, Inc., 1971), p. xxvii.

Chapter 2

[1] See Albert B. Cleage, Jr., *The Black Messiah* (New York: Sheed and Ward, 1968), pp. 4, 110; also *Black Christian Nationalism: New Directions for the Black Church* (New York: William Morrow & Co. Inc., 1972), p. xxxviii.

[2] James H. Cone, *A Black Theology of Liberation*, The C. Eric Lincoln Series in Black Religion (Philadelphia: J. B. Lippincott Co., 1970), p. 68.

[3] See Frederic Godet, *Commentary on St. Paul's First Epistle to the Corinthians,* Clark's Foreign Theological Library, trans. A. Cusin. 27 vols. (Edinburgh: T. & T. Clark, 1893), volume 1; Charles K. Barrett, *A Commentary on the First Epistle to the Corinthians,* Harper's New Testament Commentaries, ed. Henry Chadwick (New York: Harper & Row, Publishers, Inc., 1968); and Hans Conzelmann, *First Corinthians,* Hermeneia: A Critical and Historical Commentary on the Bible Series, trans. James W. Leitch, ed. George W. MacRae, S. J. (Philadelphia: Fortress Press, 1975).

[4] See Godet, *Commentary,* p. 14. See also Willi Marxsen, *Introduction to the New Testament,* trans. Geoffrey Buswell (Philadelphia: Fortress Press, 1968), pp. 71, 76.

[5] There are suggestions that 1 Corinthians 1:2b and 14:33b-35 are interpolations. Some New Testament scholars have raised the question of integrity based on the discontinuity of thought and various contradictions in the letter. Because of the reference to other letters written by Paul (see 1 Corinthians 5:9; 2 Corinthians 2:4), it has been surmised that more than the two Corinthian letters were written and that 1 and 2 Corinthians represent the compilation of those letters. For this discussion, see Conzelmann, *First Corinthians,* pp. 2ff.; and Werner Georg Kümmel, *Introduction to the New Testament,* trans. A. J. Mattill, Jr. 14th. rev. ed. (Nashville: Abingdon Press, 1966), pp. 203-204.

[6] See Kurt Aland, Matthew Black, Carlo M. Martini, Bruce M. Metzger, and Allen Wikgren, ed., *The Greek New Testament* (Stuttgart: Württemberg Bible Society, 1966), p. 593.

[7] See Wayne A. Meeks, ed., *The Writings of St. Paul,* A Norton Critical Edition (New York: W. W. Norton & Co., Inc., 1972), pp. 435-444.

[8] See Clement of Alexandria, *Exhortation,* X, 107, 3; Ignatius, *To Polycarp,* 4; *The Didache,* IV, 10-12; and St. Augustine, *The City of God,* XIX, 15-16.

[9] See John Calvin, *The First Epistle of Paul the Apostle to the Corinthians,* trans. John W. Fraser (Grand Rapids: Wm. B. Eerdmans Publishing Co., 1960), p. 154.

[10] Quoted from the Anglican Bishop of London's letter of May 19, 1727 to "Masters and Mistresses." See Peter G. Mode, *Source Book and Bibliographical Guide for American History* (Menasha, Wis.: George Banta Publishing Co., 1921), p. 551.

[11] Howard Thurman, *Jesus and the Disinherited* (Nashville: Abingdon Press, Apex Books, 1949), pp. 30-31.

[12] Albert Schweitzer, *The Mysticism of Paul the Apostle,* trans. William Montgomery (New York: The Seabury Press, 1968), p. 194.

[13] *Ibid.,* p. 195.

[14] Leander E. Keck, *Paul and His Letters,* Proclamation Commentaries: The New Testament Witnesses for Preaching, ed. Gerhard Krodel (Philadelphia: Fortress Press, 1979), p. 95.

[15] Lucas Grollenberg, *Paul,* trans. John Bowden (Philadelphia: The Westminster Press, 1978), p. 117.

[16] Rudolf Schnackenburg, *The Moral Teaching of the New Testament,* trans. J. Holland-Smith and W. J. O'Hare (New York: The Seabury Press, 1965), pp. 258-259.

[17] Günther Bornkamm, *Paul,* trans. D. M. G. Stalker (New York: Harper & Row, Publishers, Inc., 1971), p. 175.

[18] Conzelmann, *First Corinthians,* p. 127.

[19] Barrett, *Commentary,* p. 169.

[20] Conzelmann, *First Corinthians,* p. 126.

[21] *Ibid.,* p. 127.

[22]Barrett, *Commentary*, p. 170. A similar view appears in Karl Barth's statement on what Paul meant by saying that slaves should remain in the state they were called; see *Church Dogmatics*, ed. G. W. Bromiley and T. F. Torrance (Edinburgh: T. & T. Clark, 1961), vol. III, pt. 4, p. 605. See also Johannes Weiss, *Earliest Christianity: A History of the Period A. D. 30-150*, ed. Frederick C. Grant (Gloucester, Mass.: Peter Smith, 1970), 2, pp. 588-589; and Archibald Robertson and Alfred Plummer, *A Critical and Exegetical Commentary on the First Epistle of St. Paul to the Corinthians*, The International Critical Commentary, 2nd. ed. (Edinburgh: T. & T. Clark, 1914), p. 147; also Schnackenburg, *Moral Teaching*.

[23]Godet, *Commentary*, p. 356.

[24]*Ibid.*

[25]*Ibid.*

[26]K. L. Schmidt, "Keleo, Klesis, Kletos, antikaleo, egkaleo, egklema, eiskaleo, metakalea, Proskaleo, sugkaleo, epikaleo, ekklesia," *Theological Dictionary of the New Testament*, ed. Gerhard Kittel and Gerhard Friedrich, trans. Geoffrey W. Bromiley, 7 vols. (Grand Rapids: Wm. B. Eerdmans Publishing Co., 1965), 3, pp. 491-492.

[27]Walter Bauer, *A Greek-English Lexicon of the New Testament and Other Early Christian Literature*, ed. William F. Arndt and F. Wilbur Gingrich. 4th. rev. and augmented ed. (Chicago: University of Chicago Press, 1957), pp. 436-437.

[28]The term "kingdom of God" appears only seven times in genuine Pauline writings (cf. Romans 14:17; 1 Corinthians 4:20; 6:9; 15:24; 15:50; Galatians 5:21; 1 Thessalonians 2:12). In light of the fact that the central theme of the preaching of Jesus was the kingdom of God (cf. Mark 1:14-15; Matthew 4:17), the question must be raised, why did Paul not follow in the tradition of his Lord? Was it that the term bore an explicit political meaning and suggested a rival kingdom to that of the Roman Empire, a situation with which Paul and nascent believing communities were not prepared to cope? This is a crucially important theological question, but one that cannot be pursued here.

[29]Barrett, *Commentary*, p. 32.

[30]*Ibid.*, p. 261.

[31]Conzelmann, *First Corinthians*, p. 22. The reference to the Greek origin of *ekklesia* here is implied, cf. note 26.

[32]Godet, *Commentary*, p. 41.

[33]Bauer, *A Greek-English Lexicon*, p. 240; Acts 19:32; also Schmidt, "Keleo . . . ," pp. 513ff.

[34]See Paul S. Minear, "Idea of Church," *The Interpreter's Dictionary of the Bible*, ed. George A. Buttrick. 4 vols. (Nashville: Abingdon Press, 1962), 1, pp. 607-617. See also J. G. Simpson and F. C. Grant, "Church," *Dictionary of the Bible*, ed. James Hastings, rev. Frederick G. Grant and H. H. Rowley (New York: Charles Scribner's Sons, 1963), pp. 160-162.

[35]For this discussion, see Rudolf Bultmann, *Theology of the New Testament*, Scribner's Studies in Contemporary Theology, trans. Kendrick Grobel (New York: Charles Scribner's Sons, 1951; copyright renewed 1979 Antje B. Lemke), 1, pp. 92-108.

[36]If this succinct historical analysis of the term *ekklesia* and its possible meaning to Paul is substantial, the fact of *ekklesia* characterizing early believers for Paul as "the people of God" rather than a "church," as Western theology has interpreted it, would prove Albert Cleage and others wrong and negate the charge that Paul forsook the development of a "nation" or "people" and established churches. The term "church" primarily is the Western version of the more technical term *ekklesia*, cf. "church" (English), "kirche" (German), or "kerke" (Dutch). See *The Oxford Dictionary of the Christian Church*, ed. F. L. Cross, rev. F. L. Cross and E. A. Livingstone. 2nd. ed. (London: Oxford University Press, 1974), pp. 286-287. These terms for church miss the intention Paul had for *ekklesia*.

[37]Conzelmann, *First Corinthians*, p. 22.

[38]Bultmann, *Theology*, p. 308. Reprinted with the permission of Charles Scribner's Sons.

[39]*Ibid.*, p. 99.

[40]*Ibid.*, cf. p. 309.

[41]In making the larger point of separation of the church from the world, Paul strings together several Old Testament passages, e.g. Leviticus 26:11; Isaiah 52:11; Ezekiel 37:27, 20:43; Jeremiah 51:45, 31:9; Zephaniah 3:20; 2 Samuel 7:8, 14; and Hosea 2:1. The significance of this seems to be that Paul adopted the Old Testament tradition of separation of the holy from the profane, cf. Leviticus 20:23, 24b, 26. Here, again, Albert Cleage's allegation that Paul failed to carry forward the concept of "nation" falls flatly on its face.

[42]William W. Buckland, *A Textbook of Roman Law* (Cambridge: University Press, 1932), p. 177.

[43]Andrew William Lintolt, *Violence in Republican Rome* (Oxford: The Clarendon Press, 1968), p. 78.

[44]*Ibid.*, p. 82.

[45]*Ibid.*, p. 81. See also R. H. Barrow, *Slavery in the Roman Empire* (London: Methuen & Co., Ltd., 1928), p. 166.

[46]Lintoldt, *Violence*, p. 78. See also A. R. Hands, *Charities and Social Aid in Greece and Rome* (Ithaca, N. Y.: Cornell University Press, 1968), p. 81.

[47]Lintoldt, *Violence*, p. 123.

[48]We are told by Suetonius that the Jews, probably meaning Christians, were expelled from Rome by Emperor Claudius (ca. 41-54 A.D.) because of disturbances due to the instigations of Chrestus (another form of Christus). See Suetonius, *The Lives of the Caesars*, V, xxv. See also Pliny's remarks about the resemblance of Christianity to a *collegium*, *The Letters of Pliny*, x, xcvi; cf. X. xxxiv.

[49]See *The Annals of Tacitus*, XV, xliv.

[50]Under Domitian, Christians suffered exile and martyrdom because of the faith, cf. The Book of Revelation; so also under Trajan (ca. 112 A.D.). For a discussion of charges, trials, and punishment of Christians during these times, see Eusebius, *Ecclesiastical History*, IV, xv; V. i.

[51]Edgar J. Goodspeed, *Key to Ephesians* (Chicago: University of Chicago Press, 1933), p. 7, note 4.

[52]W. G. Rollins, "Slavery in the New Testament," *Interpreter's Dictionary of the Bible*, ed. Keith Crim. Supplementary Volume (Nashville: Abingdon Press, 1976), pp. 830-832.

[53]Robertson and Plummer, *Critical and Exegetical Commentary*, p. 147.

[54]Inasmuch as Corinth was a port city, it stands to reason that it was a center for slave traffic and enjoyed a sizeable slave population. It was obvious that the Corinthian congregation had former slaves within it (cf. 1 Corinthians 1:26, "Not many were powerful, not many were of noble birth . . ."). The faction referred to in 1 Corinthians 11:18-19 could very well have been the result of attempted discrimination against former slave members of the *ekklesia*. The reference to Stephanas's household, the first converts in Achaia, suggests that not only Stephanas's family became members of the *ekklesia* but his slaves did as well (see 1 Corinthians 16:15).

[55]Plato, *The Republic*, trans. B. Jowett (New York: Alfred A. Knopf, Inc., n.d.), pp. 83, 96.

[56]Aristotle, *Politics*, I, v. 1254a. Aristotle (384-322 B.C.) argued that because slaves had little or no power of rationalization, they were slaves by nature (*Politics*, I, v, 1254b). But more (or less) than this, slaves were things, not persons. Slaves became one of the instruments, or tools, by which the free man acquired wealth and comfort: ". . . in the arrangement of the family, a slave is a living possession, and property . . ." (*Politics*,

I, iv, 1253b). Essentially, slaves belonged to their master, body and soul; they had no rights that their master was obligated to respect.

⁵⁷Cato, *On Agriculture*, preface.

⁵⁸*Ibid.*, LVI.

⁵⁹Plutarch, "Marcus Cato," *The Lives of the Noble Grecians and Romans*, trans. John Dryden, rev. Arthur Hugh Clough (New York: The Modern Library, 1864), p. 427.

⁶⁰For a discussion of slaves' importance to Roman luxury, see Michael Grant, *The World of Rome* (New York: The New American Library, Inc., A Mentor Book, 1960), pp. 121-148.

⁶¹See J. P. Balsdon, *Life and Leisure in Ancient Rome* (New York: McGraw-Hill Book Co., 1969), p. 107. See also R. H. Barrow, *Slavery in the Roman Empire*, pp. 25ff., 43.

⁶²See J. A. Crook, "Law and Life of Rome," *Aspects of Greek and Roman Life*, ed. H. H. Scullard (London: Thames & Hudson, 1967), pp. 55-56; also W. W. Buckland, *The Roman Law of Slavery* (New York: AMS Press Inc., 1969), pp. 1, 3, 10.

⁶³Juvenal, *Satires*, VI, ll. 217-221.

⁶⁴See Tacitus, *Annals*, IV, 54.

⁶⁵See Tacitus, *History*, II, 72.

⁶⁶See Tacitus, *Annals*, II, 30. Another example of torture is cited in Balsdon, *Life and Leisure in Ancient Rome*, p. 52, when a household slave breaks some precious glassware and is thrown into a fish pond to feed man-eating lampreys.

⁶⁷Buckland, *Roman Law of Slavery*, p. 182.

⁶⁸Barrow, *Slavery in the Roman Empire*, p. 29.

⁶⁹See Suetonius, *Nero*, II. For other examples of atrocities inflicted upon slaves in the Roman Empire during Paul's time, see the citations from Tacitus and Suetonius in Appendix I in Barrow, *Slavery in the Roman Empire*, pp. 237ff.

⁷⁰Could it be concluded from the use of *andrapodistais*, "men stealers, kidnappers, slave dealers," in 1 Timothy 1:10 that the early church was threatened from without by intruders looking for runaway slaves or even from within by men greedy enough for money to sell their brother and sister back into slavery? Either possibility would have been traumatic for members of the *ekklesia* who were former slaves.

⁷¹There was a vast difference between a freeborn Roman citizen and a freedman. The freeborn Roman citizen gained citizenship by means of birth. The freedman, who was once a slave, gained citizenship by means of emancipation. In spite of achieving citizenship via emancipation, the freedman was not equal to a freeborn Roman citizen (see Barbara Levick, *Roman Colonies in Southern Asia Minor* [Oxford: The Clarendon Press, 1967], p. 36).

A slave could gain freedom in at least three ways: 1) *Censu*, placing his or her name on the censor's list of citizens (under oath before a magistrate); however this did not mean that he or she became a citizen of the Roman Empire. 2) *Vindicta*, taking an oath before a magistrate to the effect that manumission would not mean a change of citizenship. 3) *Testamenta*, being freed by means of a will upon the death of the *dominus*, lord. Once a slave gained liberty, certain obligations to the master, *dominus*, (who still was to be regarded as sacred) were still expected: 1) *obsequim* (respect); 2) *opera* (an oath at manumission agreeing to a certain number of days of free labor for the former master); and 3) *bona*, the patron was assured of certain property rights at the freedman's death. There was also the notion that freedmen were to give *munera*, i.e., gifts to their patrons. For a discussion of the various ramifications of freedmen's continuing obligations to their masters, see Buckland, *Roman Law of Slavery*, pp. 185-231 and Levick, *Roman Colonies*, pp. 36-44.

⁷²In a published dissertation, S. Scott Bartchy argues that Paul was indifferent toward slavery. See S. Scott Bartchy, *Mallon Chresai: First Century Slavery and the Interpre-*

tation of 1 Corinthians 7:21 (Missoula, Mont.: University of Montana, 1973), pp. 103-104.

[73] Bartchy insists that slavery was so accepted in Paul's day that no one gave a thought to it. *Ibid.*

[74] See Conzelmann, *First Corinthians*, p. 127 and Godet, *Commentary*, p. 357.

[75] For example, Godet deals extensively with whether *ei kai* should be translated "even if," "although," or "if therefore." He even suggests that *kai* might be substituted for *de* to read *ei de*, "but if." Godet, *Commentary*, pp. 358-359.

[76] This is one point at which there is agreement with Bartchy. He argues convincingly that exegesis of 1 Corinthians 7:21 is not contingent on proper grammatical analysis. Unfortunately, he concludes that the exegetical key to 1 Corinthians 7:21 is the understanding of slavery in the Roman Empire before, during, and after Paul's time. He insists that attitudes, laws, and customs pertaining to slavery affected Paul's attitude. This is in no way convincing. He does seem to be right to conclude, however, that 1 Corinthians 7:21 is not understood best in the light of grammatical excellence.

[77] Conzelmann, *First Corinthians*, p. 127.

[78] Barrett, *Commentary*, pp. 170-171.

[79] Conzelmann, *First Corinthians*, p. 127. For a similar position, see Ernst Käsemann, *New Testament Questions of Today*, trans. W. J. Montague (Philadelphia: Fortress Press, 1969), p. 208.

[80] Barrett, *Commentary*, p. 171.

[81] One can allude to several racist interpretations of Paul's attitude toward slavery based on 1 Corinthians 7:20-24. In every age, there have been strong representations of such racist interpretations. I am reminded of the instructions of 1727 A.D., which came from the Anglican Bishop of London, as they related to the Christian status of black slaves in America. Weiss, *Earliest Christianity*, 2, pp. 588ff., is another example from another era. Kenneth C. Russell is a representative of some segments of Roman Catholic thought on the subject of Paul and slavery, according to 1 Corinthians 7:20-24. Commenting on the passage he says,

> Is he not suggesting that this individual who is a slave is so because God has permitted it and that this man, slave as he is, has been called in the total situation of his life to be a Christian? His secular condition cannot be separated from his divine call and, indeed, it is in the context of his worldly position that he must live out the divine summons to the Christian life.

In a statement that sounds unreal coming from someone living in the latter half of the twentieth century, Russell says,

> The Christian vocation must be translated into the ordinary acts of everyday life, and the slave cannot escape this obligation. Hard as it sounds, the only answer for the slave is that he will be a good Christian by being a good slave.

See Kenneth C. Russell, *Slavery As Reality and Metaphor in the Pauline Letters* (Rome: Catholic Book Agency-Officium Libri Catholici, 1968), pp. 45-46.

[82] C. F. D. Moule, *An Idiom-Book of New Testament Greek*. 2nd. ed. (Cambridge: University Press, 1968), p. 21.

[83] *Ibid.*

[84] It is my conclusion that the freedom Paul talks about, which was acquired by the slave, was obtained as a result of the call. If this is true, I would be compelled to differ with Bartchy who suggests that the freedom in question was obtained as a result of the beneficence of a compassionate slave master. In his conclusion on the meaning of 1 Corinthians 7:21c, he says, "I conclude that Paul in 7:21c was speaking of any situation in which a Christian slave became a freedman. Thus his advice in 7:21d presupposes that the person addressed is a slave who has been set free by his owner." See Bartchy, *Mallon Chresai*, p. 208. Nowhere in the text at hand does Paul imply that the slave's freedom comes as a result of a gratuitous act of a master. According to Paul, freedom

for the slave comes as a result of the liberating act of Jesus on the cross (cf. v. 23) and his call to the slave to enter into the *ekklesia*.

[85] See Heinrich Schlier, "Eleutheros," *Theological Dictionary of the New Testament*, ed. Gerhard Kittel and Gerhard Friedrich, trans. Geoffrey W. Bromily, 7 vols. (Grand Rapids: Wm. B. Eerdmans Publishing Co., 1964), 2, pp. 487-492.

[86] *Ibid.*, pp. 496-502.

[87] Conzelmann, *First Corinthians*, p. 128. Conzelmann does not really tell us what freedom from sin meant for Paul as it related to slavery, whether it meant freedom from sin internally and morally or freedom from sin externally and socially or both. For what seems to be Conzelmann's position here, see the earlier discussion of verse 21 in this chapter.

[88] Barrett, *Commentary*, p. 171.

[89] Godet, *Commentary*, p. 363.

[90] Bauer, *A Greek-English Lexicon*, p. 83.

[91] Schlier, "Eleutheras," p. 501.

[92] F. Lyall, "Roman Law in the Writing of Paul—The Slave and the Freedman," *New Testament Studies*, 17 (Oct. 1970), p. 79. For the complete discussion, see pp. 73-79.

[93] *Adelphos*, "brother," denotes the mutual physical and spiritual relationship of all members of the *ekklesia*. See Hans Freiherr von Soden, "adelphos," *Theological Dictionary of the New Testament*, 1, pp. 144-146.

[94] Paul's concept of *agape* is that it is the new and vital power which prevails in the *ekklesia* and holds it captive (2 Corinthians 5:14). See Ethelbert Stauffer, "agapao," *Theological Dictionary of the New Testament*, 1, pp. 49ff.

[95] von Soden, "adelphos."

[96] Stauffer, "agapao."

[97] Theo Preiss, *Life in Christ*, Studies in Biblical Theology No. 13., trans. Harold Knight (Chicago: Alec R. Allenson, Inc., 1954), p. 40. For a refreshing commentary on Philemon, see Edward Lohse, *Colossians and Philemon*, Hermeneia: A Critical and Historical Commentary on the Bible Series, trans. Wm. R. Poehlmann and Robert J. Karrig, ed. Helmut Koester (Philadelphia: Fortress Press, 1971).

[98] Barrett, *Commentary*, p. 171.

[99] Barrow, *Slavery in the Roman Empire*, p. 12.

[100] Conzelmann, *First Corinthians*, p. 128. For a description of the practice of slaves being liberated by being sold to the gods, see Adolf Deissmann, *Light from the Ancient East*, trans. Lionel R. M. Strachen. 2nd. ed. (New York: Hodder and Staughton, 1911), p. 326.

[101] Godet, *Commentary*.

[102] See Rudolf Bultmann, *Primitive Christianity in Its Contemporary Setting*, trans. R. H. Fuller (Cleveland: The World Publishing Company, 1956), p. 185.

[103] Philo of Alexandria, a contemporary of Paul and a Jewish philosopher, seems to describe precisely Paul's psychological freedom. He argued that every good man is free. However, for Philo, freedom was not the work of Jesus' death on the cross, as Paul believed, but the result of a stoic kind of wisdom. See *Philo*, trans F. H. Colson, The Loeb Classical Library (Cambridge, Mass.: Harvard University Press, 1941), 9, pp. 2-102.

Chapter 3

[1] Hans Deiter Betz, *Galatians*, Hermeneia: A Critical and Historical Commentary on the Bible Series (Philadelphia: Fortress Press, 1979), pp. 2, 24ff.

[2] J. B. Lightfoot, *Commentary on St. Paul's Epistle to the Galatians*, A Zondervan Commentary (Grand Rapids: The Zondervan Corp., 1957), p. 6.

[3] Julius Caesar, *Gallic Wars and Other Writings*, trans. Moses Hadas (New York: Random House, Inc., 1957), VI, 24.

[4]Lightfoot, *Epistle*, p. 13.

[5]Epictetus, *Discourses*, II, xx, 17.

[6]Lightfoot, *Epistle*, p. 14.

[7]*Ibid.*, pp. 13, 15.

[8]Caesar, *Gallic Wars*, II, 1; see also III, 10.

[9]*Ibid.*, IV, 5.

[10]Gerhard Herm, *The Celts: The People Who Came out of the Darkness* (New York: St. Martin's Press, Inc., 1976), pp. 141-163. This is a well-written and documented research of ancient Celtic life and religion.

[11]Caesar, *Gallic Wars*, VI, 16.

[12]Epictetus, *Discourses*, II, xx, 17. See also Lightfoot, *Epistle*, pp. 16-17.

[13]Lightfoot, *Epistle*, p. 17; see Galatians 5:8.

[14]Herm, *The Celts*, p. 143.

[15]*Ibid.*, pp. 150-163.

[16]The dating of Galatians ranges from 48 to 58 A.D. Following are the dates some scholars give: George S. Duncan, *Galatians* (Chicago: Alec R. Allenson, Inc., 1934)—48 A.D.; Ernest DeWitt Burton, *The Epistle to the Galatians*, The International Critical Commentary (Edinburgh: T. & T. Clark, 1920)—54-55 A.D.; Reginald H. Fuller, *A Critical Introduction to the New Testament* (Chicago: Alec R. Allenson, Inc., 1966)—52-54 A.D.; Betz, *Galatians*—50-55 A.D.; Lightfoot, *Epistle*—57-58 A.D.; Wayne A. Meeks, ed., *The Writings of St. Paul*, A Norton Critical Edition (New York: W. W. Norton & Co., Inc., 1972)—54 A.D.

[17]Ferdinand Christian Baur, *Paul: The Apostle of Jesus Christ*, trans. and ed. Eduard Zeller, rev. A. Menzies. 2nd. ed. (London: Williams and Norgate, 1876), p. 253.

[18]A. Lukyn Williams, ed., *The Epistle of Paul the Apostle to the Galatians*, The Cambridge Bible for Schools and Colleges (Cambridge: University Press, 1936), pp. xxxix-x.

[19]Herman N. Ridderbos, *The Epistle of Paul to the Churches of Galatia*, The New International Commentary on the New Testament, trans. Henry Zylstra (Grand Rapids: Wm. B. Eerdmans Publishing Co., 1953), p. 18.

[20]Werner Georg Kümmel, *Introduction to the New Testament*, trans. A. J. Mattill, Jr. 14th rev. ed. (Nashville: Abingdon Press, 1966), p. 195.

[21]Eduard Meyer, *Ursprung und Anfänge des Christentums* (Sttutgart und Berlin: J. G. Cotta, 1923), 3, p. 434.

[22]Hans Lietzmann, *An die Galater* (Tubingen: Mohr, 1932), p. 38.

[23]James Hardy Ropes, *The Singular Problem of the Epistle to the Galatians*, Harvard Theological Studies XIV (Cambridge, Mass.: Harvard University Press, 1929).

[24]Walter Schmithals, *Paul and the Gnostics*, trans. John E. Steely (Nashville: Abingdon Press, 1972), pp. 13-64.

[25]Willi Marxsen, *Introduction to the New Testament*, trans. Geoffrey Buswell (Philadelphia: Fortress Press, 1970), p. 56.

[26]J. A. MacCulloch, *The Celtic and Scandinavian Religions* (London: Hutchinson's University Library, 1948), p. 9.

[27]J. A. MacCulloch, *The Religion of the Ancient Celts* (Edinburgh: T. & T. Clark, 1911), p. 19. Reprinted by courtesy of Charles Scribner's Sons.

[28]*Ibid.*, p. 14.

[29]Quote taken from Daniel J. Boorstin, *The Americans: The Colonial Experience* (New York: Random House, Inc., Vintage Books, 1978), p. 3.

[30]Perry Miller and Thomas H. Johnson, eds., *The Puritans: A Sourcebook of Their Writings*. Rev. ed. (New York: Harper & Row, Publishers, Inc., 1963), 1, p. 191.

[31]*Ibid.*, p. 4. Terrific stress was placed on the education of the Puritan clergy. It was incumbent for the clergy to have command of the teachings and doctrines of the Bible, since the Bible provided the guidelines of life, as well as other supportive disciplines,

such as philosophy, logic, and law. Hence, it is not unusual when one reads Benjamin Brook, *Lives of the Puritans* (London: York-Street, Covent-Garden, 1913), volume 3, to note that each biography begins with a citation of the clergyman's educational training and the school he attended.

[32]*Ibid.*, p. 184.

[33]*Ibid.*, p. 185.

[34]Miller and Johnson, *The Puritans*, 2, pp. 734-735.

[35]Benjamin Brook, *The Lives of the Puritans*, 3 vols. (London: James Black, 1813).

[36]Miller and Johnson, *The Puritans*, 1, p. 56.

[37]Cotton Mather, "The Negro Christianized: An Essay to Excite and Assist that Good Work, the Instruction of Negro-Servants in Christianity," in Gilbert Osofsky, *The Burden of Race: A Documentary History of Negro-White Relations in America* (New York: Harper & Row, Publishers, Inc., 1967), pp. 38-39.

[38]John Chester Miller, *The Wolf by the Ears: Thomas Jefferson and Slavery* (New York: The Free Press, 1977), *passim*. Miller's work is very well written and documented. Miller portrays Jefferson as one of the nation's most tragic personalities, a founder of the nation who was caught in the currents of fickleness, knowing what to do but not having the will to do it.

[39]Marcus G. Raskin, "Progressive Liberalism for the '80s," *The Nation* (May 17, 1980), p. 587.

[40]Gardner Taylor, "Some Musings on a Nation 'Under God,'" *Interpretation* (January, 1976), pp. 42-43. Used by permission. A similar position is taken by Taylor in an article written in 1976, "Baptists and Human Rights," in James E. Wood, Jr., ed., *Baptists and the American Experience* (Valley Forge, Judson Press, 1976), pp. 57-71.

[41]Reinhold Niebuhr, *The Irony of American History* (New York: Charles Scribner's Sons, 1952). While Niebuhr never really deals with American slavery and the nation's failure to extirpate it as its initial hindrance to reaching its goal of freedom, he does set out America's failure to live up to its notion of innocence and virtue.

[42]Lerone Bennett, *Before the Mayflower: A History of the Negro in America 1619-1964*. Rev. ed. (Baltimore: Penguin Books, 1966).

[43]John Hope Franklin, *From Slavery to Freedom: A History of American Negroes* (New York: Alfred A. Knopf, Inc., 1947).

[44]Frederick Douglass, *My Bondage and My Freedom* (Gloucester, Mass.: Peter Smith, 1969).

[45]Booker T. Washington, *Up from Slavery* (New York: Bantam Books, 1963).

[46]W. E. B. DuBois, *The Souls of Black Folk* (New York: New American Library, 1961), pp. 68ff.

[47]Günther Bornkamm, *Paul*, trans. D. M. G. Stalker (New York: Harper & Row, Publishers, Inc., 1971), p. xxvi.

Chapter 4

[1]Arnold Ehrhardt, "An Unknown Orphic Writing in the Demosthenes Scholia and St. Paul," *ZNW*, 48 (1957), pp. 101-110.

[2]Nicholaos Yalouris, ed., *The Eternal Olympics* (New Rochelle, N.Y: Caratzas Brothers, Publishers, 1979), p. 70.

[3]*Ibid.*

[4]*Ibid.*

[5]Lucian, *Anarcharsis*, 10.

[6]Robert Nisbet, *History of the Idea of Progress* (New York: Basic Books, Inc., 1979), p. 4.

[7]Herman Kahn and Anthony J. Wiener, "A Framework for Speculation" *Daedalus* (Summer, 1967), pp. 711-716.

[8]*Ibid.*, p. 717.

⁹Alvin Toffler, *Future Shock* (New York: Bantam Books, 1971), p. 11.

¹⁰John Kenneth Galbraith, *The Age of Uncertainty* (Boston: Houghton Mifflin Company, 1977).

¹¹Christopher Lasch, *The Culture of Narcissism: American Life in an Age of Diminishing Expectations* (New York: W. W. Norton & Co., Inc., 1979), p. 21.

¹²Daniel Yankelovich, "New Rules in American Life: Searching for Self-Fulfillment in a World Turned Upside Down," *Psychology Today* (April, 1981), p. 36.

¹³Howard J. Ruff, *How to Prosper During the Coming Bad Years* (New York: Times Books, 1979), p. 14. Copyright © 1980 by Howard Ruff. Reprinted by permission of Times Books/The New York Times Book Co., Inc. NOTE: The author specifically disclaims any personal liability, loss, or risk incurred as a consequence of the use and application, either directly or indirectly, of any advice or information presented herein.

¹⁴Reference is made to the ten-month period of training for the Greek athletes in Hans Conzelmann, *First Corinthians*, Hermeneia: A Critical and Historical Commentary on the Bible, trans. James W. Leitch, ed. George W. MacRae, S. J. (Philadelphia: Fortress Press, 1975), p. 162. See also Archibald Robertson and Alfred Plummer, *A Critical and Exegetical Commentary on the First Epistle of St. Paul to the Corinthians*, The International Critical Commentary, 2nd. ed. (Edinburgh: T. & T. Clark, 1914), p. 194.

¹⁵Yalouris, *The Eternal Olympics*, p. 114.

¹⁶Plato, *The Laws*, 8, 833.

¹⁷Yalouris, *The Eternal Olympics*, p. 118.

¹⁸Lucian, *Anarcharsis, passim.*

¹⁹Plato, *The Laws*, 8, 840.

²⁰Clarence M. Wagner, *Profiles of Black Georgia Baptists* (Atlanta: Bennett Brothers Printing Company, 1980), *passim.*

²¹Rudolf Bultmann, *Theology of the New Testament*, trans. Kendrick Grobel, Scribner's Studies in Contemporary Theology (New York: Charles Scribner's Sons, 1951; copyright renewed 1979 Antje B. Lemke), 1, pp. 330-352.

²²*Ibid.*, p. 335.

²³*Ibid.*

²⁴Albert Schweitzer, *The Mysticism of Paul the Apostle*, trans. William Montgomery (New York: The Seabury Press, 1968), *passim.*

²⁵*Ibid.*, p. 1.

²⁶*Ibid.*, p. 3.

²⁷Bultmann, *Theology of the New Testament*, p. 343. Reprinted with the permission of Charles Scribner's Sons.

²⁸Schweitzer, *Mysticism*, p. 195.

²⁹Jürgen Moltmann, *Theology of Hope*, trans. James W. Leitch (New York: Harper & Row, Publishers, Inc., 1967), p. 21.

³⁰Paul uses the term "power" (*dunamis*, the same root used for dynamite) almost half as many times as it is used in the entire New Testament (26). He understands the gospel, the kingdom of God, the resurrection, and other terms in terms of power.

³¹Virgil, *The Aeneid*, 5, 375.

³²Virgil, *Georgics*, 3, 234. See also Ovid, *Metamorphoses*, 7, 780 and Homer. *The Iliad*, 20, 446.

³³Günther Bornkamm, *Paul*, trans. D. M. G. Stalker (New York: Harper & Row, Publishers, Inc., 1971), p. xxvi.

Chapter 5

¹Adolf Harnack, *Expansion of Christianity in the First Three Centuries*, trans. and ed. James Moffat (Gloucester, Mass.: Peter Smith, 1972), p. 431.

²*Ibid.*, p. 432. See also p. 433.

³*Ibid.*, p. 433.

⁴*Ibid.*, p. 432.

⁵*Ibid.*, p. 434.

⁶Johannes Weiss, *Earliest Christianity: A History of the Period A. D. 30-150*, trans. Frederick C. Grant (Gloucester, Mass.: Peter Smith, 1970), pp. 45-82.

⁷Rudolf Schnackenburg, *The Church in the New Testament* (New York: The Seabury Press, 1965), pp. 165-176 and Eduard Schweizer, *The Church as the Body of Christ* (Atlanta: John Knox Press, 1964).

⁸Eduard Schweizer, "Soma," *Theological Dictionary of the New Testament,* ed. Gerhard Friedrich, trans. and ed. Geoffrey W. Bromily (Grand Rapids: Wm. B. Eerdmans Publishing Co., 1971), 7, pp. 1041-1044.

⁹H. Richard Niebuhr, *The Social Sources of Denominationalism* (Cleveland: The World Publishing Company, 1929), p. 21.

¹⁰William Warren Sweet, *The Story of Religion in America* (New York: Harper & Row, Publishers, Inc., 1930), p. 412.

¹¹See Robert G. Torbet, *A History of the Baptists.* Rev. ed. (Valley Forge: Judson Press, 1950), pp. 293-294. For a similar discussion, see Sydney E. Ahlstron, *A Religious History of the American People* (New Haven: Yale University Press, 1972), pp. 648-697. For the devastating division of white churches of the South, see H. Shelton Smith, *In His Image, But: Racism in Southern Religion* (Durham, N.C.: Duke University Press, 1972) and Lestern B. Scherer, *Slavery and the Churches in Early America* (Grand Rapids: Wm. B. Eerdmans Publishing Co., 1975).

¹²Carter G. Woodson, *The History of the Negro Church.* 3rd. ed. (Washington, D.C.: The Associated Publishers, 1921).

¹³Benjamin E. Mays and Joseph William Nicholson, *The Negro's Church* (New York: Negro University Press, 1933); E. Franklin Frazier, *The Negro Church in America* (New York: Schocken Books, 1963); James H. Cone, *Black Theology and Black Power* (New York: The Seabury Press, 1969); Gayraud S. Wilmore, *Black Religion and Black Radicalism* (New York: Doubleday & Co., Inc., 1972).

¹⁴Eduard Schweizer, *The Church as the Body of Christ* (Atlanta: John Knox Press, 1964), p. 55.

¹⁵Hans Küng, *The Church* (New York: Doubleday & Co., Inc., 1976), p. 335.

¹⁶Jürgen Moltmann, *The Church in the Power of the Spirit,* trans. Margaret Kohl (New York: Harper & Row, Publishers, Inc., 1977), p. 316.

¹⁷*Ibid.*, p. 317.

Chapter 6

¹James H. Cone, *Black Theology and Black Power* (New York: The Seabury Press, 1969); Albert B. Cleage, Jr., *The Black Messiah* (New York: Sheed and Ward, 1968) and *Black Christian Nationalism: New Directions for the Black Church* (New York: William Morrow & Company, Inc., 1972); James J. Gardiner, S.A., and J. Deotis Roberts, Sr., *Quest for a Black Theology* (Philadelphia: United Church Press, 1971).

²Gayraud S. Wilmore, *Last Things First* (Philadelphia: The Westminster Press, 1982), p. 38.

³Oddly enough, here I am following the argument of the Jewish scholar, Samuel Sandmel, who suggests that all of the writings of the New Testament were influenced by Paul. See Samuel Sandmel, *The Genius of Paul: A Study in History* (New York: Schocken Books, 1970).

⁴This position is taken by Ernst Haenchen in his commentary on The Acts of the Apostles. See Ernst Haenchen, *The Acts of the Apostles: A Commentary,* trans. Bernard Noble and Gerald Shinn (Philadelphia: The Westminster Press, 1971), p. 561.

⁵Ernest W. Saunders, *First and Second Thessalonians, Philippians, Philemon,* ed. John H. Hayes (Atlanta: John Knox Press, 1981), p. 1.

⁶See James Everett Frame, *Epistles of St. Paul to the Thessalonians,* The International Critical Commentary (Edinburgh: T. & T. Clark, 1979), p. 157.

[7] The majority of commentaries conclude that no such letter was sent to Paul from the church at Thessalonica; for example, Ernest Best, *The First and Second Epistles to the Thessalonians* (London: Adam and Charles Black, 1972), p. 171, and G. G. Findlay, *The Epistles of Paul to the Thessalonians*, Thornapple Commentaries (Grand Rapids: Baker Book House, 1982), p. 90. If such a letter had been written, Paul probably would have mentioned it (cf. 1 Corinthians 7:1).

[8] Best, *Epistles to the Thessalonians*, p. 175.

[9] Frame, *Epistles;* Best, *ibid.*, p. 176.

[10] Georg Bertram, "Ergon," *Theological Dictionary of the New Testament*, ed. Gerhard Kittel and Gerhard Friedrich, trans. Geoffrey W. Bromily, 7 vols. (Grand Rapids: Wm. B. Eerdmans Publishing Co., 1964), p. 649.

[11] *Ibid.*

[12] *Ibid.*

[13] Suetonius, *The Lives of the Caesars,* V. xxv.

[14] *Ibid.*, VI. xvi.

[15] *The Annals of Tacitus,* XV. xliv.

[16] *The Letters of Pliny,* X. xcvi, 7.

[17] See Adolf Harnack, *The Mission and Expansion of Christianity in the First Three Centuries,* trans. James Moffatt (Gloucester, Mass.: Peter Smith, 1972), p. 162.

[18] Harnack, *Mission and Expansion*, pp. 147-198.

[19] Shirley Jackson Case, *The Social Triumph of the Ancient Church* (New York: Harper & Row, Publishers, Inc., 1933), pp. 41-93. Case's statement of the early church's accumulation of wealth is very well written. But one of his glaring weaknesses is his failure to show that the early church disposed of the status of slaves in the church and possibly used its wealth to gain the slaves freedom as they came into the church.

[20] *Ibid.*, p. 9.

DATE DUE